THE
Westminster Pulpit

VOLUME VIII

THE Westminster Pulpit

VOLUME VIII

The Preaching of

G. CAMPBELL MORGAN

WIPF & STOCK · Eugene, Oregon

Wipf and Stock Publishers
199 W 8th Ave, Suite 3
Eugene, OR 97401

The Westminster Pulpit vol. VIII
The Preaching of G. Campbell Morgan
By Morgan, G. Campbell
Copyright©1954 by The Morgan Trust
ISBN 13: 978-1-60899-317-8
Publication date 1/15/2012
Previously published by Fleming H. Revell, Co., 1954

G. Campbell Morgan Reprint Series

Foreword

IF IT is true that the measure of a person's greatness is their influence, not only on his own time but on future generations, G. Campbell Morgan must be regarded as a great person. His greatness is seen not only in the wide impact of his ministry on both sides of the Atlantic, but in the fact that his books are still read and studied sixty-five years after his death. Named one of the ten greatest preachers of the twentieth-century by the contributing board of *Preaching* magazine, Morgan made the Bible a new and living book not only to the congregations who listened to him, but the vast multitude of persons who read his books.

Fox sixty-seven years Morgan preached and taught the Scriptures and served churches in England and the United States. What is remarkable is that his commentaries and expositions of the Bible still speak to persons of a new millennium. There have been many changes in the world since he faithfully preached and taught the Scriptures, but the wide appeal of his books testify to the timelessness of his message.

Although he held pastorates in the Congregational and Presbyterian denominations, he had an ecumenical appeal to persons of all denominations and traditions. The mystic

Thomas á Kempis once wrote, "He to whom the eternal word speaks is delivered from many opinions." In one of his sermons, he referred to the words of Amos that there would be a famine for hearing the word of God (Amos 8:11). The timeless work of G. Campbell Morgan addresses that hunger, as his books enable his readers to get beyond opinions to the living Word.

Wipf and Stock Publishers have rendered a great gift to the religious world in reprinting dozens of Morgan's books. This growing collection makes his books more available, so that readers have an option other than searching the internet for used, and often expensive, copies. Among this collection is the classic *The Great Physician* and commentaries on the Gospel of Matthew and John. Persons seeking a living faith and a meaningful encounter with God would profit from reading any of these Morgan books.

Near the end of his ministry, in a sermon entitled "But One Thing," Morgan commented on how Portugal changed the words of a coin after Christopher Columbus discovered America. No longer did the inscription say, *Ne Plus Ultra* (nothing more beyond) but *Plus Ultra* (more beyond). It is the hope of the G. Campbell Morgan Trust that the reprinting of these books will bring readers to the "more beyond," and an even deeper encounter with the Word in Scripture.

THE MORGAN TRUST
Richard L. Morgan
Howard C. Morgan
John C. Morgan

CONTENTS

CHAPTER		PAGE
I	THE CHURCH THE PILLAR AND GROUND OF THE TRUTH	9
II	THE ONE OFFERING	21
III	FALSE FIRE	35
IV	SPIRITUAL LEPROSY	48
V	SIN, SORROW, SILENCE	61
VI	HOPE	75
VII	A GOOD FRIDAY MEDITATION	87
VIII	AN EASTER MEDITATION	100
IX	THE CONDITIONS OF RENEWAL	114
X	THE PRIESTLY BENEDICTION	128
XI	THE RESPONSIBILITIES OF SALVATION	141
XII	BORN BLIND: THE DISCIPLES' PROBLEM—THE MASTER'S ANSWER	154
XIII	SANCTIFICATION	168
XIV	THE FILLING OF THE SPIRIT	181
XV	NEHUSHTAN	194
XVI	THE POSSIBILITY OF RESTORATION	207
XVII	DANIEL, A MAN OF EXCELLENT SPIRIT	221
XVIII	THE TOUCH OF FAITH	233
XIX	OUR ALTAR	246
XX	THE PRESENCE NEEDED	257
XXI	THE FRUIT-BEARING FRIENDS OF JESUS	270
XXII	THE POWER OF THE GOSPEL	284
XXIII	WINNING SOULS	297

CHAPTER		PAGE
XXIV	BE STRONG—AND WORK!	310
XXV	THE WAY TO THE ALTAR	324
XXVI	THE FIRST-BORN	337

THE
Westminster
Pulpit

VOLUME VIII

CHAPTER I

THE CHURCH THE PILLAR AND GROUND OF THE TRUTH

The Church of the living God, the pillar and ground of the truth.
                                    I TIMOTHY 3:15.

THIS IS A TEXT. IT IS NOT A STATEMENT. IT MAKES NO DEFINITE declaration. It is, nevertheless, full of light and suggestiveness. The words constitute an arresting figure of speech, setting forth inclusively the function of the Christian Church in the world. Paul was writing to Timothy concerning his responsibilities in the city of Ephesus. He had exhorted Timothy to tarry there for a very definite purpose. This purpose is found in the opening of the letter in these words: "As I exhorted thee to tarry at Ephesus, when I was going into Macedonia, that thou mightest charge certain men not to teach a different doctrine, neither to give heed to fables and endless genealogies, the which minister questionings rather than a dispensation of God which is in faith."

The passage from which the text is taken contains Paul's statement of the reason of his writing yet more particularly: "These things write I unto thee, hoping to come unto thee shortly, but if I tarry long, that thou mayest know how men ought to behave themselves in the house of God, which is the church of the living God, the pillar and ground of the truth.

And without controversy, great is the mystery of godliness, He Who was manifested in the flesh, justified in the spirit, seen of angels, preached among the nations, believed on in the world, received up in glory."

Let us glance at that paragraph in reverse order. It concludes with a declaration of the whole content of Christian truth: "Great is the mystery of godliness; He Who was manifested in the flesh, justified in the spirit, seen of angels, preached among the nations, believed on in the world, received up in glory."

The mystery of godliness is the truth of which the Church is the pillar and the ground.

I have said that this is an arresting figure. Let us, first, then, briefly but carefully consider the figure in itself, in order that we may proceed to examine the function of the Church as it is set forth by the figure.

It may be that when Paul wrote these words, he was looking out on the monuments of some city. It is almost certain that when Timothy read it, it would be easy for him to look out on Ephesus. Here and there in the city in the day of its wealth, great memorial columns were to be seen. Let us have the structure clearly in mind. The word "pillar" describes an elevated column, sometimes one solid block of masonry, as for instance, Cleopatra's Needle on the Thames Embankment; very often one column built of many parts, of different stones or bricks. The idea is that of an upright column giving elevation.

The word "ground" simply refers to that on which the column rests—what an architect would probably describe as the plinth. It may be well to say that the foundation is never the final thing in a building. The Church is not built on a rock foundation, in spite of all our hymns and our expositions. The Church is built on the foundation of apostles and prophets, and that foundation is based on rock, which is the eternal underlying strength. Paul was dealing here with the foundation, and not with that on which the foundation rests. Such is the structure.

Given any such structure, what is its purpose? It is always the instrument by which some object or truth is elevated in order that it may be clearly seen, in order that the attention of men may be drawn to it. Sometimes what is to be seen is a statue, as, for instance, in Trafalgar Square, where the great column is the pillar and the plinth, elevating Nelson.

Sometimes it is not the statue of a person that is to be seen, but a light. Those of you who have passed along our southern shores in the dark and seen the flashing light of Eddystone will have an illustration. The building is a pillar, erected on a foundation, resting finally on the rock; but the purpose of elevation is the flashing of a light. Sometimes both ideas are combined. Those who have sailed up the Hudson into New York City have looked at the Statue of Liberty facing out toward the ocean. It was some very unkind Englishman who said that Liberty had turned its back on America and was looking homeward again. As you looked at that statue, two things arrested your attention. First, the figure of Liberty; and when the night came, lo, from the brow flashed an electric light. There we have the two things, the elevation of a person, the flashing of a light. Sometimes the purpose is the proclamation of a truth, a historic truth, as in the weird and wonderful Cleopatra's Needle to which I have already made reference, whereupon is written the history of ancient kings and dynasties and deeds of prowess. The idea is always that of the elevation of a person, of a light, of a truth, that these things may be seen.

Mark, then, I pray you, still thinking of the structure in all simplicity, the interrelationship. First, the pillar and the ground are of no value apart from what they reveal. Second, the statue, the light, the word, need the pillar, the ground, in order that they may be seen. A column built for a statue is a laughingstock if the statue is not placed on it, and seen. When Eddystone ceases to flash its light across the waters for the sake of mariners it may be destroyed. When the writing of the pillar is obliterated, though out of sentiment we may still keep it there, it will have no real value. But it is also true that the statue cannot be seen unless it be elevated. Place it on the level, and only a few can see it. It must be lifted up, if it is to utter its message. The light on the ground flings no radiance to the distance, and the mariner will not be helped. It must be elevated, if the light is to be seen. The word simply written is of no value. It must be proclaimed, published.

Such is the figure in itself, and I am inclined to think that this simple and childlike examination of the figure has already preached the sermon. "The Church of the Living God, which is the pillar and the ground of the truth." Immediately, we see how the figure illustrates, in consonance with other Scriptures, one phase of the function of the Church.

The first mention of the Church in the New Testament is found in those inclusive words of Jesus, so brief and yet so full of meaning, spoken at Cæsarea Philippi: "I will build My Church." A structure which the Lord Himself builds is suggested. When, later on, Paul came to write of the Church he made use of the same figure: "Built upon the foundation of the apostles and prophets, Christ Jesus Himself being the Chief Corner Stone." Here he speaks of that structure, as the pillar and the ground of the truth. The Church is the medium by which the truth is to be proclaimed, to be elevated to a height that men may see it, to be published to the city, to the nation, to the world at large. In the Christian Faith we have centrally a Person, resultantly a Light, finally a Word. If the Person is to be seen He must be lifted up; if the light is to flash across the darkness it must have height; if the word is to be proclaimed it must have an instrument for its proclamation; and the Church is the pillar and ground of the truth; its one business is to reveal the Person, to flash the light, to proclaim the word.

Passing from the figure to the fact, mark the interrelation between these matters. The Church of God apart from the Person of Christ is a useless structure. However ornate it may be in its organization, however perfect in all its arrangements, however rich and increased with goods, if the Church is not revealing the Person, lifting Him to the height where all men can see Him, then the Church becomes an impertinence and a sham, a blasphemy and a fraud, and the sooner the world is rid of it, the better. The Church, apart from the shining of a light, is a lampstand, dark, valueless, effete. The Church that fails to proclaim the Word is a sound, a voice without articulation, sounding brass and a clanging cymbal; of no value.

With all reverence, let me state the other side, which is to my own heart full of grave solemnity. That supernal Person, apart from the Church, is hidden. Jesus Christ has no means of showing Himself save through His Church. The light that flashes from His eyes cannot be seen save as it beams and shines and burns and flashes and flames from the eyes of His people. The tenderness and strength of His teaching can be felt only as the Church becomes the instrument through which He speaks to humanity to direct, instruct, and bless it. The great central Person is hidden unless the Church reveals Him. The Light that lighteth every man, and which came into the world, and was focused, centralized for a brief period in a Person, has passed out of human sight, and is no longer shining save through the Church. The Word of God today has no voice apart from the Christian Church.

Now, from these more general statements let us come to particular considerations. The moment we do so it is necessary that we remember that, finally, the figure must be interpreted by the fact. A fact is always greater than the figure that represents it. We may take it as an axiom that whenever we have a figure it is because a fact is so fine that there is no apprehending it apart from the figure. Consequently, the figure presently must vanish away in the presence of the fact.

In this case it is pre-eminently so. This is seen in Paul's use of the figure. He had already defined what is the pillar and the ground of the Truth by two words: "House" and "Church." In each case, moreover, he had qualified his definition: "The House of God," "the Church of the living God."

Paul first called it "The House of God." This word "House" means, first, a dwelling place; then, a family; then, a householder; and, finally, a dynasty; the word is employed in all these senses in the New Testament. It is God's dwelling place, family, household, and Kingdom. That is the pillar and ground of the Truth. Paul also called it the Church of the living God. The Church is the theocracy, the whole company of souls governed by God; and, consequently, it is God's governing body in the midst of human history, that through which He makes known His will, enunciates His law, reveals His purpose, communicates His life, marches ever onward toward the ultimate goal of His determined purpose. Paul, in his last letter concerning the Church, the letter to the Colossians, speaks of a mystery, the Church; and, a few sentences later, refers to "the mystery of Christ in you, the hope of glory"; and yet a few sentences later, speaks of "the mystery which is Christ." To reverse the order. First, there is the unfathomable and infinite mystery of Christ Himself, God manifest in the flesh, the One in Whom all the fulness of Godhead dwelt corporeally. Then follows the mystery of Christ formed in the heart of individual souls. Multiply the number of such units and we have the mystery of the Church; and that is the pillar and ground of the truth. The Person can be seen only through that company of men and women; the light can flash only through them; the

Word of God can be proclaimed only through them. Their one responsibility in the world, then—individually and in their corporate capacity—is the revelation of the Person, the shining of the Light, the proclamation of the Word. When we pass into our New Testament and breathe its rare and spacious atmosphere, the trivialities that divide us perish, and we gain the sense of God's great Church of all souls that are born anew, that share the Life Divine, in whom Christ is formed, the very hope of glory; upon that multitude of every tongue and kindred and nation rests one supreme responsibility; that Church of the Living God is the pillar and the ground of the Truth.

How is the Church to fulfil that responsibility? The Church is to fulfil the responsibility of revealing a Person, flashing a light, proclaiming a word, by Incarnation, and by proclamation. In considering these we must remember the Divine order: that the whole Church is called to the ministry; and that within the Church there is a ministry, the business of which is to perfect the whole Church that it may fulfil its ministry.

First, the Church of God is to fulfil its obligation by Incarnation. In one of the very last conversations I had with D. L. Moody, in his own beautiful home in the Connecticut Valley, we were talking of the Bible, of its importance in the life of the nation, and in the life of the world; and with that short, sharp, quick manner in which he often said great things, he said this: "Never forget that the Christian man is the world's Bible, and in the majority of cases a Revised Version is needed." I am not proposing now to discuss the second part of his declaration. I am afraid it is too true, but I leave it. I am interested in the first part of his declaration. The Christian man is the world's Bible. How is this nation of ours to know this Bible? The printing of it, and the scattering of it is not enough. That is most important, most valuable; but the letter killeth; it is the spirit that maketh alive. The spirit of the Bible is never revealed to the unregenerate man until it is incarnate in the lives of men and women who believe it. That is the perpetual principle of God's methods with men. God might have adopted some other method; but God has chosen this method, and I believe that His choice is based upon infinite wisdom. Man hears the Word of God through man. That tremendous truth underlies the central mystery of our holy faith, that of the Incarnation. God had spoken to the fathers in times past through their prophets in divers portions, by divers methods; but there was no final, prevailing and pervasive power in the Word of God until He spoke in His Son. It was when the Word became flesh and tabernacled among men, and men beheld His glory, that the Word of God became prevailing. There is a sense in which that great Incarnation of God and of the Word of God in Jesus of Nazareth was central and final and inclusive; but the principle obtains, and persists. Ere He left the little group of men that had gathered about Him, He said to them, Ye shall be My witnesses. By this, He did not mean merely, Ye shall be men who talk about Me; but ye shall be My evidences, My credentials, My examples. The early victories of the Church were won by men who believed the story of Jesus, by men telling the story of Jesus; but also by men illustrating the story that they told in what they were in themselves. In proportion as the Word was incarnate, the Word ran and had free course and was glorified. This is persistently so. It is so today. The Church is the pillar and ground of the truth. Through her, the Person is to be seen, the Light is to shine, the Word is to be proclaimed; but she can fulfil her sacred duty only as the word which she hears, the light which is granted her, the Person known to her, is revealed in her individual members. The Church is in the world to proclaim a great Evangel. The Church is in the world to make protest against all things that are unlike God. The Church is in the world to be the instrument of the Divine philanthropy. The Church is in the world to pronounce the ethic of heaven and to insist that men shall hear it and obey it.

How is the Church to proclaim her evangel? She will send her evangelists; but the evangelists have no power in their message save as that message is backed by the testimony of men and women who are pardoned. It is the pardoned man who preaches the Gospel, the man who lives in the power of God's forgiveness; the man who is forever humble, never forgetting the hole of the pit from which he was digged, marching to the end of life's journey with the subdued and reverent demeanor of a man who owes everything to the Divine grace; and yet, marching with his head erect, knowing the forgiveness of his own sins. That man is proclaiming the Word, is flashing the Light, is revealing the Saviour. That man is preaching the Gospel, and it is by that preaching that the evangel is to be proclaimed.

The church is in the world to make eternal protest against all the things that spoil humanity. How is she to do it? By preaching? God has chosen the foolishness of preaching for the accomplishment of His great and infinite purpose; but preaching is powerless save as it is reinforced by the lives of men and women whose lives are a perpetual protest against evil things. God's Church sends out to every Pool of Bethesda where are gathered the withered and the maimed, men and women who are against the things that wither, that maim, that spoil; Crusaders that have lifted their hands in the sight of heaven, and sworn beneath the Cross of Calvary, that they will make no truce with evil. As the Church sends these men and women out, she is making her protest.

The Church is in the world, a great instrument of Divine Philanthropy. There is a great word of the Church that we Protestants have nearly lost: Mother Church! She is, or ought to be, the great Mother, picking up the crippled child and nursing it back to life, finding the starved and feeding them, taking hold of the imbecile and saying: We will see to it that you are guarded while life's lamp still burns. That is the Church's business, and, thank God, she has done wonderful work. All the great philanthropies that care for the unfit have resulted from the incarnation of the Love of God in the Christian Church.

The Church is in the world to proclaim the great ethic of God. How shall she do it? By enunciating moral codes? No, they have been enunciated once and forever, and we can add nothing to the Decalogue and the Sermon on the Mount. The Church is to proclaim the ethic by sending into the highways and byways, into the places of commerce, and the places of professional life, men and women who themselves observe the Divine Law, and reveal to men the infinite love that has inspired it.

But there is also a corporate revelation by incarnation. By her fellowship with God and by the consequent fellowship within her borders the Church of God ought to speak to the whole world of the realization of the Divine ideal. The Church ought to be revealing to the world the Kingdom of God and the will of God for humanity. In order to do this, the Christian Church has a ministry, a ministry of those on whom God has bestowed His great gifts. "He gave some apostles, . . . some pastors and teachers." The business of those within the Church is to teach the word of truth in such form and fashion that the Church will be able to incarnate the Word, and flash the light on the world's darkness. The apostolic function, which, technically is expressing truth in its balanced form and proportion, is always to that end. The pastoral function is breaking the Bread of Life, feeding the flock of God, leading individual souls to new appreciation, in order that by obedience thereto they may proclaim the truth. These gifts within the Church are bestowed in order that the Church may fulfil her function of being the pillar and the ground of the truth.

The Church must not only fulfil its function by incarnation, she must do it also by proclamation. In order to do this, she has her prophets and evangelists. The function of the prophet is to proclaim the evangel, call men to repentance and faith. The prophet and the evangelist must speak on behalf of the Church, explaining the secrets of the Church's experience. If there be no experience to explain, the declaration of a theory is of no avail. For one brief moment let us go back to the Day of Pentecost. Think of the significant and important fact, that Peter's preaching was made possible by the Church's enthusiasm. What attracted the crowd? A Church with its eyes aflame with light and its lips filled with song! All Jerusalem gathered together, and they were amazed, and they were perplexed, and they said, What meaneth this? The Church attracted the crowd by its enthusiasm, and so the opportunity of the preacher was created. This is the supreme work of the Christian Church, and it is only as she does her work that men and nations and the world will live by the Bible.

In the midst of the chaos and the uncertainty and the perplexity there is nothing at this moment more important, than that the Church of God should proclaim the Word of God to the nation. This she must do by life in harmony with the Word, by the messages of her apostles and prophets and evangelists and pastors and teachers. The message lacks all force, unless it have behind it the witness of the souls that have proved its power.

The Church of the Living God is the pillar and ground of the truth. If the Church is to do this work she must know the Word of God for herself. If the men appointed to minister within her borders are to assist the Church to the fulfilment of her function, they must know the Word of God themselves.

There is a Person the world needs to see. Am I helping to show Him to the world? There are dark and troubled and storm-tossed waters on which mariners are being wrecked, and there is a Light for them. Am I helping to flash the light across the dark waters? There is famine for the Word of God everywhere, and men are wandering away and dying, and there is a Word of God that meets the need of such hungry souls. Am I doing anything to make it known?

CHAPTER II

THE ONE OFFERING

For by one offering He hath perfected for ever them that are sanctified.
HEBREWS 10:14.

THE BIBLICAL CONCEPTION OF RELIGION IS RIGHT RELATIONship between God and man. The Biblical doctrine of man is, essentially, that he is the offspring of God, whose relation to God, therefore, is threefold: first, that he has the right of personal access to God; second, that there the possibility of direct, immediate intercourse with God is given to him; finally, that the privilege and responsibility of co-operation with God in carrying out God's designs rests on him. After the briefest declarations concerning the origin and nature of man, the Bible introduces the subject of sin. Sin, according to its teaching, results in the exclusion of man from God, the cessation of communion with Him, and the consequent inability to realize the privilege and fulfil the responsibility of co-operation with Him.

The ultimate message of the Bible, however, is neither that of the essential nature of man nor that of his sin. The final message of the Bible is that of redemption. It is the literature of redemption. It is therefore a message to sinning men, to those who are excluded from their birthright by sin; excluded from the consciousness of the presence of God, denied fellowship with Him, and unable to fulfil their responsibility to Him either personally or relatively. To that state the Bible appeals. The Bible has been written for sinning and not for sinless men. If I may venture to put into brief words that which shall express the whole message of the Bible, then I shall employ the very words of the Lord Himself, for that which is the truth concerning the Word incarnate by His own declaration is true concerning this written word: "I came not to call the righteous but sinners to repentance."

The burden of the Bible was perfectly expressed in the words of the wise woman of Tekoa to King David when he was fleeing from Absalom, in which she uttered the profound truth, "God . . . deviseth means that he that is banished be not outcast from Him." So far as the Biblical revelation is concerned, this great declaration has been made in two stages, both of which are referred to by the writer in the opening words of the treatise from which our text is taken: "God, having of old time spoken unto the fathers in the prophets by divers portions and in divers manners, hath at the end of these days spoken unto us in His Son." The first stage was that of the revelation to the fathers in the prophets by divers portions in divers manners. The final stage is that of to-day, the revelation in the Son.

The method of the old economy was suggestion, prediction, illustration. That of to-day is the method of finality, fulfilment, realization. In the Hebrew system one phase of the necessity for human redemption, and one phase of the way of its provision was revealed in all that splendid ritual of the Hebrew people, revealed particularly in the offerings as they shadowed forth the way of approach to God by sinning man. It is the way of complete dedication, accompanied by sacrifice and propitiation, with the resulting elements of atonement and forgiveness. In that pictorial system there were five offerings, named, respectively, the Burnt Offering, the Meal Offering, the Peace Offering, the Sin Offering, and the Trespass Offering.

These may be divided into two groups, the first consisting of three offerings, the Burnt, the Meal, the Peace: the Burnt, the symbol of the dedication of the entire life to God; the Meal, the symbol of the dedication of the service of the life to God; and the Peace, the symbol of that fellowship with God which is possible on the basis of the dedication of life and of service. In each case there was the element of sacrifice connected with the offering.

The second group consisted of two offerings: the Sin Offering, which suggested the necessity for, and the method of, putting away sins in order that man might be brought back to his birthright of access to God, intercourse with God, and co-operation with God; and the Trespass Offering, which dealt with certain definite acts of sin.

The writer of this letter to the Hebrews declared that these offerings were not in themselves efficacious, and in that declaration he wrote in harmony with the teaching of the great Hebrew prophets. In his argument he quoted from the ancient Hebrew Scriptures, and his quotations might be multiplied, for they are manifold. The declaration of the seers of the old economy was persistently that in themselves these sacrifices, these offerings, had no value, no efficacy, but that they pointed to something profounder, were adumbrations of something greater, shadows of it demonstrating its reality. In this chapter the word of the writer of this letter, is a striking, suggestive one, "The law having a *shadow* of the good things to come, not the very image of the things." While he recognized that there can be no power, no dynamic, no saving virtue in the shadow, he did nevertheless recognize that there can be no shadow without the substance. There was infinitely more in these ancient sacrifices than feasting and fasting; they were evidences of the existing purpose and power of Deity, to be yet more perfectly manifested. The whole argument of the writer of the letter was that the deepest, profoundest meaning of all those offerings of the ancient ritual was fulfilled in human history in the Person and work of the Son of God, "For by one offering He hath perfected for ever them that are sanctified." We must be true to the conception of the writer if we would understand his meaning. To whom, then, was the writer referring? Who is it that by one offering can perfect forever them that are sanctified? The answer is found in the opening declaration of the letter, "God . . . hath spoken unto us in His Son, Whom He appointed heir of all things, through Whom also He made the worlds; Who being the effulgence of His glory, and the very image of His substance, and upholding all things by the word of His power, when He had made purification of sins, sat down on the right hand of the Majesty on high." In that august and remarkable introduction of the central Person in the mind of the writer we find relationships with all the arguments that follow. When I read that He, this wondrous Son of God, perfects forever them that are sanctified, I remember that associated with the description of His inherent being and glory and beauty is the declaration that He has made purification of sins.

The declaration of our text, then, is that in and through Him the Son of God man may be restored to right relationship with God, and that in every way. If the Biblical conception of religion be that of man in right relationship with God; if the Bible teaches that sin has excluded man from access to God, from intercourse and from co-operation, the ultimate word of the Bible is that God has devised means by which the banished shall not be outcast, the means being that in His Son God has wrought the work through which man may be restored to his right of access, restored to his communion and fellowship, restored to both the responsibility and privilege of co-operation with God.

Let us, then, consider this declaration of the text as it deals with the one offering provided in Christ, with the perfection provided for men, and with the condition of appropriation.

"By one offering." Let us think of that offering in itself, in its sufficiency, and in its exclusiveness.

First, in itself. Directly we begin to attempt to think of this one offering in itself there are so many aspects of the matter that we are in difficulty. Let us follow the simplest method and consider the *offering*, using the word as a noun, that which was offered; and then consider the *offering*, using the word as a verb, the act of offering, the way of the offering.

What, then, is this one offering through which Christ hath perfected forever them that are sanctified? We are not left to any speculation; we follow the statement of the writer and we have a clear and distinct declaration of what that offering was. From verse fourteen, which constitutes the text, I glance back to verse ten, and there I read these words: "By which will we have been sanctified through the offering of the body of Jesus Christ once for all." Ere I am able to comprehend the meaning of that utterance, I move backward still a little further, and notice a very remarkable and significant quotation from one of the psalms,

> Sacrifice and offering Thou wouldest not,
> But a body didst Thou prepare for Me.

By the offering of that body of Jesus Christ, that body prepared for Jesus Christ, He perfects forever them that are sanctified. We must briefly give attention to one matter of detail, and perhaps of difficulty. The quotation of the psalm here by the writer is a quotation from the Septuagint, and not from the Hebrew Scriptures. In the Hebrew the psalm reads:

> Sacrifice and offering Thou wouldest not,
> But Mine ear hast Thou opened.

I draw attention to the difference because it has created difficulty as to whether the translators of what we speak of as the Septuagint version thought for some reason that there was a mistake in the Hebrew, or whether the text as it is in the Hebrew to-day is correct. There is a sense in which the vital, underlying spiritual value is not changed in either case, for the word as we have it in the Hebrew text and in the Bible, "Mine ear hast Thou opened," has no reference whatever to that ancient rite or ceremony by which the servant coming to the doorpost had his ear pierced in order that he might demonstrate his fidelity. The thought is that rather of making the ear absolutely attentive in order that the soul may be mastered by the Divine will. That is the whole story of the human life of Jesus. I have no doubt that the Septuagint version is the true one. I build my view on the fact that the New Testament writer quoted the psalm in this way, as I believe, under the inspiration of the Holy Spirit, thus distinguishing between the true and the false and giving us a most remarkable statement concerning that offering which our Lord made: "A body didst Thou prepare for Me." Under the guidance of the Holy Spirit, this word was fastened on by the writer of the New Testament to show that the sacrifice of our Lord by which we are redeemed, even on the physical side, was that of a body especially prepared by God for His Son. Thus the One Who hung on the Cross is differentiated from all other men, even in the matter of His physical life. In that word, "a body didst Thou prepare for Me," is involved the mysterious method of incarnation which is recorded by two of the evangelists, that of the virgin birth of our Lord. In an activity, wholly within the compass of the Divine power, God did purify human flesh and through that purification gave to us the immaculate

Son of His love in human form and human being. He was in Himself the sinless One, not a member of our sinning race, but a member of our race, brought into it by a Divine overruling and activity of love and power so as to share that which is essential in humanity and be separate from sinners and from all things which have ruined and spoiled humanity.

Then we must remember that His living body fulfilled its true function, that of being an instrument of the spirit. The body of a human being is but the earthly instrument of the spirit, which is the essential fact in the life of that human being. Thus reverting to the original economy and ideal of creation, this Man of Nazareth fulfilled the Divine purpose, and His body, prepared for the specific purpose, was the perfect instrument of His spirit. His spirit was never imprisoned within His body, was never mastered by the appetites of the body, was never deflected from the course of rightness by the allurements of the body, was never clouded in its vision of God by illicit answer to the cry of the body. It was the instrument of the spirit; and as in His spirit life this Man of Nazareth was separate from sinners, holy, undefiled, so also in all His bodily life He was separate from sinners, holy, undefiled. Therefore, when we think of the Man of Nazareth, and in those hours in which we properly rejoice at His nearness to us by reason of His humanity, let us with equal propriety and solemnity tremble and wonder as we recognize that He was alone, distanced from us in Himself in spiritual life and in bodily life; that He stands alone, unique in all the centuries, a lonely Man by virtue of His purity and uninterrupted adjustment to the holiness, purity, and rightness of God.

If these things be remembered we shall never fall into the unutterable blunder of imagining that the evangelical doctrine is that one man died for other men, we shall never fall into the unutterable mistake of imagining that on the Cross some one member of our own race did persuade God to a change of mind and a change of relationship concerning men. We shall watch through all the process for the movements of God, for which He first did prepare a body for the Son of His love; and we shall watch Him as He moves along the way of men, ever recognizing His entire separation from humanity, even in the hours of close, mysterious identification.

In the Hebrew economy the Burnt Offering was symbolic of the dedication of the whole life to God; the Meal Offering was symbolic of the dedication of the service, for in that offering men brought what they themselves had wrought, the result of their own toil; the Peace Offering was the symbol of the unbroken fellowship with God which results from the dedication of the life and the service. We immediately see how that wonderful kindergarten of the old economy found its fulfilment in Jesus. On all the pathway of His pilgrimage the supreme note was that of the dedication of His whole life to God. I reverently quote in this connection from the Roman epistle: "I beseech you therefore, brethren, by the mercies of God, to present your bodies a living sacrifice, holy, acceptable to God, which is your spiritual worship." That was the apostolic appeal to redeemed men, that they should make the body the sacramental symbol of the spiritual attitude. Reverently I declare that this is exactly the story of the life of Jesus; His spirit was ever yielded to God in perfect obedience, and the body perpetually expressed that attitude of the spirit, so that every journey the body took was a journey God-ordained, and every activity of those gentle hands was an activity God-inspired, and every glance of His eye was the outlooking of the purpose and will and intention of God. All the body of the Lord expressed the fact of the dedication of His whole life and being to God. It was also the medium of a dedicated service, for all that He did He did under the Divine authority; I do nothing of Myself; I speak nothing of Myself; what My Father gives Me that I do; what My Father gives Me that I speak. All His service was God-inspired. I see Him with the children about Him, angry with the disciples who would prevent them coming, and I hear the thunder of His love, "Suffer the little children, and forbid them not, to come unto Me: for of such is the Kingdom of heaven." That is a Man acting under Divine impulse and Divine authority. I see Him on another day, when, looking into the eyes of the false rulers of His people, He says to them, Woe unto you! scribes, hypocrites, whited sepulchres, full of dead men's bones. That was not a passing spasm of human passion; it was God speaking out of His holiness and His wrath to the men who oppressed other men. Therefore He realized the meaning of the Peace Offering. He was always at peace with God, always in fellowship with God. He spoke with august and reverent familiarity of His Father at all times and in all circumstances, feeling that no sanctity was violated when He linked God to flowers, to sparrows, and to children.

Consider, then, the worth of that One, and mark the worth of that body, prepared in infinite mystery and by infinite power, the perfected and unharmed instrument of the spirit, perfectly adjusted to God. There has been nothing like it in human history.

We pass now to the word "offering" as a verb. The intention of the offering was symbolized in the two remaining offerings of the Hebrew economy, the Sin Offering and the Trespass Offering. Its method was co-operation with God, and its purpose, reconciliation of man with God, making peace, or, again to take up the august word of the Old Testament and of the Christian Church, making atonement.

In Jesus, fulfilment of the symbolism of the Burnt, the Meal, and the Peace Offerings, we see the sacrificial element. Have I spoken of the Burnt Offering of a dedicated life? He was a Man of sorrows and acquainted with grief. Have I spoken of the Meal Offering of dedicated service? In all His service there was the element of vicarious suffering. With infinite ease He healed the sick as Matthew records—no, not with infinite ease, for Matthew adds, "That it might be fulfilled which was spoken by Isaiah the prophet, saying, Himself took our infirmities, and bare our diseases." Have I spoken of the Peace Offering of fellowship? Our Lord's unbroken peace with God was challenged by the perpetual restlessness of humanity, and found expression again and again in the hot discontent of His heart with things unlike God. Take sin out of the world and Christ had known no sorrow. He might have lived a life of perfect dedication, a life of perfect dedication in service, a life of perpetual peace untroubled by sorrow, undesolated by agony. But in this world the measure of His perfection was the measure of His pain. The measure of our nearness to Christ is the measure in which we are capable of suffering with sinning men and sinning women. If we are merely righteous, cold and hard when we have sinners to deal with, we know very little about God or Christ. The measure of purity is the measure of pain in the presence of impurity. All through His life there was this sacrificial element, until at last everything was gathered up in the infinite, awe-inspiring mystery of the offering of His body on the Tree.

All the demand of the Divine character was perfectly met in that offering. In such life there ought to be no pain, no death; if pain and death were there, and that by the very will of God, pain and death were there for some wider and beneficent purpose. All the demands of the Divine character are met in that Person.

Once again, that which it is so extremely difficult to state or to comprehend, but which nevertheless is the declaration of Scripture and must be true or all our religion fails, in Christ there was the fulness of the Divine consciousness: "In Him dwelleth all the fulness of the Godhead corporeally." All the Divine consciousness was in Him, and the Divine consciousness includes the whole creation, the consciousness of all men and of all life that has consciousness. All was focused in Him. That body prepared by infinite power and in infinite mystery, and yet of my very nature, was the central instrument of the spirit which in co-operation with God was conscious of the fulness of the Divine consciousness.

Not only did it please the Father that all the fulness should dwell in Him as to consciousness, but also as to resources. The supply of Deity was vested in Him in order to co-operate in the Divine work.

So, in the light of these unfathomable things and of these Divine facts that defy our mathematical terms, I read my text again: "For by one offering He hath perfected for ever them that are sanctified."

I say in the presence of God that I am not astonished now, when I think of Who Christ is, and what that body really meant, even though I cannot fathom the mystery. If there are depths too deep for me and heights too vastly removed for my climbing, still I feel that here is the place of my refuge:

> Rock of ages, cleft for me,
> Let me hide myself in Thee.

That one offering excludes all human activity which is insufficient to realize the restoration which man seeks. It excludes the value of human merit, for human merit is worthless. It excludes the necessity for all human intervention which, in its presence, becomes blasphemous and impertinent.

In considering the perfection provided through the offering we go back to the initial words of our meditation. The perfection provided is the restoration of everything lost. Through that one offering we have perfection of access to

God, for we come to God now by way of a cleansing which is immediate and continuous. We come to God by the way of a renewal of our spiritual life which is progressive. We come to God by way of a reconciliation which is constant.

It is the perfection of communion with God. Communion with God is, first, the sense that we have no secrets from Him, that He knows everything, all our sin and our failure:

> Thy kind but searching glance can scan
> The very wounds that shame would hide.

Do you know the restfulness of getting alone with someone to whom you have not to say anything about yourself because that someone knows? You do not, unless you know God. Do you know the awful agonizing awkwardness of attempting to make yourself known to your nearest and dearest? Fellowship with God means that there is no such agony, no such awkwardness; all things are naked and open before the eyes of Him with Whom I have to do. That is the doctrine that fills the soul with fear until the soul is reconciled; but it is the doctrine of infinite comfort to the soul that has rested on Christ.

It is not only a sense that we have no secrets from Him, this communion with God; it is also the desire and capacity to know His secrets, and the fact that He tells us His secrets. "The secret of the Lord is with them that fear Him."

Fellowship means, moreover, the appropriation in intercourse with Him of His wisdom, so that we need no longer blunder our way through darkness—He will direct; it means appropriation of His might, so that we need no longer struggle helplessly against difficulties—He will energize; it means appropriation of His love, so that we are never alone. In fellowship with our Lord we can say with our Lord, My Father doth not leave me alone!

All that issues in perfection of ability. Restored likeness to God is renewed fitness for co-operation with God, and that is in itself regained power.

The condition for appropriating the perfection provided is sanctification. There are different aspects of sanctification. Sanctification is separation to the will of God. It is wrought in the soul of man by the ministry of the Spirit. It is made possible by the work of the Son.

The reference to sanctification in this text is to that act of the Spirit, in response to faith, whereby we are accepted in the beloved. All such are adjusted to the will of God, perfect but not yet perfected; perfect in standing, relationship, and resources, but yet to be perfected in experience, in finality and complete realization.

The dwelling place of the saints is the holy place. They sit at the table of shewbread and have communion with God; they trim the golden lampstand and bear their testimony to the world; they stand before the golden altar of incense, God's remembrancers and intercessors; and, most wonderful of all, they pass beyond the holy place into the holy of holies, and, standing face to face with God hold communion unafraid, because on the mercy seat are the tokens of that one offering whereby He hath perfected for ever them that are sanctified.

This is our only perfection. Let us not presume upon it. Let us not repose our confidence in anything else, not in our Christian service, not in our preaching, or our work; for at the last we shall come home, and we shall do, saying:

> Nothing in my hand I bring;
> Simply to Thy Cross I cling!
> Naked, come to Thee for dress;
> Helpless, look to Thee for grace:
> Foul, I to the fountain fly;
> Wash me, Saviour, or I die!

I think that will be the last prayer I shall ever pray, and it will be answered, "For by one offering He hath perfected for ever them that are sanctified"!

This is not only our only perfection, it is our sufficient perfection. Let us perfectly trust it. Let us answer all its demands, that we may realize all its power. Let no doubt of the efficacy of the one offering lurk in the heart, and so we shall enter into the very peace of God.

CHAPTER III

FALSE FIRE

And Nadab and Abihu, the sons of Aaron, took each of them his censer, and put fire therein, and laid incense thereon, and offered strange fire before the Lord, which He had not commanded them. And there came forth fire from before the Lord, and devoured them, and they died before the Lord. Then Moses said unto Aaron, This is it that the Lord spake, saying, I will be sanctified in them that come nigh Me, and before all the people I will be glorified. And Aaron held his peace.
LEVITICUS 10: 1-3.

To understand the story of Nadab and Abihu, so far as it has any value for us, it is necessary to recognize the situation in its widest aspect. While the preacher of olden times declared that the eyes of the fool are in the ends of the earth, and thereby indicated the unutterable folly of gazing at the far distances while the near and the immediate is neglected, it is nevertheless true that the near things may be most woefully misinterpreted unless we take in the wider range of vision and see them in relation thereto.

That is particularly the case in such a story as that of Nadab and Abihu, intermixed as it is with the code of laws, and being a brief historical narrative telling how, when the people were coming to consciousness of their national existence, and at the very commencement of the observance of all the symbolic ritual which had been provided for them, two men ministering in the holy place were suddenly smitten with death.

We must begin at the Divine standpoint, and in order to understand this swift and fiery judgment we must see not merely Aaron and his sons, not merely the encamped tribes of the children of Israel, but the whole wide world, and we must see that world as loved by God. We must remind ourselves as we approach this Old Testament story that the declaration of the New Testament revelation was as true then as when the New Testament writer penned it, the declaration that "God so loved the world that He gave His only-begotten Son." All the peoples were loved by God, and of all of them He thought, and for all of them He wrought in all His dealings with the Hebrew people.

This nation had been created by God for the blessing of that world which He loved. Through strange and devious ways had the Hebrew people been brought to this hour. With the infinite majesty of perfect workmanship, which we sometimes count almost unutterable slowness, God had moved to that moment; from the hour in which He spoke in the soul of one man in Ur of the Chaldees and called him to the high venture of faith, to become a pilgrim seeking the establishment of the Divine order in the world and the building of the city of God; through those strange and troublous times of the history of his son, through the long sojourn in Egypt, and now in bringing the people unto Himself and so creating a nation, not in order to have some one people upon which to lavish His love, but in order to have a nation through which He might manifest His love for all the nations of the world.

Thus we come to the third circle, an inner circle, the circle of the priesthood, the circle of those who in this wonderful economy had been set apart for specific work, the work of mediating between these people comprising the new-created nation and their God, the men whose work should be that of intercession, the men who were to be admitted to the holy place to stand in the presence of God and there to intercede on behalf of men, the men who were to move out from the holy place into the presence of the multitudes, and there intercede with men on behalf of God. Thus we see the mediating priesthood at the center of the national life, the national life at the center of all the world; the nation created for the world, the priesthood created for the nation.

The world needed one thing supremely, to live by the law of God. "All souls are Mine," said a later prophet of these people: His by creation and by preservation. All men are perfectly known to His heart; His heart is the heart of love; His law for men is the only perfect law of their lives; the world therefore needs, and waits for the law of God. Within that wider world there now existed the nation; its specific equipment for the fulfilment of the Divine purpose lay in the fact that the law of God had been given directly to them, that they might know it, that they might obey it, that they might be transformed by it into the very likeness of their God, and so reveal to the world the breath, beauty, and beneficence of the Divine Kingdom.

Yet, again, at the heart of the nation, associated with its symbolic ritual and worship, there existed this priesthood, having as its final responsibility the necessity for the strictest observance of the law of God, the most entire abandonment to the will of God, in order that it might mediate between God and His own nation, and that in order that the nation incarnating His will might be the means of blessing to the nations lying beyond.

What Nadab and Abihu did that day must be measured by these larger issues, for a disobedient priesthood means a corrupted nation, and a corrupted nation means a wronged world. This indeed is the story of the ultimate temporary failure of the Hebrew people: corrupted in its priesthood, therefore in its national life, therefore failing to fulfil its mission in the world. The final example of the failure is that of the refusal of the Messiah. The whole story of it is written in those brief, striking words of John, "He came unto His own, and His own received Him not." A corrupted priesthood, Sadducean, demoralized, departed from the place of loyalty to God; a corrupted nation under the influence of such a priesthood resulted in the refusal of the One toward Whom the whole economy had moved, and, therefore, so far as the Hebrew people were concerned, the world was wronged and robbed and degraded. The world triumph of Messiah will not result from Israel's realization, but from God's overruling grace, whereby Israel itself will presently be restored. The triumph will be the triumph of grace.

In view of these wider responsibilities we can understand the immediateness and severity of this swift judgment at the very commencement of the national life. As to the exact form of the strange fire which was offered speculation is unnecessary and valueless. The facts are sufficiently patent for our instruction. They "offered strange fire before the Lord, which He had not commanded them. And there came forth fire from before the Lord, and devoured them, and they died before the Lord." Men appointed to the most sacred service, rendered the service, but rendered the service in disobedience, and were consumed.

We are far removed from the Hebrew ritual; the chapter which was read in our hearing was a little wearisome to some of us; it seemed almost meaningless—a chapter of offerings, goats and rams, ritual and ceremonial; and we sighed with relief that we had escaped these things, and in some senses quite properly so; but let us not forget the illuminative word of the New Testament concerning these things, for they were the "shadow of the good things to come." While it is perfectly true that they were only shadows, and that when that is come which is substance, the shadow is of no value; nevertheless, the shadow demonstrates the substance. There can be no shadow apart from substance. The photograph demonstrates the person of whom it is but a shadow; you will hold the photograph and look on it, and love to look on it, until he comes of whom it is the shadow, and then you are independent of the shadow; but the shadow demonstrates the substance, for there could have been no such picture apart from the person. We are living under the Covenant of the Substance. We have nothing to do with this ritual, these ceremonies, censers, fires, and this material incense.

We are unconsciously inclined, it may be, to boast our freedom from these things. Let our boasting be intelligent. We are set free from the shadows only because the substance has come; those who live in the presence of the Substance have a far greater responsibility than those who live in the shadow. All of which means, not that the teaching of this Old Testament story has no application to us, but that the service which we are called on to render is more sacred, and the responsibilities are more solemn, and, consequently, the impact of this story on the soul of an honest man will be a forceful one. As Christ is greater than Moses, so is the responsibility of the priests of the new covenant greater than that of Nadab and Abihu.

Let us, then, with all solemnity consider the teaching of this story in regard to two matters: first, the sin which was thus judged as the fire of the Lord came out and devoured Nadab and Abihu; and, second, the responsibility which that judgment reveals.

Let us consider what the sin of Nadab and Abihu was externally, actually; what it was inspirationally; and, finally, what it was influentially.

What was it externally? Let us at once admit that it is most difficult to answer that question. These men were in the holy place, arrayed in holy garments for actual service, for that is the meaning of the phrase, "they drew near, and carried them in their coats out of the camp"—and they were rendering holy service. It was a great hour in the religious life of the nation, when the glory of the Lord was manifested; and the people were hushed and awed into the very solemnity of worship. It was then, in the holy place, arrayed in holy garments, occupied in holy service, that these men sinned the sin which was immediately punished by death. How are we to account for it? Let us glance on to a later chapter in this book of Leviticus.

In the sixteenth chapter we have an account of the ceremonial arrangements for the great Day of Atonement, and in the course of that account we find instructions given to the priests concerning their entering into the holy place and the burning of incense: "He shall take a censer full of coals of fire off the altar before the Lord, and his hands full of sweet incense beaten small, and bring it within the veil." A remarkable fact is that the chapter thus giving instructions concerning the Day of Atonement and how the High Priest must enter in and offer incense is prefaced with these words, "And the Lord spake unto Moses, after the death of the two sons of Aaron, when they drew near before the Lord, and died." Here, then, perhaps we have some light on what happened that day. I think it is not an inaccurate deduction that in that hour of religious enthusiasm these men placed on their censers fire that they obtained from somewhere other than the altar of God. They did a right thing in a wrong way. An amazing fact! So amazing that we are at first inclined to revolt against the judgment. Let us, however, ponder the matter more carefully. How came it that these men did a right thing in a wrong way? It is never the act that is the important thing, but rather the reason that lies behind the act. God is a God of justice, and He weighs actions by investigating motives. What lay behind this strange act that seems to be so harmless? The fact that in high enthusiasm these men rushed in their holy garments into the holy place and took fire other than that which came from the altar of God shows that they were yielding to wrong motives. I crave your very patient following or we shall miss the very core of this matter. Was it a wrong motive to desire to burn incense before the Lord? It depends on the reason for the desire. Perhaps it was excitement that made them careless of the moment of the Divine provision and the Divine requirement.

There is a dark hint in this story. I would not care to overemphasize it, but there is no escape from the suggestiveness of the fact that subsequently "the Lord spake unto Aaron, saying, Drink no wine nor strong drink, thou, nor thy sons with thee, when ye go into the tent of meeting, that ye die not: it shall be a statute for ever." It is at least significant that the solemn warning is placed in immediate relation with the story of the death of Nadab and Abihu. It at least suggests that when they went in they may have done so under the influence of some false stimulant; that they may not have been drunk but had been drinking wine, forgetting the necessity in the exercise of their holy office of having their spirits clear of everything that could influence them in any direction, save under the complete control of the God Whom they served. In the excitement of passionate desire to take part in the awful hour of Divine manifestation they snatched strange fire and offered it; and fire from God consumed them. It may be that it was merely carelessness, that they did not pay sufficient attention to the Divine requirements. Or, again, it may be that it was a matter of convenience, adaptation, that word which may tell the story of the ruin of the work of God in the world as well as the story of its victory. All seemed so harmless, whatever the motive, whether of excitement, carelessness, or adaptation and convenience. But these men were acting on their own initiative, and not under the control of God. God was dethroned, all unconsciously to themselves it may be; and self was enthroned, and that in the holy place. At the center of the religious life of the nation the priest himself had failed to believe and obey. It is not said that Nadab and Abihu were lost. In all probability they went straight into heaven. We have nothing to do with the matter of their individual salvation. At the heart of the national life it was necessary that the lesson should immediately be impressed on the priest and on the people, that men must do God's work in God's way; there must be no deflection from the Divine appointment and arrangement.

Sin in the priesthood must produce sin in the people. If the priesthood yield to the false authority of some excitement, some expediency, then they will exercise false authority and inspire false activity. All the subsequent history of these people is full of illustrations of that great principle, and we may tell the story of the Hebrew people by declaring that they sought the Divine goal in a wrong way and consequently never found the goal they sought.

The story speaks eloquently to us. It deals, first of all, with the question of the end and the means. It exposes and gives the lie to the whole heresy which is the heart and soul of Jesuitry, that the end justifies the means, that in order to reach the Divine goal we may travel any way, that in order to accomplish the Divine purposes we are allowed to choose any method. The essential lie of that heresy is that the right end is ever reached by the wrong means. It never can be, it never has been, it never will be. For the moment it may seem that deflection from the strict path of the Divinely marked out economy may not matter much, because we are arriving; but wait the long issues, and we discover that there has been no arrival. We cannot build the temple of truth on a foundation of fraud. We cannot erect the palace of purity on a foundation of corruption. We cannot accomplish the building of the city of God save as we are true to the Divinely prepared plan. We cannot glorify God by incense whose smoke arises from false fire, from fire which has not been taken from the altar of sacrifice. Therefore, to adopt any method in worship or in work which is a departure by a hairbreadth from the Divine is to defeat the purpose of effort.

We learn from this story, therefore, that the test of means is motive. The motive of reaching God's goal is not enough. The motive which permits an action which in itself is born of thinking or planning or arranging which leaves God out of account is in itself untrue, and though it looks toward God's goal it never travels there. There are thousands of men to-day in England who actually desire the coming of the Kingdom of God, but they are doing nothing to bring it about. They pray for it. They would be willing to vote for it if we could have an election on the basis of its propositions. But in their own lives, in their own planning and arrangements of business, of dwelling places, of friendships, they forget God. Then no voting will help God, and no effort that they may make will bring the Kingdom of God any nearer. God refuses to be distanced to the ultimate from putting forth energy in the life of any man; He must be there at the moment, must be consulted immediately. It is not enough to join with the multitudes on the great day and offer any fire in order to glorify God; the fire must be fire God-appointed, it must be fire that comes from the altar.

To us in this age the will of God is being revealed, not by laws written on tables of stone, not by sign or symbol or ritual, not by an order of priests within the church, nor by an order of prophets. Within the sacred enclosure of the Church to-day there are those whom God has called to prophetic work, but it is ever that of interpretation of the last and final speech of God to men through His incarnate Son. Therefore, I say, to us the will of God is revealed, not even by the prophet, but by the ever-present Spirit Who takes of the things of Christ which are the things of God and interprets them to us. We are not to be bound by the hard and fast requirements of an ecclesiastical system; we are not to be bound to some particular form of ritual; we are to wait before every action, and before every enterprise, and to inquire in the very moment of our desire to serve God, What is the mind of the Lord? and we are to seek the answer from the ever-present Spirit of God. To us to cease to wait is to cease to go. To go without waiting before the Lord for instruction is never to go at all. Moreover, it is to fall under the displeasure of God and to be in danger of being consumed by fire from God, and that in the interest of the world for which Christ died, and which God loves.

To state the responsibility which that swift judgment reveals to us is to take the story and look at it from the standpoint which is revealed in the last words of my text. This is the lesson which the judgment teaches.

"Then Moses said unto Aaron, This is it that the Lord spake, saying, I will be sanctified in them that come nigh Me, and before all the people I will be glorified."

All I have been trying to say is there involved. Before all people He will be glorified; that is the ultimate purpose, and therefore He will be sanctified in them that come nigh Him. Those who stand in His presence for service must be those who have enthroned Him, those who inquire at His gates, those who obey His behests. He will be sanctified in them. They shall be the sanctuary in which He dwells. Within them He will be sanctified, enthroned, inquired of, obeyed. And for what purpose? "Before all the people I will be glorified." God must be glorified in the priests who represent Him. God must be glorified in the service which the priest is rendering. God must be glorified in His own work, which must be done in His way. God must be glorified through that work which He will most assuredly do when His laws are observed. The teaching of the story of responsibility is that in our worship and in our work, we are not merely to seek for the ultimate, far-distant realization of the Divine glory, we are to seek that glory in the methods we employ. We believe in the "far-off Divine event to which the whole creation moves," but it is not enough to desire that event, and then proceed to attempt to realize it in our own way and by our own wit and wisdom. The one far-off Divine event to which the whole creation moves can be realized by God only in fellowship with men, by men in fellowship with God. The deflection of the servant of God by a single hairbreadth from the Divinely marked path becomes ultimately an infinite and abysmal distance between that worker and God. When the skilful engineer would drive his tunnel through the mountain, the deflection of half an inch at the commencement, what matters it? Everything! For the next half inch will conform to the first one, and the third to the second. So here, at the beginning, two sons of Aaron, in undue excitement of wine, or carelessly, or for convenience and greater speed, did enthrone their thinking above the Divine command, and fire from the Lord consumed them in order that the priests might know forever that they themselves must believe and obey if the work of God is to be completed work.

    This teaching may be applied by all Christian workers. Suffer me the broadest of all applications. The Church of God must not only be true to the work of God in the world as to the general conception; she must also be true to the work of God in the world as to the particular methods which He did ordain. So surely as we imagine that we can improve on the Divine method in the instructions left us by our Lord Himself and by His holy apostles in these sacred writings of the Scriptures, so surely we shall find that while we are desiring the accomplishment of the Divine purpose, yet all the while we are preventing it. That is the solemn lesson concerning our responsibility.

This is without question a story full of solemnity. It gives pause to all who are called to service, as it reminds us of the necessity for a constant and sustained loyalty to God in our methods of service. It calls the Christian Church ever and anon to halt in her progress in order that she may readjust her relationships with her Lord. It calls us to examine every organization that is springing up, lest haply we find that they are not in accordance with the Divine method, even though they desire the realization of the Divine purpose. I am not at all sure that if the Church would give herself to such solemn consideration and readjustment, she would not find many organizations which are merely fungus growths, sapping her life, and contributing nothing to the work of God.

When we turn from the larger outlook to the more particular, with what awful solemnity does this word speak to us of our work for God, and of the sources of the inspiration of our work for God. The dark appalling hint of the story needs emphasizing in all its applications; the worker for God must never touch God's work in the strength of any false stimulant. To attempt God's work under the stimulus of passion for fame, or desire for notoriety, is to burn false fire on the altar. To us, I repeat, prescribed forms are no more; but the living and ever-present Spirit of God is with us, and the greatest matter in all our Christian service is that we seek to know His will and submit ourselves to His direction.

Yet I cannot end at that point. There is one other word that must be uttered. So solemn is the story that not only is it calculated to give us pause, it is liable to make us so full of fear that we hardly dare touch our work. That is exactly how Ithamar and Eleazar felt, that they dared not continue their work. Moses instituted investigation, inquired why they had been disobedient and had failed to observe things of privilege within the holy place; and the answer was that the day had been so appalling that they were afraid; and in grace, on that explanation, they were excused for the failure. But I think the story of Ithamar and Eleazar is told that we may be warned that though it is a terrible thing in many senses to do God's work in the world we must not neglect it. We have no right to say that because the responsibility is terrific we dare not approach it. He has made us a kingdom of priests, and it is not merely the saving of our own souls that is in His view, but the need of the world beyond. Therefore, with all solemnity and with hushed spirits, we must take up our work, praying ever to be delivered from the sin of burning false fire in the presence of God.

CHAPTER IV

SPIRITUAL LEPROSY

And the Lord spake unto Moses, saying, This shall be the law of the leper in the day of his cleansing.
LEVITICUS 14:1, 2.

LEPROSY REMAINS UNTIL THIS HOUR MORE OR LESS A MYStery to medical science.* In the New Year's Honors List a name included was that of Dr. George Turnei, now Sir George Turner, whose story is one of splendid heroism and of pathetic interest. In Pretoria he did arduous work among the lepers, and on reaching the age limit gave himself to bacteriological research in the laboratories of this country, inspired by the ambition to find some remedy for the disease. Suddenly he discovered that he had contracted the disease himself, and now for over two years has been working in seclusion toward the same end.

Dr. Gerhard H. A. Hansen, of Bergen, Norway, who died last year, discovered the bacillus of leprosy, which was previously unknown. The exact value of the discovery cannot yet be known, but it is recognized as an important contribution.

These preliminary references are made in order to emphasize the mystery of the disease. It is, to say the least,

* Medical science has made great strides toward the conquest of leprosy since this was written. It is now widely known as Hansen's disease from the name of the discoverer of its bacillus.

SPIRITUAL LEPROSY

an interesting fact, to which attention was drawn in *The Times* in an article on Sir George Turner, that the problem of the remedy for leprosy is an exceedingly difficult one because of the fact that none of the lower animals has yet been found to be capable of contracting the disease.

The Hebrew word for leprosy is derived from a root which means to strike down. It was looked upon as a stroke of God. There was, however, nothing in the law itself to give any ground for the view that it was always such. In the thirteenth and fourteenth chapters of Leviticus, which contain the law of the leper, leprosy is dealt with on the ground of health, simply as a disease; yet it is quite evident that its mysterious character—its unknown origin and its insidious and resistless progress—made it the fit type or symbol of sin.

Lange graphically describes it as "a speaking picture of sin, and of evil the punishment of sin—the plastic manifestation, the medical phantom, or representation of all the misery of sin."

Jewish expositors of these Scriptures were quite explicit as to their spiritual suggestiveness. In dealing with these particular laws, one of them said, "If a man considers this, he will be humbled and ashamed on account of his sin; since every sin is a leprosy; a spot upon his soul."

The study of the law of the leper has for us a twofold value. Its first teaching has to do with the actual fact of the Divine interest in the physical well-being of men. The general good of humanity was sought by the segregation of the leper. The individual interest was safeguarded in the extreme caution observed in order that no person should thus be cut off from communion with the people unless he were actually leprous. I am not now dealing with that aspect of the teaching of these two chapters. I should, however, like to say so much as this in passing, that in each of these matters we have very much yet to learn. We are a long way behind the Hebrew economy in the recognition of God's interest in the affairs of man's physical well-being, and in the application of the principles to which I have referred—the necessity for the separation of all those in the grip of a disease which constitutes a danger to the community. We are slowly moving toward it, but very slowly. There are some who describe legislation along these lines as grandmotherly. If it be grandmotherly, then may God increase it! We need to learn a good deal also before we arrive at the full realization of the importance of the second of these principles, that there must be strict justice: no person must be cut off from fellowship unless he actually is a peril to society.

However, when we turn from these general principles to the actual disease of leprosy, the only application possible to us is the symbolic, and that is supreme. There can be no reading of these chapters, especially of the fourteenth, without realizing that while in these laws there was provision for the physical well-being of the community, there was also a remarkable recognition of the spiritual.

It is important, therefore, that we consider quite briefly, and yet most carefully, the relation between the two parts of this law of the leper as we find it in Leviticus, chapters thirteen and fourteen. The thirteenth chapter is diagnostic. There is nothing more in it than instructions by which the priest was to discover whether what appeared to be leprosy was actually leprosy. In the thirteenth chapter there is no gleam of hope for the leper. The symbolic value of the chapter, therefore, is that sin demands the separation of the sinner, and is incurable by human agency.

Chapter fourteen opens with the words of my text: "And the Lord spake unto Moses, saying, This shall be the law of the leper in the day of his cleansing." The careful reader will immediately be arrested by the assumption that the leper can be cleansed. The thirteenth chapter contains no gleam of hope for the leper; but the fourteenth opens in the full flood of the light of hope. In the thirteenth the priest is to distinguish and differentiate and separate, and make possible the return to the camp of the man who is not suffering from leprosy. The fourteenth says, "This shall be the law of the leper in the day of his cleansing." This is an admission of the possibility of what is not in the power of man to provide or produce. The chapter then contains instructions for that ceremonial procedure by which the cleansed man is to be restored to the privileges of the camp and of the tabernacle, the privileges of the economy of the theocracy, and fellowship with God in personal and direct worship. So far as the two chapters constitute a part of the Levitical code, we see that this code distinctly taught that leprosy is entirely incurable by human action; but it also recognized the fact that it may be cured by Divine action. As these chapters are viewed as symbolic, their suggestion concerning sin is the same: sin is incurable by any human process, but it is curable within the Divine economy.

We at once recognize a gap between the two chapters, and the gap is great. Between the thirteenth and fourteenth chapters of this shadow of the old economy stands our great Christ, our great High Priest. In the thirteenth we have the unveiling of sin under the figure of leprosy, and in the fourteenth we have an unveiling of the way of salvation in the picturesque, and suggestive if vanishing, ritual of the old economy.

Let us, then, consider what these chapters suggest pictorially. Our line of consideration will be twofold: first, leprosy as the symbol of sin; and, second, the way of cleansing from sin as revealed in the symbolic ceremonial.

Leprosy stands as a symbol of sin in four distinct particulars: first, in the mystery of its origin; second, in the method of its manifestation; third, in the nature of its effects; and, finally, in its treatment in this Hebrew economy.

First, in the mystery of its origin. So far as leprosy is concerned, that may be dismissed by the simplest of statements already made, that even until this hour of scientific advancement, man has not been able to discover the origin of leprosy. There is nothing more appalling, shall I say, nothing more perplexing, nothing more certain, than the mystery of sin. I know we have our doctrine of original sin—in passing I should like to say that original sin is not a Scriptural phrase and therefore I hold no brief for it. But, granted the doctrine, believing in the doctrine in certain senses as I most certainly do, let it be remembered that it does not explain the nature of the persistent presence of sin in every human being; it states only the fact that sin is there, that in some form, sin is discovered in every human being. Moreover, it admits the fundamental truth that in human life sin is superinduced. The poetic declaration, "To err is human," is not true, though it is perfectly true if by human we mean humanity as we find it to-day. But if we think of humanity as in the purpose and economy of God, it is not human to err, not human to sin. Sin is a poison, sin is something within the soul that atrophies its powers and prevents the realization of all the deep and profound meaning of life. It is not part of essential humanity. Whatever terms we may employ in dealing with sin, we must remember that sin is superinduced.

Sin is a spiritual malady, the physical is but the expression of it; behind every physical act of sin is the spiritual attitude. There is no sin of the flesh which is not inspired by sin of the spirit. I cannot sin with my hand until I have sinned with my heart. I cannot sin physically, save as I have sinned spiritually.

Then is it inherited? If so, how? The Bible teaches that every man is offspring of God in his first creation, in his spirit life. Or is the spiritual malady of sin contracted in man? If so, when? I would have you clearly to understand that I am asking questions I do not propose to answer, for the simple reason that I cannot answer them. I ask them in order to affirm that there is no answer. Neither the theologian nor the philosopher has ever answered either of these questions. If sin is inherited, how is sin transmitted in the spirit realm? I am not spiritually the son of the man whose name I bear. "We had the *fathers of our flesh* to chasten us, and we gave them reverence, shall we not much rather be in subjection unto *the Father of spirits* and live?" Mark the clear distinction. If sin is of the spirit, and in the spirit, then some evil bacillus has been introduced poisoning the spirit.

The nature of that poison is discovered in Biblical definitions. Paul speaks of "the mystery of lawlessness"; John declares "sin is lawlessness." In the first we have the admission of the mystery. In the second we have a statement as to the true nature of sin. The sins which we denounce are but symptoms; sin lies deeper. Sin is "lawlessness," which does not mean being without law, but being in revolt against law. This evil germ within the spirit of man that affects all his mind and heart and soul is lawlessness; it has a thousand manifestations, but it is always the same in essence. It is indeed the *mystery* of lawlessness. How is it, why is it, that all men find this principle at work within the soul? I recognize the mystery; but I face the fact. As leprosy is a mystery as to its origin, so also is sin; but it is an appalling fact.

Leprosy is a symbol of sin in the method of its manifestation. The first appearance is at times discoverable only by the trained eye. Dr. Turner was a specialist, having a trained eye, yet the disease was on him and manifesting itself before he knew it. One morning, while shaving, he caught sight of marks on his hands that arrested him; he was a leper! The first symptoms are discoverable only to the trained eye. In the little child there may be a thousand things that you count sin that are not proofs of sin at all; a child romancing up to a certain age is not sinning. It is exercising a faculty of mind which belongs to it.

The time comes when the first sign of sin is manifested in the child; it is lawlessness.

This leprosy of lawlessness is invariably progressive, never halting; it steals insidiously forward with varying degrees of speed, until, at last, the whole man is corrupt, mastered—strange paradox—by lawlessness; the whole life is in revolt against authority, against government.

Leprosy is the symbol of sin in the nature of its effects. It excludes from fellowship with our fellow men. It renders the victim loathsome even to his fellow men. Not always in the more vulgar forms of sensuality, but with cold, hard, cynical, devilish self-centeredness, infinitely more loathsome than vulgar forms of sensuality. Sin, like leprosy, ultimately renders its victim insensible to the pain of his own disease. We have in the Scriptures of Truth such arresting phrases as "hardened," "a conscience seared," "past feeling"! Leprosy ultimately completely destroys the physical frame; so also sin ultimately completely destroys the spirit life, and all its powers.

Once again, leprosy is the symbol of sin in its treatment in the Hebrew economy. Why was the leper separated not only from man but from God also as to outward worship? Surely because that in itself it was a symbol of sin, and there must be recognition of the fact that sin cuts a man off from fellowship with God, dims the vision, makes him insensible to the fact of God. That necessarily means separation from the camp, exclusion from the fellowship of those who see the City of God and strive for its building; and that without respect of persons.

Sin is an appalling mystery as to its origin in the individual soul and life; in itself it is lawlessness, revolt against the law of God; and it expresses itself in a thousand ways as revolt against the law of man. Our age is particularly characterized by the restless spirit of lawlessness. Everywhere there are signs of mental, moral, social, theological, lawlessness; the refusal to recognize authority, or to be bound even by contracts which men make between themselves. Lawlessness is of the very essence of sin, a poison at the heart of man, a virus at the center of human life, that which prevents the realization of high ideals in individuals and in humanity. It is that which ultimately destroys man and destroys nations. I have never yet heard of a person being asked to sign a pledge against it. This is a very significant fact, revealing, first of all, that men do not as a rule deal with sin, but with sins; not with the malady but with the symptoms; we are always in danger of dealing with the surface of things, instead of getting down to the central trouble. On the other hand, perhaps, no pledge has ever been asked against it because of the subconscious conviction of humanity that it is something with which humanity cannot deal.

Is there a way of cleansing for the leper? Is there a way of cleansing for the sinner? Here we turn to the New Testament. I referred to a gap between the thirteenth and fourteenth chapters of Leviticus, and I declared that Christ stands in that gap, in the spiritual realm. In the fourteenth chapter we have the poetic symbols of His work, quite simple figures intended for that kindergarten period in the history of the people of God, yet all eloquent.

Passing into the New Testament, I find lepers, but I also find Christ; and the first general remark I desire to make is that never under any circumstances do we read in the New Testament of Christ *healing* a leper; never under any circumstances do we read of any writer describing a leper as being *healed*. The one word uniformly used is *cleansed*. That there is a distinction is evident from the fact when John asked, "Art Thou He that cometh, or look we for another?" Jesus said, Tell John the things you have seen, that "the blind receive their sight, and the lame walk, the lepers are *cleansed*, and the deaf hear, and the dead are raised up, and the poor have good tidings preached to them." At the foot of the mountain of beatitudes, when the Lord had uttered the ethic that remains to this day startling and awful in its white holiness, He was immediately met by a leper, who said to Him, "Lord, if Thou wilt, Thou canst make me clean." The hand of Christ was immediately stretched out, and the leper who could not be touched, was touched, the word was spoken, "I will; be thou made clean," and the leper was cleansed of his leprosy. Exactly the same scene was repeated later in one of the cities to which Jesus went. Again a band of ten lepers came, and He cleansed them all. These stories of the cleansing of the lepers must be interpreted as all the stories of healing are interpreted. According to New Testament teaching, Jesus never wrought a physical miracle wholly within the realm of the physical; such wonders were always associated with a spiritual activity far more wonderful. "Son, thy sins are forgiven," said He to the man sick of the palsy; and the people complained, "Why doth this man thus speak? he blasphemeth; who can forgive sins but One, even God." Jesus replied to them, "Whether is easier, to say to the sick of the palsy, Thy sins are forgiven; or to say, Arise, and take up thy bed, and walk? But that ye may know that the Son of man hath power on earth to forgive sins . . . I say unto thee, Arise, take up thy bed, and go unto thy house." In the ministry of Jesus there was perpetual relationship between the physical and the spiritual; every physical miracle of healing or of cleansing was an outward sign of the spiritual marvel that He was able to work in the souls of men.

I glance back to Leviticus, to the fourteenth chapter, with which I am not proposing to deal in detail. Therein two great movements are revealed in the law of the leper on the day of his cleansing; they may thus be summarized. First, the priest meets the leper without the camp and leads him back into the camp. Second, the priest within the camp offers on behalf of the leper certain offerings, and anoints him with oil, and sets him at the door of the tent of meeting, the place of fellowship with God. The symbolism is perfect.

In the old economy the priest went without the camp where the leper had been driven on account of his leprosy, to certify the leper's cleansing, not to cleanse him; he could do no more than that. He then observed the ceremony which symbolized the way of his spiritual cleansing, and in doing so employed two birds, one to be sacrificed, the other to be set free, and cedarwood, scarlet, and hyssop. Do not be afraid of these pictures, they are very suggestive. The birds were for sacrifice, the cedarwood was the symbol of strength, for it was incorruptible wood; the scarlet, forevermore the color of earthly glory, spoke of life and health and beauty; the hyssop was the plant of fragrance and of healing. All these things in the old economy were brought by the leper; but none of them cleansed him, neither did the priest cleanse him; but the man, having been cleansed by some act of God, was now to celebrate the physical cleansing, and that by such ceremony as suggested the method of spiritual cleansing. The disparity between all this and the method of Christ is more eloquent than the comparison. Our High Priest does not come without the camp to certify the leper cleansed; He comes without the camp to cleanse the leper. He comes to the place where the leper is cast out, the place where the leper is alone, excommunicated from the holy place, ostracized by all his familiar friends, shut out in his own loathsomeness for the sake of the health of those left behind. Coming to the leper there, in some infinite and amazing mystery, Christ takes into His own heart and nature the virus and poison of the leprosy, cancels it and by passion, by blood, the outward symbol of the profounder spiritual passion makes it not to be; and, lo, the leper is cleansed. His flesh comes again as the flesh of a little child, and the spirit that was lawless utters its first word, and it is a word of submission: "Lord, what wilt Thou have me to do?" That is the death of lawlessness and the beginning of the law-abiding life. Our High Priest comes not to certify the leper cleansed, but to cleanse the leper, and to bring that leper back into the camp, into the theocratic economy, into right relationship with God, into the Kingdom of God.

The priest not only brings the cleansed man back into the camp, he sets him at the door of the tent of meeting. Again we have the pictorial suggestions. In the old economy the priest offered the guilt offering, speaking of the reparation the man was making to God; he anointed the man with oil on ear and hand and foot, indicating his new consecration, then presented the Sin Offering and the Burnt Offering and the Meal Offering for him. Mark again the disparity: in the old economy the leper himself had to provide the offerings and bring the oil. In the new economy the one and only Priest, provides against every aspect of human sin, all which aspects were suggested in these offerings of the old pictorial method. Sin is fraud; the man who is lawless is robbing God, defrauding God of His rights, rights that are always beneficent in purpose toward man himself, so that man robbing God of His rights is destroying himself in the infinite mystery of his being. For that the Guilt Offering or the Trespass Offering was provided. Sin is not only fraud, it is defilement finding its way into the life with its pollution and vileness. The Sin Offering provided for the removal of defilement. Sin is also failure in life, failure in the realization of the real meaning of life. The Burnt Offering suggests sacrifice that puts away the defilement, and issues in new dedication of the life. Sin is also failure in service. The Meal Offering covers it.

Let the shadows pass and summarize the whole suggestiveness by declaring that our High Priest in His one offering for sin meets every aspect of human sin and deals with it. In this strange and wonderful economy of grace the offerings and the oil are provided by the Priest, forfeited life for life forfeit, spiritual power for spiritual death. A man is not a Christian merely because Christ has stood between him and some ultimate punishment. A man is a Christian when he has received from Christ the gift of life whereby lawlessness is checked, halted, mastered, dealt with, and life is related anew to God.

There is another mystery, the mystery of godliness. The New Testament speaks of both. The mystery of lawlessness has many manifestations. It manifests itself in one man in reckless sensuality, in the plunge into the vulgar and bestial. It manifests itself in another man in cynical selfishness, selfishness which is so absolutely selfish that it dare not sin vulgarly, has not the courage to do it. Lawlessness expresses itself in one man in actual murder, and in another man in a cynical contempt for suffering and indifference to the agonies of men. As God is my witness I do not know which is the more terrible manifestation of lawlessness, but the latter I think. I can understand the rush of blood, the red passion that strikes a blow; that is lawlessness, and it is terrible; but, oh, the terror of the form of lawlessness which has so little recognition of the throne of God, and so little recognition of the claims of humanity, that it is content to live for self and minister to self, shutting its doors that it may never see the objectionable things outside. There may be all the perfumes of Arabia, and all the upholstery of Damascus; but in the sight of heaven whose God is love, and Who is prepared to die for humanity, it is the very ultimate of hell, and the most terrible form of lawlessness. The self-centered cynical man will say hard things about the sensualist and the murderer. We still measure ourselves among ourselves, and compare ourselves as with ourselves; and we find satisfaction while thus we put the little measurements of dust on our lives; but all the while God sees the leprosy of lawlessness and the rottenness of our godless culture.

But there is another mystery. "Great is the mystery of

godliness; He Who was manifested in the flesh, justified in the spirit, seen of angels [messengers], preached among the nations, believed on in the world, received up in glory." This mystery of godliness is also spiritual. There has been one manifestation of it in human history. Jesus Christ lived and wrought and served, not independently, but dependently on God. He manifested in the midst of human history the glory and beauty of true life, law-abiding and submissive. But He did infinitely more, He went outside the camp to meet the leper, and in some wonderful mystery of infinite compassion to place His pure life at the disposal of the impure man, so that being communicated to him his leprosy may be cleansed, and the man made to live.

That mystery of godliness has been given to us as the norm of life, the type of what God would have other men to be; but more, blessed be God, or I am left a leper: not the norm alone but the germ also, and that communicated to my soul, so that the lawlessness is subdued, made not to be; and my feet are turned into the way of the Divine commandment, and my life at last conformed to the good and perfect and acceptable will of God. There is no other name given under heaven among men whereby we can be saved.

CHAPTER V

SIN, SORROW, SILENCE

Scripture: PSALM 32.

WHOEVER WROTE THIS PSALM KNEW MUCH OF SPIRITUAL experience on ordinary human levels. It is difficult sometimes to understand how some of these psalms were written so long before the coming of Christ. They seem to have been written by men who were almost as familiar as we are with all the great facts of the grace of God, as that grace was made known in Christ Jesus.

Among all of them, I do not know one that has more of the evangelical spirit than this, the thirty-second. Who that knows anything of the abounding and abundant grace of God has not at some time or another found a suitable vehicle of expression in its language? Observe the experiences that thrill throughout it. Sin is here, not as a theory, but as an experience. It was written by a man who knew sin, who knew it in his own life, who knew its bitterness, its burden, its hatefulness; who had been very profoundly under conviction of sin.

Here, also, is the experience of sorrow, sorrow described in figurative language as the overflowing of waters; described, although not in words, yet inferentially, as the sweeping of a great storm; described, again, by inference as a prison house. All these figures are here, not actually named, but suggested by the terms that the psalmist used to describe his victory over sorrow.

The psalmist knew also that desolating experience of ignorance with which we are all familiar. I do not mean merely intellectual ignorance, but spiritual ignorance, the ignorance of not knowing which way to take, the ignorance of perplexity about the things of life created by the problems that vex the soul. All these experiences of the soul are grouped and referred to in this psalm.

Yet observe again that the things to which I have referred, sin as an experience, sorrow as an experience, ignorance or perplexity, or, if you will, silence—for I think the word "silence" is a most eloquent word to express what we feel when we do not see the way, or know the way, when there is no light upon the pathway, or voice speaking to us —sin, sorrow, silence; all the experiences of the human heart are here in order that over against them may be placed the things that correct them, the things that cancel them. If this man knew sin he knew forgiveness. If this man was familiar with sorrow he had experienced a wonderful succor. If this man was conscious of silence he had been brought into the place of instruction, and of a speech that had become to him the very guide and counsel of all his days.

Therefore, this is a psalm that thrills to tireless music, and makes its perpetual appeal to the heart of those who share these common human experiences.

Now, let us look a little more closely. First of all, observe its opening exclamation and its closing appeal. Between these we shall find a very definite movement of experience. When this man sat down to write this psalm he began with a doxology. It is the fashion of the Church to-day to close services with doxologies. The fashion of the Bible is to begin with the doxology. We find it in the psalms and in the epistles. There are doxologies at the close also, but the great writers of the Bible constantly began with a note of praise and gave their reasons for praise afterwards.

The first verse of the psalm reads thus:

> Blessed is he whose transgression is forgiven, whose sin is covered.

Whereas that may be a very accurate and beautiful sentence, in the Hebrew it reads somewhat differently; this is what the psalmist wrote:

> O the blessings of transgression forgiven, and sin covered.

As a matter of fact, in that first verse there is no personal pronoun. The psalmist was not describing an experience in which man has any place, or any part, except as the result of something that God has done for him, and provided for him.

It is an exclamation resulting from contemplation and meditation. All the experience which he was about to describe in the psalm found its vent in his opening doxology. The blessings are two: transgressing forgiven, and sin covered. Every form of sin is recognized in the course of the psalm. Presently there is a reference to iniquity. All these are different words, conveying different ideas of sin.

The Hebrew word, "transgression," means the actual, wilful wrongdoing of which a man is conscious, and of which he is guilty. "Sin" is the common Hebrew word which has the same significance as the common Greek word, namely, missing the mark. No day passes in my life in which I do not sin, which does not necessarily mean that I sin wilfully but that I come short of the glory, I fail of the highest, I do not attain unto the best. After thirty years at least of the experience of following Jesus Christ, the apostle had to say, "Not that I have already obtained, or am already made perfect. . . . I count not myself yet to have apprehended." In so much as I have not attained, in so much as I am not yet made perfect, in so much as I have not yet apprehended, I am a sinner, I miss the mark, I come short, I do not reach the standard.

There are thus two ideas in this opening doxology: one wilful and positive sin, the other, missing the mark, in which will may have no part. Both are dealt with; the transgression is forgiven, and missing the mark is covered. That is the opening exclamation. It is that of a man, conscious of God's infinite grace, of what someone has spoken of, and I think wonderfully spoken of, as "the incredible mercy of God."

O the blessings of transgression forgiven, and sin covered.

The psalm ends with an appeal.

Be glad in the Lord, and rejoice, ye righteous;
And shout for joy all ye that are upright in heart.

The opening exclamation and the closing appeal are closely linked. "Oh the blessings of transgression forgiven." "Be glad in the Lord, and rejoice, ye righteous." "Of sin covered." "Shout for joy, all ye that are upright in heart." The blessings of the forgiveness of transgression and of the covering of sin come from God, and in response to those blessings we are called on to be glad in the Lord, and to shout for joy.

Between that opening exclamation and that closing appeal we have the general movement of the psalm, a record of the experiences of life in sin, in sorrow, and in those silences in which the soul is ignorant as to the right way to go and the right thing to do.

First, as to sin. Everything is founded on a right relationship with God, which results from the activity of grace as expressed in the first verse. Moving out from that provision of grace, the psalmist deals with the individual. "Blessed is *the man*." In the first verse is an exclamation: "O the blessings," the blessings that God provides for the race; and consequently, of course, for individual men; but now, from that

SIN, SORROW, SILENCE

contemplation of the whole economy of God's grace, he passes to the individual soul.

> Blessed is the man unto whom the Lord imputeth not iniquity,
> And in whose spirit there is no guile.

Here the psalmist describes a man standing before a judge, the judge being the Lord, the judge being Jehovah. Here the psalmist describes a man acquitted by his judge: the Lord imputeth not iniquity. Here, moreover, the psalmist reveals the condition on which that judge will acquit the man, "in whose spirit there is no guile." Let it be remembered that we cannot have this second blessing apart from the first. There must be, first, the fact of the infinite blessings in the economy of God, of transgression forgiven, and of sin covered. That is taken for granted in the first outburst of praise. This psalm was written, if not consciously, yet most surely, under the shadow of the Cross. It could not have been written anywhere else. Nowhere else can we find the possibility of transgression being forgiven and sin being covered. Calvary, dark Calvary, with all its mystery of darkness and of light, of sin and of salvation, of the unveiling of sin in the light of the glory of God, and the unveiling of the grace of God against the dark background of sin. All that is expressed in the first verse; then we get to the second verse, and we find how God is prepared to deal with a man who is conscious of sin, of iniquity, which is perverseness, crookedness, the life out of the straight.

This verse always comforts my heart, because the psalmist said: "Blessed is the man unto whom the Lord imputeth not iniquity." He did not say, Blessed is the man unto whom his neighbor imputeth not iniquity. I am very thankful for that. He did not say, Blessed is the man unto whom those to whom he ministers impute not iniquity. The man stands at no judgment bar save that of God, and, believe me, it is far easier to please God than anybody else. I would much rather have to please God for one day than anybody else in the world. It is far easier to please Him, for He is far more reasonable, more patient than are men, for His reasonableness and patience are based on His perfect knowledge. I think one of the most wonderful things in the Bible is that in speaking of the ultimate rule of the earth by God's anointed King it declares that He shall not judge by the sight of His eyes or by the hearing of His ears. Think of judgment in England to-day, think of law in England to-day, think of any law court into which you may go—everything is based on the sight of the eyes and the hearing of the ears, and there is no other way in which men can judge. In every court of law witnesses give evidence of what they saw and heard, and the jury listen and find their verdict, and the judge passes his sentence, on the sight of the eyes and the hearing of the ears. God does not judge by the sight of the eyes or by the hearing of the ears. How, then, does He judge? His judgments are righteous. They are so because they are based on His knowledge of all the underlying facts of the case. There is an old saying, To know all is to forgive all. It may be falsely used, but there is a vast amount of truth in it, and we may depend on it: if we knew all we should be far more likely to forgive most men than to condemn them.

"Blessed is the man unto whom the Lord imputeth not iniquity." There is a grandeur about this statement in that it shuts the man up to God, excludes all other judges and juries, and says: Stand before God, and let Him judge you!

And what will He do if a man will stand there? It depends on the man. God will not impute iniquity to him if there is no guile in his spirit. That is the condition. What is guile? Deceit, cloaking over, trying to hide! We are inclined to say that no man can practice guile in the presence of God. Think again. Oh, how constantly we do it by arguing in God's presence that some evil thing is not so very evil, or we try to find an excuse for sin. That is guile. God imputes iniquity, fastens the guilt on the soul that is hiding it; but if the sin be confessed, He puts away the guilt which the man cannot himself put away. If there be no guile, if there be no cloaking, no hiding, if the moment has come in which I am constrained to say, Oh, God, I have hidden this thing long enough by trying to excuse it; I have done with it; God be merciful to me a sinner; then, in a moment, swift as the lightning's flash and swifter, sweet and gentle as the daybreak, the guile is no longer imputed, the man is acquitted; God immediately pronounces on that man the verdict of guiltless, and the man says, "Happy is the man unto whom Jehovah imputeth not iniquity, in whose spirit there is no guile." That is how God deals with sin.

In order that this may be clearer, the psalmist immediately described the contrary experience, showing exactly what happened in his own soul when there was guile there, when he was cloaking something evil, and hiding it.

> When I kept silence, my bones waxed old
> Through my roaring all the day long.
> For day and night Thy hand was heavy upon me;
> My moisture was changed as with the drought of summer.

I do not think there is any language in all the Bible more wonderful in its clear, concise, graphic, startling revelation of the experience of a soul trying to hide sin from God. When I kept silence, when I knew, knew in the deepest of me that something was wrong but would not own it, I tried to put a brave face on it and excuse it to myself, and to make myself believe —strange and devilish deceit—that God did not disapprove, which was only another way of trying to make myself believe God did not know. Then

> My bones waxed old through my roaring all the day long;
> My moisture was changed into the drought of summer.

There was no life; there was no sap. What that means may be learned by quotation from another psalm, "The trees of the Lord are full of sap." The Hebrew does not say "sap." The word has been added by translators, and it is very full of beauty. Yet another psalm will help us, the one which declares that those who put their trust in God are like trees planted by the rivers of water. A tree planted by the rivers of water is a tree whose roots run down and under, and find their way to the water. In the case of such a tree, a living, healthy tree, we may take the utmost bough and break it, or take a leaf and break it in twain, and sap exudes. The trees of the Lord are full.

My moisture was turned into the drought of summer. There was no sap, no life. The godly man is like the tree planted by the rivers of water. There is sap, he is full of it. In business he is full of life; and in everything full of strength. But the man with sin unconfessed is like a tree in the desert, having no water; it is dry, scorched, burnt up. His faith in God fails. The death of faith in God expresses itself in the death of faith in one's fellow man. The man who believes in God believes in humanity. The man who loses his faith in God begins to question humanity, is suspicious of everyone. That is the condition of those who keep silence.

The psalmist then tells us why his bones waxed old and moisture was changed into drought:

For day and night Thy hand was heavy upon me.

That sounds severe, and so it is, but it is full of beauty. Not only is the severity of God in it, but also His goodness. It is as though the psalmist had said: In those days when I kept silence and tried to hide my sin Thou didst give me no peace, Thy hand was always on me, always troubling me; the thing I tried to hide Thou didst keep alive within me as a consciousness. That habit of life, that friendship that God condemned, that thing we persisted in, how it haunted us! That was God's hand on us! He will not let us escape. We argue it out and think it is settled, and go on, and, suddenly, it rises before us again: the controversy with God is continued, and God never rests until it ends in our submission, if we are His children:

> Day and night Thy hand was heavy upon me.

Now take the opposite:

> I acknowledged my sin unto Thee, and mine iniquity have I not hid.

Then the psalmist goes yet further back to show how quickly God answered, and how quickly God acted. Whereas the psalmist did acknowledge the sin and ceased to hide the iniquity, God did not wait for the actual acknowledgment, but in the moment when the psalmist decided he would do so God met him;

> I said, I will confess my transgressions unto the Lord;
> And Thou forgavest the iniquity of my sin.

I said I would do it, and the moment I made up my mind Thou didst act. That is a true picture of God. Some child of God may be burdened with sin, sin persisted in; if such a one at this moment will say, I will confess my sin, then, in the moment in which the heart has taken the attitude of confession, God will forgive the iniquity of the sin.

How truly the prophet described Him as "a God ready to pardon." Oh for some figure of speech to help men to understand the meaning of that "ready to pardon." There is no figure of speech finer than that of this psalm: He is so ready to pardon that when man makes up his mind to confess, he is forgiven before he does confess. God does not wait for your formalities; He deals with your attitudes. He does not wait until the Sabbath day comes round. He does not wait until the human confessional is open. He does not wait until the special Inquiry Meeting is called at the end of the service. He does not wait for an hour. This is not ancient history; it is present fact. At this moment, without sigh or sound that mortal ear can detect, or attitude that the eye of man can observe even before the thing is said, when I make up my mind to confess, "Thou forgavest the iniquity of my sin!" Do you wonder that when this man was going to write a psalm about this matter he had to begin:

> O the blessings of transgression forgiven, and sin covered.

In the moment in which a man ceases guile and makes his soul naked in the eyes of God he is forgiven. God, in an awe-inspiring mystery, respects the veil that a man tries to fling over himself, and excludes Himself from communion with the man until the man tears the veil and says, I am going to be before God what I really am, when, in that moment, God makes him what He would have the man to be.

> Thou forgavest the iniquity of my sin.

Then follow the matters of sorrow and silence. "For this let everyone that is Godly pray." "For this" means because of this or for this cause. It does not mean we are to pray for forgiveness. There is no need to do that. All we have to do to obtain forgiveness is to quit hypocrisy, and to make our souls naked, and confess. So it is not that we are to pray for forgiveness, but because of it. The questions of sin and sorrow are intimately related, and the place of prayer is thus guarded. It is only when a man is guileless before God, and sin is dealt with by God, that he has free access to the place of prayer. Having that access, a man finds that the way of prayer is the way of deliverance in sorrow.

> Surely when the great waters overflow they shall not reach unto him.

That is an apparent contradiction. When the great waters overflow they shall not reach him! That is a paradox indeed. It is the picture of a man in the middle of overflowing waters, but the waters do not reach him. The same thought is in the next figure:

> Thou art my hiding place; Thou shalt preserve me from trouble.

Not keep me from going into trouble, but preserve me from it when I am in it.

> Thou wilt compass me about with songs of deliverance.

Not keep me from going into prison, nor even necessarily bring me out of prison; but enable me to sing in prison! The psalmist does not declare that the Godly man is to be immune from sorrow, but that he is to be triumphant over it, that sorrow is not to be allowed to harm him. Great waves and billows will overflow him, so that the Godly man of all godly men, God's own Son, could perfectly say, All Thy waves and Thy billows have gone over Me! Oh, the waves and the billows that have gone over our heads, floods of great waters; and yet, even though at the moment we felt as though we were about to be drowned, we were not drowned! The great waters have not reached, they have not harmed, they have not destroyed us, because we had access to God by prayer, and so sin was dealt with. We prayed to Him in the time when the proud waters went over our souls, and we were delivered.

> Thou art my hiding place; Thou wilt preserve me from trouble.

Quite literally, Thou wilt preserve me in a tight place. Oh, yes, we may often be in a tight place, but we shall be preserved; for nearer to us than all the pressure of circumstances is God, and though circumstances press until we think we shall be ground to powder, we never are, because the resistance of God against the pressure of circumstances keeps us safe.

And yet again,

> Thou wilt compass me about with songs of deliverance.

Such songs are sung in prison. We are familiar with the New Testament illustration. Paul and Silas sang praises when they got out of prison? No! After the thunder, after the earthquake that shook their feet loose from the stocks? No. They sang with feet fast in the stocks, with backs sore from Philippian rods. That is the place of song to the forgiven soul. The psalmist knew sorrows, knew the sweeping of the storm, knew the rolling of the waters, knew the loneliness of the prison house; but he knew deliverance, he knew a hiding place in which he was safe, and therefore he could sing in the midst of the sorrowful hours.

Then he passed to the matter of silence, and now he seems to have been so full of the consciousness of God that he adopted the language of God, changed the methods of his speech, and did not sing of God, but wrote as though God were singing to him:

> I will instruct thee and teach thee in the way which thou shalt go;
> I will counsel thee with Mine eye upon thee.
> Be ye not as the horse, or as the mule, which have no understanding;
> Whose trappings must be bit and bridle to hold them in,
> Else they will not come near unto thee.
> Many sorrows shall be to the wicked:
> But he that trusteth in the Lord, mercy shall compass him about.

"I will instruct thee," that is, I will make thee circumspect, I will make thee intelligent. "I will teach thee in the way which thou shalt go," that is, I will point out thy way with the finger. This is a picture of God dealing with a soul troubled, perplexed. The sorrow of silence is the worst of all, the appalling perplexity of hearing no voice in the hour of greatest need. God says, I will make thee intelligent, and then with My finger I will point out the way. It is as though God bent over the soul perplexed and in difficulty about the way, and said, I will give thee the capacity for understanding Me, and having done it, I will show you the right way. And, more, I will counsel thee; not, I will guide thee with mine eye, but, I will talk to you, and give you counsel with My eye on you. I will never lose sight of you.

Then follows a loving word, which is most arresting. It may thus be expressed bluntly: Do not be a mule! The horse and the mule need to be kept near to their drivers, with bit and bridle, so that they may be controlled. God says, I do not want to put a bit in your mouth; I want to keep you near Me in other ways. If we will not yield to the constraint of His guidance, then He will put bits into our mouths; but He would rather that we waited for Him, watched for the pointing of His finger, listened for the whisper of His word, and followed the light in His eye.

What wonder that the psalmist finished as he did:

Be glad in the Lord, and rejoice, ye righteous!

If we have done with our hypocrisy, He will put away our sin; that being settled, if we pray, He will guard us from all the evil of our sorrows; He will guide us with His counsel. Then let us be glad in the Lord, and let us not be content with being glad, let us obey the further command:

Shout for joy, all ye that are upright in heart.

When men really know God, they become hilarious, full of laughter and merriment and song and perpetual gladness.

So may He in His grace lead us into the secrets of communion.

CHAPTER VI

HOPE

By hope were we saved.

ROMANS 8:24.

THE EXPERIENCE OF HOPE IS THAT OF TRIUMPH OVER CONditions and circumstances which are calculated to produce despair. Where there is no place for despair there is none for hope. If there is no danger of despair there is no possibility or necessity for hope. The old English word "hope," in all its mutations, has retained the sense of expectation, of something desired and not yet attained. The Greek word, of which it is a translation in my text, coming to us as it does from a primitive word meaning anticipation, and almost always anticipation with pleasure, has exactly the same significance. Indeed, the word is used in the New Testament invariably in the sense of anticipation with pleasure, and in the sense of desire. When that which is anticipated is realized, there is room neither for despair nor hope; when faith is lost to sight, then hope in full fruition dies; or, as the writer of this letter says in immediate connection with my text, "Hope that is seen is not hope; for who hopeth for that which he seeth?" This, then, is peculiarly a word for days of stress and strain. Hope comes to its brightest shining in the presence of the deepest darkness. The function of hope is conditioned by the prevalence of conditions making for despair. We need not enter into any lengthy consideration of the distinction between faith and hope. Hope is an aspect of faith. According to the Biblical presentation of faith, it will be perfectly safe to say that the soul of man, looking upward in faith, is conscious of perfect confidence; that the soul of man, looking onward in faith, is conscious of hope; that the soul, looking around in faith, is conscious of peace. Faith is an attitude of the soul, hope is the experience which that attitude creates with regard to the future.

The apostolic declaration is made in connection with an argument in the course of which conditions calculated to produce despair were most clearly recognized, and, indeed, described. The whole passage is one in which, in broad statement, the Apostle recognizes those things which persist until this hour: the trouble, the turmoil, the travail, the groaning of the world. "The whole creation groaneth and travaileth in pain together; . . . we ourselves groan within ourselves; . . . the Spirit Himself maketh intercession for us with groanings which cannot be uttered."

The way in which hope saves will best be apprehended if we consider, first, the nature of the hope which is referred to by the Apostle; second, the foundation of that hope; and, third, the effects which that hope produces.

If we are to understand the nature of the hope referred to, we must begin by a yet more careful examination of the need for this ministry of hope. It is important that we recognize that it is discovered in the very conditions causing despair. By repetition of the quotations already made in a slightly different language I think we shall discover these conditions. "The whole creation groaneth and travaileth in pain together until now." "Ourselves also groan within ourselves." "The Spirit Himself maketh intercession with groanings which cannot be uttered."

The first of these declarations was the Apostle's recognition of the fact that the whole problem of pain and suffering, of evil in the widest sense is the problem which constantly assaults the soul of the man of faith in God. It may be well that we remind ourselves that pain presents no *problem* to any man except to the man who believes in God. Pain becomes a problem only in the presence of faith. When, ever and anon, some believer, it may be one whose faith at the moment is trembling, challenges the world's agony, the challenge is always uttered in the presence of the consciousness of God. When the soul cries out in revolt in the presence of the abounding suffering of men, the cry is always born of the wonder how God can permit this. There is no other problem. Blot God out of His universe and you will still have pain, but no problem to assault the soul. It is only faith that has to face this perplexity. It is Habakkuk who suffers most in the day of the declension of the people of God. It is Habakkuk who says, "Oh, Lord, how long?" I cry murder and Thou dost not hear. I cry violence and there is no answer. What is God doing?

It was Carlyle, rough, rugged, peculiar in many ways, and yet a man of the greatest faith, who, when Froude attempted to comfort him by telling him that God is in His heaven, said, "Yes, but He is doing nothing." I never repeat that without being inclined to say to believing souls, Do not be angry with Carlyle. It was not true, God *was* doing something, but there is neither man nor woman in this house who has ever come very near, and remained near to the world's agony, who has not had that thought at some time or another. The whole creation groaneth and travaileth together in pain, and the proportion of our nearness to God is the proportion of our sense of this problem of pain, for it is the love of God shed abroad in the heart that renders the heart keen and sensitive to the world's agony. The heart of man, taught by the Divine love, questions the Divine love, until, presently, the heart of the man discovers that the very agony he feels which makes him question is the result of the presence in his soul of the God of love, and, indeed, it is an expression of God's own agony. It is when we become sensible of that prevalent pain that we need hope; and unless hope shall save us, then we shall indeed be lost.

The second state of the apostolic description, "We ourselves groan within ourselves, waiting for our adoption, the redemption of our body," is one of the most illuminating sentences on personal Christian experience in all this writing. The Apostle here describes the increasing sense of failure and shortcomings, the cry and the sob that come out of life with intenser meaning as the years go on: "Wretched man that I am! Who shall deliver me out of the body of this death?" It is the man who comes into the closest association with Christ who also comes to the acutest sense of his own defilement. We groan within ourselves in the baffling defeat of the soul in its attempt to reach the heights; we wait for the redemption of the body, conscious that the tabernacle in which the spirit dwells is the instrument of defilement for the spirit. It is in hours when the under side of our nature wins its victories that we cry out in agony and almost in despair. It is then that we need the gospel of hope.

Then we come to the last and highest word, most mystic and most difficult of interpretation, "The Spirit Himself maketh intercession for us with groanings that cannot be uttered." In that word we have a description, not merely of our sense of the general pain of the world, not merely of our sense of our own particular limitations and defeats, but of the Divine discontent which, within the soul of a man, makes him angry and puts him in agony; that knowledge of God which generates restlessness with everything that is unlike Him and unlike His peace; that hot turbulent protest of the soul against every form of wrong and of tyranny, against the conditions that blight and spoil the universe of God. The Spirit Who knoweth the deep things of God, the profound emotions of the Divine heart, touches the heart and spirit of a man with the selfsame feelings until the man himself rises unconsciously to a plane of prayer on which he expresses to God the things which God Himself is feeling.

Now, it is this sense of the world's pain, of our own pain, this sense of anger and agony born of our communion with God, that makes hope necessary. These are the things that fill the heart with despair.

What, then, is the hope? This, again, is a most necessary question for consideration, for if it be true that we are saved by hope, it is equally true that men are lost by hope. Unless the hope be true it destroys. The will-of-the-wisp creates a hope in the heart of the wanderer over the marshes, but it destroys him because it is not a true light. The lights lit by the wreckers along the Cornish shore in the olden days created hope in the heart of many a mariner, but they destroyed. And so, unless hope be true, it will not save, it will destroy.

The Bishop of Durham, Dr. Moule, in his "Commentary on Romans" in the Expositors' Bible, has suggested a translation of this text which is certainly illuminative. What he suggests is a fair implication of the text. He suggests that, instead of "We were saved by hope," we render here, "It is as to our hope that we were saved," as if the text should mean that we are saved as Christian men by hope because of the nature of the hope that is presented to us. What, then, is the Christian hope? If we go over these passages again, we shall find that in every case the hope is declared. What is our hope for creation? That it shall be delivered from the bondage of corruption into the liberty of the children of God. That is one of the greatest sentences in all the writings of the Apostle. It presents a vision of the whole creation, ultimately led out from the bondage or corruption, of that which disintegrates, spoils, mars, ruins, into the liberty of the children of God. A doctrine of the world is involved in that statement, and it is the Biblical doctrine, the doctrine of the cosmos as under the dominion of man. The cosmos is seen suffering pain and tribulation, because its lord and master, man, has lost his scepter and his power to govern. That same cosmos will come at last to the realization of all its beauty and all its glory, because the children of God, men and women after the Divine image and likeness, and fulfilling the Divine relationship, will govern it, so that the creation will realize itself and pass out of corruption into full and complete realization.

The feeling of the poets helps us here. There lay the dead sea mew, and Elizabeth Barrett Browning sang,

> Our human touch did on him pass,
> And with our touch, our agony.

It was the symbol of the whole creation groaning and travailing together in pain.

Thomas Blake, the father of our Nature poetry, sang:

> A robin redbreast in a cage
> Puts all heaven in a rage;
> A dog starved at his master's gate
> Predicts the ruin of the State.

Superlative language, you say. The superlatives of earth are the positives of eternity. At last there will be no starved dog anywhere, no caged robin, no mauled sea mew, nothing left in creation which results from the misgovernment of men. Creation will escape its corruption and enter into the liberty of the glory of the sons of God.

We groan within ourselves, waiting—for what? The adoption, the redemption of the body, the ultimate mastering of the body that it may become the fitting instrument of the spirit. Or as Paul put it when writing to the Philippians of his personal experiences: He "shall fashion a new body of our humiliation, that it may be conformed to the body of His glory."

Concerning that groaning of the spirit, that restlessness

of God interpreted to the soul and creating the agony and the power of prayer, what is our hope? The ultimate rest and joy of God in His completed work, which, perhaps, we most clearly express when we quote the prophecy and the promise concerning the Messiah Himself, that at last He shall see of the travail of His soul and be satisfied.

What are the foundations of this hope? Inclusively, we may say that our hope is set on God, and that through the unveilings of Himself and of His activity which have been granted to us in Christ. To say that is to say everything. God is our hope in the presence of the problem of pain. Our fellowship with Him has created the problem. Who is God? What is God doing? Is God doing anything? Does God care? These are all questions arising out of faith in God. Blot God out of the heavens, blot God out of the intellectual concept, say there is no God! What then? Ah! but our faith has created our problem, and we shall not solve our problem by denying the God Who created our problem. We have seen a universe in which pain is a wrong, but we should not have seen that if we had not seen God. Therefore, inquiring still more deeply, turning the soul back upon itself, facing the problem, we affirm that the very ultimate ground of hope is God, and that the unveiling of Himself which He has given us in Christ is the very inspiration of hope. It is out of that unveiling that hope comes back to us.

Let us inquire a little more particularly about the aspects of these unveilings which inspire hope. And, again, we will confine ourselves to this very passage, for in it the very foundations of hope are laid bare. I base my hope, first on the suffering of God, on the fact that the Spirit maketh intercession for us with groanings which cannot be uttered; second, on the suffering of the saints, that they, who have the first-fruits of the Spirit, suffer; and, finally, on the suffering of creation itself. In regard to the creation, the Apostle has linked another word to the word "groaning": "Groaneth and travaileth." It is the word that suggests birth rather than death. This is the wondrous alchemy of Christianity: pain is the ground of confidence that pain will end.

The first ground of hope is that of the suffering of God. "The Spirit maketh intercession for us with groanings that cannot be uttered." "He that searcheth the hearts knoweth what is the mind of the Spirit." "The Spirit searcheth the deep things of God." When we speak here of the Spirit we are thinking of God, and included in the thought is that of infinite wisdom, infinite love, infinite power. God, infinite in wisdom, therefore making no mistake; infinite in love, therefore never failing in love, for "Love is not love which alters when it alteration finds"; infinite in power, therefore able to do all that wisdom reveals and love dictates.

The revelation that is given to us of God in our Lord and Saviour Jesus Christ is that He is conscious of this agony and is active in the midst of it. He, being the sum total of all things, and being more than all the things in which pain is to be found, has gathered the whole within Himself and knows it to its depths. When I look next on the problem of the suffering of the innocent with the guilty, let me remember I am looking on the problem of God's suffering. I admit that this is a problem, a profounder problem than anything London presents, or Europe presents, or the world presents. The problem of a suffering God is indeed profound! But there is a solution. It is the solution of a loving God expressing Himself in a thousand ways in every generation if men had but eyes to see, and ears to hear, and hearts to understand; expressing Himself assuredly in the suffering of every innocent soul that consents to suffering on behalf of the guilty; expressing Himself centrally, and this in some senses finally, in the Cross! You talk to me of the problem of evil in London. I take you to the Cross. There it is focused. You talk to me of the problem of those who suffer. It is centralized in the Cross. You talk to me of the problem of evil, evil winning, evil crushing good, evil mauling that which is high and noble. I take you to the Cross. There it is, in its vulgar tragedy, focused, centralized, made vulgar, as it is vulgar!

In that unveiling God has revealed the fact that wherever there is suffering, there is He also. He, the infinitely wise and loving and powerful, is conscious and active in the midst of all suffering.

On that I build my palace of hope. I stand in the midst of the world's agony, and I say this is also the Divine agony, and therefore my heart believes that at last, how, I cannot tell, by what methods, I do not know, but at last the very creation will be delivered from its corruption and find its way into the glory of the liberty of the children of that God Who has not absented Himself from human sorrow, but Who remains within it, gathering its most poignant power into His own being, and vicariously suffering in the midst of the universe blighted by sin.

If I pass from that wider outlook and look again at the saints, I build my hope on their suffering far more than on their rejoicing, for in their pain they are sharers of the Divine pain, making up that which is behind in the suffering of Christ, and having fellowship with His suffering. They are also sharers of the Divine power and of the Divine patience.

Who are the saints? Take any one Christian man or woman in the life of this city, or far away on the mission field; take an isolated case for the illumination of the general fact. What is this man? What is this woman? This is humanity reborn and regained for God. To use the word of Jesus, this individual is the seed of the Kingdom. New born souls constitute in earth's soil the seed of the coming Kingdom. Then I hear the word of the Lord spoken on another occasion, and I link it to this declaration: "Except a grain of wheat fall into the earth and die, it abideth by itself alone." By the suffering of the saints the Kingdom is to come.

This is very well as a general statement. Its particular and personal application must be reserved for loneliness. Let us get away presently, somewhere quite alone, those of us who are suffering in the cause of the Kingdom, or in fellowship with the Kingdom, or as the result of our loyalty to the Kingdom. Does there seem to be no connection between such suffering and the Kingdom? It is false seeming, for by that suffering, by that pain, by that anguish, we are in fellowship with God; and by that fellowship in pain the victory is to be won and the Kingdom is to come.

So with the whole creation. I remind you again in a passing sentence only of the suggestiveness of the word, "groaneth and travaileth together in pain." It is the word of birth pangs! The sobbing of creation, its sigh and its agony, are the declaration of its rebirth. "Behold, I make all things new," is the perpetual word of God. He makes all things new by the way of travail. Thus our hope is born of the transmutation of the causes of our despair.

What are the effects of this hope? I will speak of two only, one named in the immediate context, and one named by the Apostle John. The effects are patience and purity. "We with patience wait." "He that hath his hope set on Him purifieth himself, even as He is pure." What is patience? Patience is simply remaining under. Remaining under in order to bear. To attempt to withdraw is to leave God. If I am to be in co-operation with God in the processes that are to lead to the final restoration, I must stay in the midst, I must remain under; fellowship with God in service is patience, remaining under, not merely to bear but to lift. To save the life is to lose it, because to withhold the life from pouring out is to exclude God, Who is ever pouring Himself out in sacrifice. The mental experience of such fellowship is patience with God, patience with ourselves, patience with creation.

Patience means staying underneath, in fellowship with God, because of the assurance, not that at last I shall climb the height, but that at last He will perfect that which concerneth me.

The second effect of this hope is that of purity. "Everyone that hath this hope set on Him purifieth himself, even as He is pure." At your leisure, contrast the passage in John with the one in Romans, and see how close the thoughts lie to each other. Creation is waiting for the revealing of the sons of God, and we who are the children groan within ourselves waiting for the adoption, the redemption of the body, and the Spirit Himself maketh intercession for us with groanings which cannot be uttered. So run the thoughts of Romans. Then I turn to John, and I read, "Beloved, now are we the children of God, but it doth not yet appear what we shall be, for He is not yet manifested." There has been no manifestation yet of this sonship of God in all its finality and its glory and its beauty. But we know that when He shall be manifested as He is, we shall be like Him. Paul says that creation is waiting for the sons of God. John declares that the Son of God will be manifested with the sons of God. The man who has that hope set on God purifies himself, even as God is pure. The responsibility is that of purification, the type of purity is that of the purity of God.

If that were all, I hardly dare read the passage. Is there power for such purification? The Apostle goes on to declare that He was manifested to destroy the works of the devil.

And so, as we are conscious of the sorrows of the world, the perils threatening us in our home life, the perils of our prosperity, the persistence of pain everywhere, the failure and disappointment verging on despair, we are saved by hope! Our hope is built on Him Who is our God. Our hope, therefore, is based also on the very sense of defeat and despair and pain that cause our agony; for by these things men live, by these defeats they climb to the higher heights, by these bruisings and these batterings of the iron life is molded and shaped to the Divine purpose. The only man who has no hope is the man who has no God.

But that must not be the last note. The last note must be this: God is our abiding hope, and by hope we are saved.

CHAPTER VII

A GOOD FRIDAY MEDITATION

The fellowship of His sufferings.
PHILIPPIANS 3:10.

WE ARE GATHERED HERE THIS MORNING NOT SO MUCH TO observe a day as to take advantage of it. This is a day which affords us one of those opportunities, all too rare, for the display of our oneness with the whole Catholic Church of our Lord. The purpose of our assembly is pre-eminently that of meditation in the presence of the Cross of our Lord and Saviour Jesus Christ.

By the selection of this one brief phrase from the writings of Paul we take the highest level of consideration possible to us in these days of our probation and our waiting for the full manifestation of grace in the Advent of glory, that level of consideration, namely, which is occupied with the subject of the fellowship of the saints in the suffering of the Saviour.

It is quite evident that these words describe what Paul himself considered to be one of the highest possible phases of experience of Christian men and women during this period. He immediately continued, and declared that he had not yet attained, had not yet apprehended, all the fulness of his Lord's purpose for him when his Lord apprehended him; and if we read to the end of this very wonderful biographical chapter in the letter to the Philippians we find that Paul did not think it was possible for us to enter into the ultimate experience of Christianity until the very body of our humiliation should be changed and fashioned according to the body of Christ's glory? For the present, for the "little while" of this earthly, limited, straitened life, the Apostle evidently considered that in this passage he had revealed his estimate of the highest experience.

This experience he described in a threefold way. The consuming passion of his heart was, "That I may know Him, and the power of His resurrection, and the fellowship of His sufferings." That is a description of Christian experience on an ascending scale. First, "That I may know Him"; second, and therefore, "That I may know . . . the power of His resurrection"; third, and consequently, "That I may know . . . the fellowship of His sufferings."

The words immediately following reveal the condition on which the believer may enter into this threefold experience, "Becoming conformed unto His dying." Thus, in this strange and yet wonderful unveiling of Christian experience, the Cross is seen at the commencement and at the culmination. "By becoming conformed unto His dying," I know Him; and by such knowledge of Himself, I know the power of His resurrection operating in and through me; and by such knowledge of the power of His resurrection, I come back again to the Cross, not now merely for conformity to it in order that I from it may derive benefit, but rather for that highest, holiest, most mysterious experience, that I may have fellowship with His sufferings.

Notice, further, that in this description of Christian experience Paul places this fellowship in suffering last, because it is last in the experimental order; it is the final experience of the saint in this world; it is the largest, deepest, highest, broadest.

Surely, we also have to say about this that we have not yet attained, we have not yet apprehended. Gleams of the infinite and mysterious glory have we seen; passing experience of the deep, the profound, the sorrowful mystery have we known; but, oh, to know Him so that we may also know the power of His resurrection, so that we may also enter into the true, abiding fellowship of His sufferings!

For this threefold experience the Apostle had counted all things as refuse, and had resolutely turned his back on every ambition, hope, and aspiration. We may well, then, in quietness and solemnity attempt to meditate on the sacred matter.

What, then, are the sufferings of Christ in which we may have fellowship? Such an inquiry necessitates a declaration which in some senses need hardly be made, for we are all convinced of its truth, that the central, supreme, mysterious values, quantities, qualities—I know not the true word—of the sufferings of Christ we can never share. At last He trod the winepress alone, the darkness into which He passed was such as no other has ever known. It is quite alone, this Cross of Christ, if our eyes can see the central Person, for He was not merely the Man of Nazareth, He was God in Christ, quite alone by reason of the infinite reaches of it, for the Cross, so far as our calculation can carry us, is far older than creation—"The Lamb slain from the foundation of the world." Through all this strange, perplexing history which we find in the ancient Scriptures the principle is found: ever and anon high, noble souls, by heroic abandonment to the vision, were permitted to enter into some measure of sympathy and fellowship with the central mystery. Abraham on the mountain, offering his firstborn, was brought nearer to understanding the God Who "so loved the world that He gave His only begotten Son" than he could have been in any other way. Isaiah exercised a great ministry, part of the meaning of which is voiced, in the paragraphs found in the fifty-third chapter of his prophecy. The cry of Isaiah's heart was, "Who hath believed our report? and to whom hath the arm of the Lord been revealed?" Yet out of that very personal experience he rose to a higher height, portraying the picture of One in Whom all sorrows should meet and center and find their fulfilment, and through Whom all light should break on the darkness of human nature.

All the way we find the Cross, and all the way we may discover some measure of fellowship with it by those who saw the vision and yielded themselves to the will of God. All the way also there were great deeps and heights and mysteries eluding those watchers and toilers and warriors.

Now for two millenniums men have gathered about the Cross; saints and scholars have attempted to interpret its meaning to us; and here we gather again to-day, and still we have to say, It is too deep for us, too high for us. Neither theologian nor philosopher has ever yet been able to penetrate to the heart of the mystery and unveil before the eyes of men its deep processes. Therefore we once more adopt the simple and sublime language of the Bible, "Who His own self bare our sins in His own body upon the tree." There is nothing to be added to that; no final explanation of it is possible; it baffles theology, for it is too great for theology. In the vastness of it I hide; there I find rest amid the conflict with evil, within and without; and there, at last, when the sun goes westering and I pass o'er the line, I shall find my refuge, singing on the way,

> Nothing in my hands I bring,
> Simply to Thy Cross I cling.

I can have no share in the Cross, in all its profoundest meanings, save as I take from it the benefit that heals and helps and renews hope within my heart.

In what sense, then, is it possible for us to have fellowship with the suffering of our Lord? Reverently I want to suggest to you some of the things that have come to my own heart in meditating on this great matter. I must at once say that I am most conscious that I cannot exhaust even this aspect of the Cross, and there may be those of you who have known this Master of mine longer than I have, or in a briefer period have come to know Him better than I, who perchance may know the meaning of these words far better than I. Such will, I know, be patient while I attempt to interpret what I have seen of the possibility and speak of some of the things in which it is given to us to have fellowship with Christ in His suffering.

The first possibility which I see is that it is given to the saints to have fellowship with Christ in the sense of sin. This is possible only to those who have a very keen sense of the perfection and beauty of the Divine will. It is possible only to those who are living in close conformity to the ideal which Christ has revealed, in the power of the life which Christ has communicated. Of the way into the secret I will speak again; I want to speak now merely of the experience itself. I think I may venture to affirm that our Lord always suffered in the presence of sin. Wherever He saw sin, He suffered. It is given to us to have fellowship with Him in that suffering. It seems to me this morning—I speak now for myself and for none but myself—that I can interpret the thought that is in my heart only by turning my statement round and making it negative. Is it not true that familiarity with sin tends to breed contempt for sin? After all is said and done, the most callous men and women are those living nearest to sin. How easy it is to see sin, and to see it so often, and to look on it so constantly, even though we ourselves may be delivered from its power and may not be yielding to its seduction, that it ceases to make any appeal in our heart, and ceases to produce any suffering in our soul! That is the perpetual peril of familiarity with sin. If I go back and look at these pictures of the life of the Lord and watch Him reverently, I believe that whenever He looked on sinning men sin caused Him suffering. In the suffering, there was ever the mingling elements of love and of anger. Sin forevermore caused pain to the heart of the Lord because sin was the violation of the Divine order, something spoiling the Divine purpose, interfering with all the highest of the Divine conceptions. The measure in which it is difficult for us to understand this is the measure in which we fail to have fellowship with our Lord. I am almost loath to take any illustration, yet suffer me one: how a discord hurts the man of music, how disproportion wounds the artistic temperament. It is a very low level of illustration, but it is an illustration on the level of the mental. If it be possible to climb by way of it to the plane of higher spiritual conception, then we see at once that our Lord, not merely in the final, supreme hour of the Cross, but in all those days in Nazareth, in public ministry, suffered in the presence of sin. Every discord hurt His soul, all lack of proportion touched Him to the very quick of His high, holy, sensitive spiritual nature. Sin hurt, sin filled the heart of the Christ of God with pain. Not merely the cruel bloody Cross, but all that made that Cross possible in the ruin of the race and necessary for the redemption of the race gave Him pain.

We have fellowship in His suffering when sin, wherever it is manifest, brings pain to the heart. It was no idle thing that our fathers and mothers said to us when we were children, though we could hardly believe it, that our wrongdoing hurt them. It was true. When you and I have true fellowship with Christ, then when our eyes rest on a man, a woman, bruised, broken, smirched, soiled by sin, we suffer in the presence of sin. Paganism at its highest gathers its garment about it and holds sin in loathing and contempt; Christianity lays its robe aside and endures the agony in order to save the sinner. That is fellowship with Christ's sufferings.

That leads us to that which is closely connected with it, which is indeed but another phase of the experience. We may have fellowship with Christ's sufferings in the presence of man's misunderstanding of God. He knew God, and, knowing God perfectly, He suffered as everywhere He saw God misinterpreted because misunderstood. In speech which to this day scorches and burns His hot anger proceeded against men who misinterpreted God to the multitudes.

Fellowship with Him in this is possible only to such as live in the love of God. Misunderstanding too often embitters, and so ceases to cause pain; and this is almost invariably so when the misunderstanding is of ourselves. That is a very low level of illustration, from which we resolutely turn. Our Master suffered because God was misunderstood. Do we? How much do we know of pain when we take up some brilliant magazine article that libels God, that reveals the writer's absolute inability to interpret One he does not know. It is perpetual sorrow to the saint living in fellowship with Christ that God is not known, is misunderstood and misinterpreted. How much do we know of this fellowship with God which issues in fellowship with the suffering of our Lord? I apologize for my illustrations, because I recognize that no illustrations can reach the high level of the great theme we are attempting to consider. How we suffer if our friend, whom we thoroughly know and understand, is misunderstood! How we burn with indignation when something is said that libels our friend! Do we ever feel angry with an anger that grows out of a great agony when God is libeled, when God is misunderstood, when God is misinterpreted? Such pain comes out of only the closest fellowship with Christ. We cannot force the experience.

One other note, and only one. We can have fellowship with Christ in His pity for human failure. Sin in itself causes Him to suffer. The misunderstanding of God causes Him pain. But there is something beyond this, while yet related to it. I look at my Lord through life and in death, and am almost overwhelmed by the fact that He suffered in the presence of human failure, and suffered in sympathy even with the punishment that was inevitable. If I quote old and familiar words I do so because they recur naturally. "O Jerusalem, Jerusalem, which killeth the prophets, and stoneth them that are sent unto her! How often would I have gathered thy children together, even as a hen gathereth her chickens under her wings, and ye would not! Behold, your house is left unto you desolate." The awful word must be pronounced. There is no weakness in God. No violation of holiness can be permitted. "Desolate," He said, but as He said it His voice was choked with tears. That was not His will for Jerusalem. Beautiful for situation, the joy of the whole earth—that is the dream of God for Jerusalem. "Desolate" is Jerusalem's choice, and it broke Christ's heart. "Father, forgive them, for they know not what they do." "Consider Him that hath endured such gainsaying of sinners"—the old version translated, "against Himself"; the new version translates, "against themselves." When my eyes first lighted on the change I was startled and I thought I had lost something. He "endured such gainsaying of sinners against Himself"; it was a great picture, that of the Lord enduring man's attitude of hostility toward Himself. But look again: endured the gainsaying of sinners against themselves; their attitude toward Him was rebounding against themselves; their waywardness was making for their own destruction. That is what Christ endured. That was the deepest note of His suffering, the suffering of pity for human failure. A great prophetic word, uttered long ago, declared that judgment is "His strange act," necessary in the interest of love and holiness and in order to establish the universal kingdom of peace, but strange. I shall have come into some true measure of fellowship with Christ's suffering when I speak of a lost soul, not as though I rejoice, but with a breaking heart. Robert William Dale said to me when I was beginning my ministry, I have known one man who as an evangelist had the right to speak of a man being lost, and that man was D. L. Moody, because he never could do it except in tears. That is fellowship with the suffering of Christ.

We may, we ought to have, perpetual fellowship with Him in these aspects of His suffering. Sin always ought to make us suffer. I do not mean sin in our own lives merely, but sin in other lives. These streets of our city, these multitudes of fallen human beings sinning—we ought to carry the sorrow of it all perpetually on our hearts. The fact that our God is being misunderstood and misinterpreted should rest forevermore as a grief on our souls. There should be in all the declarations of the counsels of God that are vibrant with terror something of the infinite pity and sorrow of the heart of Christ, Who even while denouncing the doomed city expressed Himself in sorrow and in tears.

How is it possible to know this fellowship? We can come into fellowship with Christ in suffering only through the power of His resurrection. The sense of the Master's suffering comes only when His own life is regnant in the life of the saint. It is Christ in me that fills me with compassion. I know it to be true. I cannot—God forgive me if the confession is an unworthy one—produce within myself any pity for some sinning men; but the measure in which my Lord lives in me, masters my life, dominates me, the measure in which I dare yield myself to the impulses of His indwelling, is the measure in which I cannot look upon sinning men without suffering and desiring to help. The beauty of His life amazes and shames me as I watch Him in Judea, Galilee, and Perea; but when by the way of the Cross it is liberated, illuminating my intelligence, firing my emotion, bending my will, then I live one life with Christ and have fellowship in his suffering. The man who here wrote about the fellowship of His sufferings is the man who also wrote, "I could wish that I myself were anathema from Christ for my brethren's sake." Commentators, expositors, and exegetes who declare that Paul did not mean that do not know Paul, and they do not know

Christ. When Christ has full possession of the life, then out of the tides of His life, His risen life, surging through the life of the saint proceeds the passionate cry, I would I could be accursed from Christ for the deliverance of these others. By the power of His resurrection, and by that alone, can I know the fellowship of His sufferings.

Before it, yet hardly before it, for it is so intimately related to it, that we cannot omit it, is the phrase, "That I may know Him." The first movement of the resurrection life of Christ in the soul is the consciousness of Christ, and it is when I know Him that I know the world without; and to know Him makes me know the truth about sinning, suffering men and women. First, the knowledge of Christ, then the consciousness of the power of His resurrection in the opened vision, and the inspired emotion, and the driving will. Then I move into the great realm of fellowship with His suffering. He suffers in me, through me, for I have become part of the mystic body of Christ. He Himself is the Head, in Whom all pain is focused, but I may be part of the throbbing nerve system that has fellowship with that central pain. It is by the way of knowledge of Him and of the power of His resurrection that I can pass into fellowship with His suffering.

That leads me to the phrase just beyond my text to which I have already referred, "becoming conformed unto His death." There we really begin. Until we are conformable unto His death we cannot know Him, we cannot know the power of His resurrection, we cannot know the fellowship of His sufferings. What is it to be made conformable to His death? The whole chapter from which our text is taken gives the answer by illustration. Paul said, "I count all things to be loss for the excellency of the knowledge of Christ Jesus my Lord; for Whom I suffered the loss of all things, and do count them but refuse." What things? All the sinful pleasures of this world? Nay, they were out of sight! What things? All the things he had counted gain. What were they? Pride of birth, of religion, and of ethical attainment. All high and noble things until he had a vision of Christ, but then the things in which he had boasted, blood, religion, and ethical attainment, were dross, refuse. He gave himself entirely to the Christ, dying to all that lay behind. That is the way to know Christ. Christ is never known until He alone is desired. The highway to the upper levels of the Christ-life is the low way of the Cross, wherein we die to everything else. That is what hinders so many of us. We sing:

> Were the whole realm of nature mine . . .

Are you ever afraid that you are committing blasphemy as you sing it?

> Were the whole realm of nature mine,
> That were an offering far too small:
> Love so amazing, so divine,
> Demands my soul, my life, my all.

Yet we still cling to ambition and to high ideals which, in the deep subconsciousness of our religious thinking, make us imagine that we are not quite dependent on Christ or His Cross. To know Him everything else must be counted as refuse.

This is, it seems to me, the highest level on which it is possible for us to consider the sufferings of Christ. There is a contemplation of the lonely sufferings of Christ, the results of which we receive by grace, which is perfectly right, but which may be terribly wrong. If we gather to gaze on that Cross only to know the benefits conferred on us, only to gather them into our own souls, only to spend right, high, holy, spiritual things on our own small needs, then, after all, is not that the blasphemy of all blasphemies? Can I dare to be selfish in the presence of that Cross? If I dare, am I not sinning the sin of all sins the most deadly and most dastardly?

Is it not necessary that while I come empty-handed and God fills my hand with blessings, while I come to the Cross and receive the infinite benefit of His Cross, I should understand that my full hands are but symbols of my responsibility to press closer still to Him, in order that through me there may be made up that which is behind in the suffering of the Lord?

Yet my last word is this. Do not miss the blessedness of the fact that the fellowship of His sufferings means that He has fellowship with us. When I enter into the fellowship of His sufferings I am not alone, for He is forever with me. I can endure no pain for Him that He does not share with me. When I stand in the presence of sin and suffer—if I have climbed high enough, in that moment He is with me, He is feeling the same pain, He is suffering with me. When my heart is moved with hot anger because God is misunderstood, He is suffering with me. My fellowship with Him means His fellowship with me. When through pity born of His love my heart breaks over the awful punishment that is falling on the head of the sinner, never let Satan suggest I have reached a higher level than the Lord, for He is having fellowship with me, my pity is born of His pity, and His love is suffering with my love.

Paradox of Christianity which no man can explain—there is no joy like the fellowship of His suffering! What is the sense of sin that causes you pain, dear child of God? It is the outcome of purity. The measure of purity is the measure of suffering in the presence of sin. In the infinite mystery of pain there is the deeper heart and core of holy joy. What is that suffering of your heart in the presence of misunderstanding of God? It is born of your perfect satisfaction in God. Why are you angry when that man libels God? Because you know Him. Your hot pain and great sorrow come out of the quiet rest of intimate knowledge. What is that pity for the sinner that throbs through your soul, fills your eyes, breaks your heart? It is the outcome of the love of God shed abroad in your heart.

Oh, verily, if we can but come to the Cross now, and in its presence ". . . lay in dust life's glory dead," then, indeed "from the ground there blossoms red, life that shall endless be."

CHAPTER VIII

AN EASTER MEDITATION

Blessed be the God and Father of our Lord Jesus Christ, Who according to His great mercy begat us again unto a living hope by the resurrection of Jesus Christ from the dead.

I PETER 1:3.

THESE ARE THE FIRST DIRECT WORDS OF THIS LETTER OF Peter, following, as they do, immediately on the salutation. They constitute an outburst of praise. Undoubtedly, this letter was written by Peter in obedience to his Lord's injunction, "Do thou, when once thou hast turned again, stablish thy brethren." He wrote "to the elect who are sojourners of the Dispersion in Pontus, Galatia, Cappadocia, Asia, and Bithynia," and he wrote for the one purpose of strengthening them in the midst of severe trial and great difficulty. The letter thus intended to strengthen opens with this great doxology. One can understand how these words of Peter came from a very full heart. They are distinctly autobiographical. While expressed in that plural number which associated all the saints with himself, those to whom he wrote as well as those who had been his immediate companions in the early days of discipleship, there can be no escape from the conviction that he was writing very much out of his own experience. They were the words of one who had passed through deep waters because of manifold temptations and severe proof of faith, manifold temptations in the midst of which he had faltered and failed, severe proof of faith in the process of which his courage had failed, though his faith in his Lord personally had never failed. They were the words of a man who had passed through these experiences and had proved his Lord's power to deliver. They were words written, as we have already indicated, to such as were then passing through trial, so that he spoke to them almost immediately of the manifold temptations through which they are passing, and referred to that trial of their faith which was indeed severe, but which had its values and place in perfecting their character.

In a letter from such a man to such people we are at once arrested by the initial outburst of praise: "Blessed be the God and Father of our Lord Jesus Christ, Who according to His great mercy begat us again unto a living hope by the resurrection of Jesus Christ from the dead."

In these words we have Peter's own account of what the resurrection of Christ did for him and for the first disciples. That is the narrowest application of the text; but, in proportion as we appreciate it, we shall be prepared for the wider application. I repeat, Peter was writing out of a personal experience. He was thinking of the past, of the first meeting with Jesus, of the mystic and marvelous influence he felt when his Lord looked into his eyes and said to him, "Thou art Simon . . . thou shalt be called Rock." He was remembering how, there and then, he yielded himself to the irresistible glamor of that personality and went blunderingly but courageously after Jesus. He was remembering all the days that followed, the weeks and the months, the wonders and the teachings, the dreams, the revelations, and the aspirations; he was remembering the gathering of the shadows, and the darkness that settled on him, and the dull despair, and then that strange and mystic light which broke on his astonished spirit when—we know not where or when—his

Lord, having risen from the dead, found him all alone and talked to him. In that hour, he now declared, we were born again unto a living hope by the resurrection of Jesus Christ from the dead.

Here again we may consider Peter, as indeed we constantly have to do, as the representative man. Interpreting his declaration that he was begotten again unto a living hope by his experience as it is revealed to us in the gospel stories, we may consider in what sense this was true. Such a meditation will serve to reveal to us the true value of that glorious event which we celebrate this morning, the resurrection of our Lord.

We shall consider, then, first, Peter's experience of Christ before resurrection; and, second, the difference which the resurrection made.

First, the experience before the resurrection. We will confine our attention to the man who wrote this letter, Peter, looking upon him as a representative man. We need not dwell on the earlier incidents to which I have already made reference, but only on those of the later months of our Lord's ministry, the incidents occurring in that last, mysterious, shadowed portion of the time.

In the earliest days and months of our Lord's ministry He was the center of attraction to all sorts and conditions of men. We cannot but have observed in our reading of these gospel narratives that there was a very strange sifting process which went on from the beginning of that public ministry: gradually men and women who had been irresistibly attracted to Him withdrew from Him. Indeed, I should almost be prepared to say that they were driven away from Him by the very severity of His terms and the strange and almost appalling manner in which He repelled them. Our theme is not that of the attractive, or the repelling power of Jesus, but it is important that we remind ourselves of it. At the commencement of His public ministry multitudes crowded after Him; at the close of His life's mission not a single man stood by His side. The tragedy is ultimately expressed in words that always flame with fire when we read them, "They all forsook Him and fled," for these words refer to His own disciples. The course of the ministry was one of attraction and sifting as within the infinite wisdom of God; it was part of the Divine economy. In the course of our study of the life of the Lord we become impressed with the fact that in about two and a half years this hostility became very patent, criticism became more definite, men were evidently plotting to silence His voice, to take His life. They are seen working against Him, spreading the net, in order to capture and destroy Him.

Let us listen to three things that Peter said in that shadowed period, for in those three things I think we shall be brought face to face with his experience of his Lord. As the result of all the training, all the teaching, and all the gracious ministry of the years, he said three things, not to be undervalued, but for the moment simply to be observed. Without staying to turn to the actual passages, which are amongst the most familiar in the New Testament, let me refer to them and group them.

The first is recorded in the Gospel of John. We have the account of a certain hour of criticism, in the midst of which our Lord delivered discourses recorded by no other evangelist. In that hour of profound teaching, men drifted away from Him, and at last He asked the disciples, "Would ye also go away?" Then Peter spoke, "Lord, to whom shall we go? Thou hast the words of eternal life." That was Peter's first great confession.

A little further on, so far as one is able to follow these events in chronological order, perhaps three months later, we have that very familiar scene at Cæsarea Philippi, where Jesus, having gathered the disciples away from the multitudes, questioned them on the result of His ministry, and at last made the question personal to them: "Who say ye that I am?" In that connection we find Peter's second great confession, "Thou art Messiah, the Son of the living God."

So far as time is concerned, almost immediately following, perhaps within the next few hours, for Matthew carefully links that which follows to the story of the great confession, our Lord began to unveil to these men the method by which He would pass into His Kingdom, and told them of the coming Cross and resurrection. Then Peter looked at Him, and we have now no confession, but a voice full of anguish and anger. We have hardly dared to translate this passage accurately; that may be a somewhat bold thing to say, but those who are familiar with the Greek will agree. To catch the real significance of the word of Peter on this occasion we need to express what he said in the most colloquial language. In effect, he exclaimed in angry protest, God help you, that be far from Thee!

In those three sayings of Peter—all uttered within the space of three months, in the period when the method of ministry of our Lord was changing, and He was moving toward the ultimate passion—his experience of Christ is revealed to me.

First, "Thou hast the words of eternal life." Then, "Thou art the Messiah." Finally, God help you, not that, not the Cross, not suffering! That was as far as Peter went in experience before the resurrection, and it was a long way.

The occasion of the first was that of gathering hostility. There was a deeper tone in the teaching of Christ as He attempted to direct the attention of the crowds from the material miracle to the spiritual suggestiveness, and the very disciples were offended in Him; and of them who had followed Him, "many of His disciples went back, and walked no more with Him." Then came the hour in which Jesus looked at the twelve and said to them, "Would ye also go away?" That is, do you wish to go? He gave them the opportunity to do so. There was in that question a touch full of severity. It was as though He had said, If you wish to go, the way is open. Do you desire to go? Then Peter looked at Him and said, "Lord, to whom shall we go? Thou hast the words of eternal life." This was a remarkable reply. Oh to be able to get back into the actual atmosphere! Think of these words for a moment, not from the Christian standpoint, but from the Hebrew, remembering the mental outlook of the man who uttered them. It is only as we do so that we shall understand what he meant. In that word of Peter spoken to Jesus he declared his conviction that the teaching of the Lord was authoritative and life-giving. In other words, in that confession of Peter, I find the declaration of his conviction that in the hands of Jesus were the keys of prophetic ministry, the keys of the true interpretation of the moral order, that His word was final as the law of life. In effect, Peter said at that moment, In Thee we have found the Prophet for Whom we have long been waiting: "Thou hast the words of age-abiding life."

We pass on, a few months perhaps, to the next crisis at Cæsarea Philippi, and hear the challenge of Jesus, "Who say ye that I am?" answered by that old and familiar confession, "Thou art the Messiah," for of set purpose I adopt the Hebrew word for interpretation of the Greek word "Christ." Once again, oh, to be back in the actual atmosphere and listen to the words as they came from the lips of Peter. What was it that he really meant? What was the Hebrew idea of Messiahship? It was that of kingship. In the second psalm we find the light of the Old Testament conception focused. The Hebrew was looking for a king to sit on the throne, and administer the affairs of the kingdom in order to realize the great ideal of the Hebrew nation as a nation, to make it the Kingdom of God. Peter looked into the eyes of Jesus and said, "Thou art the Messiah"! I can never quite make up my own mind whether there and then the conviction became final, or whether some little while before he had come to this conviction. I am inclined to think that it was in that moment when he was challenged that all the thinking, all the previous processes of his mind, crystallized into conviction and he said, "Thou art the Messiah," recognizing that Christ held the scepter.

Thus Peter saw Jesus not only as the Prophet for Whom men had long been waiting, speaking the words of ultimate authority; he saw Him also as the King for Whom men had long been waiting, holding in His hand the scepter of perfect government. He had discovered in Jesus the King to Whom all the prophets had given witness. This meant that his heart was full of hope, hope for the establishment of the Kingdom, the realization of the Divine purpose, and the fulfilment of the aspiration of his own people for generations; hope that in the King-Prophet there should be the enunciation of the final, perfect ethic, hope that the Kingdom would now be established.

Immediately we pass to the third word of Peter. The third word was spoken following the two confessions: the confession of Peter of which we have been speaking, and the confession of Jesus answering that of Peter. The confession of Peter was, "Thou art the Messiah, the Son of the living God"; the confession of Jesus was, "I also say unto thee, that thou art Peter, and upon this rock I will build My church; and the gates of Hades shall not prevail against it." In this word of his Master there flamed before the surprised vision of Peter the glory of the established order, and then immediately that deeper secret of the Cross, which Christ had never explicitly mentioned before to His disciples, for the evangelists are very careful to tell us that after this Christ began to show that He must suffer. This secret He had nursed within His own heart; it was the ultimate movement of His mission, the passion, the *exodos!* Of this He had never until now been able to speak; but "from that time began Jesus to show unto His disciples, how that He must go unto Jerusalem, and suffer many things of the elders and chief priests and scribes, and be killed, and the third day be raised up."

It is well to notice in this connection that every passage in the Gospel narratives which records our Lord's foretelling of His death records also His foretelling of His resurrection. This is a matter of supreme importance, because we are sometimes told that this foretelling of death was the result of Christ's yielding to circumstances, that He was so heroic that He would not turn aside from His path although He knew that men would kill Him. That is not the New Testament teaching. The New Testament does not reveal Jesus going to death as a victim, but as a Victor.

After the confession of Peter, then He told the secret for the first time to Peter and the rest of the disciples, that He must die, and that He must rise again. It was then that Peter uttered his passionate word of protest.

The more I ponder these stories, the less I am inclined to criticize Peter, and the more perfectly I come into sympathy with his protest. I do not say that it was right, but that it was perfectly natural. The Church of God still only half believes that the way to crowning is the way of the Cross. There never yet has emerged the Christian nation that is ready to die for the sake of right in the hope of resurrection into new life.

Jesus now looked at this man and said, You have found that I am a Prophet; you have found that I am a King; now let me tell you the secret of how I am going to utter the deepest truth, and of how I am going to build the Kingdom. I must go up to the city, I must be bruised, killed, and rise again. If we put ourselves in the place of Peter we shall understand his protest, made in anguish and anger. There is no escape at all from the fact that Peter was angry. He took Jesus aside, and began to rebuke Him, that is, to chide

Him. God help you! That be far from Thee! In that moment his hope was overshadowed. If He was going to Jerusalem to suffer and to die, what about the words of age-abiding life? If the Teacher dies, the words will be dead! In that moment the shadows fell. If we read the story carefully and chronologically so far as we can, we see what happened from that moment until the Cross. Peter never came near to his Lord again. This is true of all the disciples. They followed Him all the way, they were amazed, they dared not ask Him questions. Over and over again we have the account of how He tried to tell them about His Cross, and every time—oh, the tragedy of it, and the wonderful unveiling of human nature there is in it—every time He spoke of His Cross some one of them broke in upon the conversation with practically the same question: Lord, who is the greatest among us? In those final days hope was dying. The disciples never ceased to love Him, never ceased to believe in Him and in His intention; but they lost all hope. Hope died, until at last they could bear it no longer, and they all forsook Him and fled. There at last He hung on the Cross, the brutal Roman gibbet, done to death; and the sun went out of the sky, the light faded from the horizon, and despair surged through their souls, and who can wonder?

And now let us listen to the doxology:

> Blessed be the God and Father of our Lord Jesus Christ, Who according to His great mercy begat us again unto a living hope by the resurrection of Jesus Christ from the dead.

The text tells its own story, but for a moment or two let us meditate on it, that we may discover the difference which the resurrection made. Do not forget the unutterable, immeasurable, unfathomable darkness of those days and nights, especially to these men—the Prophet dead, therefore the teaching impracticable; the King dead, therefore the Kingdom impossible.

Then came the strange news of the morning: "Certain women . . . came saying, that they had also seen a vision of angels, which said that He was alive"—I never read that without feeling that these men did not quite believe the story, because the women had told them! Then somewhere, somewhen—I am always thankful there is no record of the where or the when—Jesus found this very man Peter. When the two arrived from Emmaus eager to tell the assembled disciples that Jesus had walked and talked with them, before they could tell the story, the eleven told theirs, and this was what they had to tell: "The Lord is risen indeed, and hath appeared to Simon." When, or where we do not know. When he was massing the evidences of the resurrection of Jesus, Paul referred to it, but neither he nor the Evangelist gives any details. This is one of the sacred, powerful silences of the New Testament. Somewhere the Lord met Peter. It would be almost sacrilegious to paint the scene, yet I feel that I could paint the picture of that meeting. At least, in this doxology we find the effect produced on Peter:

> Blessed be the God and Father of our Lord Jesus Christ, Who according to His great mercy begat us again unto a living hope by the resurrection of Jesus Christ from the dead.

It was the dawning of a new day in the rebirth of hope. The resurrection began its work at the point where this man had broken down. He had discovered the Prophet; the King had been revealed to him: Prophet? yes! King? yes! Priest? no! That he had not understood. He had seen the keys of moral interpretation in the hand of Christ and had said, Thou art a Prophet. He had seen the scepter and had said, Thou art a King. But he did not understand the wearing of the ephod, he did not apprehend the need of the Priest. The Cross had filled him with fear. In that moment when he saw the risen Christ, the first effect was on his conception of the Cross; the Cross was transfigured before his eyes! He had seen the hand holding the scroll, and the brow on which rested the crown; but now he saw, not first the King, not first the Prophet, but first the Priest wearing the ephod.

We are all familiar with Watts' great hymn:

> When I survey the wondrous Cross.

In it there is a verse which is generally omitted from our hymn books today, why I do not know. It reads thus:

> His dying crimson like a robe
> Spreads o'er His body on the tree,
> And I am dead to all the globe,
> And all the globe is dead to me.

Why have we cut that verse out of our hymnbooks? If it is the sign of a theological movement, that movement was not born in heaven.

> His dying crimson like a robe
> Spreads o'er His body on the tree.

That is the robe of priesthood. Peter now looked at the Cross through the resurrection light; and the Cross that had shamed him, that had filled him with fear, flashed and gleamed with the splendor of mercy: "Blessed be the God and Father of our Lord Jesus Christ, Who according to his great mercy . . ."

The Cross was now seen as the propitiatory, the place of priesthood; there was the altar, the sacrifice, and the priest; there sin was dealt with. Before Peter was far on with this letter, he wrote: "Ye were redeemed, not with corruptible things, with silver or gold, from your vain manner of life handed down from your fathers; but with precious blood, as of a lamb without blemish and without spot, even the blood of Christ."

Go back to the other side of Resurrection and stand with Peter. Death? God help you, no! That is murder and defeat! Come to this Resurrection side and look back. The Cross is no less vulgar—the vulgarity of the Cross is the vulgarity of the sin that erected it—but the Cross flames with light. The light of the glory of the grace of God, who took sin into His own heart and canceled it in a mystery of pain that can be expressed in human history only by bloodshedding, is shining from the Tree! The Cross is transfigured: "Who according to His great mercy begat us again into a living hope." By the way of that Cross the Evangel of forgiveness, which is the moral basis of the Kingdom, is made possible. The word of the prophet is the law of the Kingdom; the scepter of the King is the government of the Kingdom; but the Kingdom is a lost Kingdom, despoiled territory, a people in rebellion. How can it be restored? Only by building on a moral basis, by reconstruction, regeneration, repentance, renewal—all great Christian words born of the fact of the Cross. In the morning after the resurrection, when the Lord sought him, Peter saw in the transfigured Cross the first gleam of hope, the hope that had perished when the Cross was erected, and he was begotten again unto a living hope. Hope springs from the Cross, it begins the flush of a new morning, it inspires the anthem of the ultimate victory, it composes the song of undying hope.

In the Cross Peter saw the throne established, and he saw the King, still holding the scepter in His hand, and knew that authority was vested in Him. Presently Peter heard Christ say, "All authority hath been given unto Me in heaven and on earth. Go ye therefore, and disciple the nations," and by the witness of Resurrection Peter knew that in the King were vested all resources of power for the establishment of the Kingdom.

When the risen Lord spoke to him that morning, Peter heard the final word of revelation. He had seen the keys in Christ's hand before; but now the truth was perfectly published. Thus the hope-restoring vision was, first, that of the Priest; second, that of the King; third, that of the Prophet enunciating the laws of the Kingdom, and every word full of force and power and life because of the victory won in the midst of the mystery of the darkness of the Cross.

Take away the resurrection, and what then? It is surely a work of supererogation to argue it in this assembly. Deny the fact which we celebrate to-day, what then? Then the Cross was the ultimate tragedy. If Christ was murdered and there was nothing in His death other than the victory of sin, then that is the severest reflection on the government of God of which I know anything; no other moral problem compares with it. If there was no resurrection, then that was of all tragedies the most tragic! No resurrection! Then that King with high vision, noble aspiration, is dead! No resurrection! Then the Prophet was mistaken when He said, "Fear not them which kill the body, and after that have no more that they can do," mistaken in all His high ideals! Then where am I? "If Christ hath not been raised, then is our preaching in vain, your faith also is vain . . . ye are yet in your sins."

It is altogether too late for arguments of that kind. The results demonstrate the resurrection. Spiritual and moral reconstruction by the way of the Cross, the fact that men have seen, and still do see, sin when they come to the Cross, and confess it when they kneel before the Cross, and know the breaking of its power when they yield themselves to the Christ of the Cross, these are the facts that prove the resurrection.

The King is alive and known, exercising His will in the hearts of individuals, creating magnificent heroisms to-day, so that men are venturing forth in obedience to Him on high and holy enterprises, counting not their lives dear unto them, that they may be obedient to His will. The prophet is vindicated in the growing victories of His teaching.

Our hope is living, for these things are the result of the resurrection, they demonstrate the resurrection.

If for a while we are in the midst of conflict, and the noise of battle is about us, we know the victory is already won. Armageddon was fought in the hour of the Cross, the prince of this world hath been judged, and at last the victory shall be complete.

So that, with this song of hope in our heart, we also, born to a living hope by the way of the resurrection, trust in the Priest, follow the King, and obey the Prophet until His Kingdom shall come.

CHAPTER IX

THE CONDITIONS OF RENEWAL

Repentance toward God, and faith toward our Lord Jesus Christ.

ACTS 20:21.

WE AT ONCE RECOGNIZE THAT THIS IS NOT A SENTENCE. AS A matter of fact, the text consists of two phrases, incidentally employed in the course of apostolic discourse. Paul halted at Miletus in order that he might meet the elders of the church at Ephesus and speak to them, as he did not expect to see them again. In the course of his address, delivered to those elders, in the interest of the church at Ephesus, and therefore as always, in the interest of Ephesus itself, he reviewed the ministry which he had conducted in that city during three years, reminding them that he had not shrunk from declaring to them anything that was profitable, teaching them publicly and from house to house, testifying to both the Jews and the Greeks of "repentance toward God, and faith toward our Lord Jesus Christ."

In these phrases the Apostle summarized the burden of his message in Ephesus in so far as that message emphasized personal and individual responsibility concerning the gospel of the grace of God which he had proclaimed there. I have taken the words because they seem to me to give the simplest formula concerning human responsibility in the presence of the preaching of that gospel of grace.

You will immediately see that the terms are those of spiritual things, spiritual relationships. It is quite easy, I think, to discover behind the words the apostolic outlook, the apostolic conception. It is quite evident that these phrases take for granted certain facts, while they reveal the immediate responsibility of men. There can be no meaning in them apart from certain facts which most evidently were present in the mind of the Apostle, facts, moreover, which he took for granted as being received and believed in by those to whom at this particular moment he was speaking.

What, then, are these underlying facts? First, the fact of God; second, the fact of man's relationship to God; third, the fact of man's being out of harmony with God; and, finally, the fact that a man out of harmony with God is a failure.

If we blot God out of our thinking or out of our belief, then there is no meaning in this text at all. It is only as we become conscious that the deep, true thing concerning ourselves is that we have relationship with God, that such relationship is at fault, and that therefore we are at fault, that there can be any appeal in such phrases as these.

Let us, then, proceed on the assumption that we take for granted the God of the Bible, the God from Whom all things have proceeded, the God by Whose power all things are upheld, from Whose government nothing can ever by any possible chance escape.

Let us take for granted, in the second place, that man is spiritual, that the deepest, profoundest truth concerning man is that he is offspring of God, that the word which Ezekiel uttered long ago for the correction of false proverbs, "All souls are Mine," is a profound truth; that the deepest thing in each individual life is not the material, is not even the moral, but the spiritual; that, therefore, the things of change in the midst of which we find ourselves to-day cannot be the things which find us in the deepest of our lives;

that, therefore, if we live only in relation to things seen and temporal, things that pass and vanish and perish even while we look on them, touch and handle them, we are ruining ourselves in that we are failing to realize the whole meaning of our lives.

Let us take for granted that we are children of the ages and not of the passing day, that we are in our essential being related to Deity and are not wholly of the dust; that to make the order of our life such as expresses itself in such words as, "Let us eat and drink, for to-morrow we die," is to fail entirely to understand ourselves. Let us further take for granted that if these things be so, then we are moving inevitably toward some change through which we shall come to a yet clearer apprehension of the reality of spiritual things and stand in the light of the Divine presence, in the nakedness of our spiritual life, stripped of all those things which to-day hide the spiritual from us, hide us so largely from each other, and hide us so perpetually from ourselves. If someone should say, Why do you not say plainly that we are all going to die? I would reply, Very well, let it be so stated—we are all approaching death! What is death? Death is but transition. Death is but the process of change by which personality passes from existence limited, hindered, probationary, into that which is larger, where the light is clearer, and the understanding perfected, and being comes to its fulness in some form or fashion. The reason for the fear of death is simply stated: "The sting of death is sin; and the power of sin is the law." Men do fear death, all their lifetime men are subject to bondage through the fear of death. The fear of death that rests on the heart of humanity is born of the fact that man is conscious that if he pass away from this life, with its limitations, into larger life, he is unprepared, he has not taken sufficient account of the larger life, has neglected the true aspiration of his nature, has not turned a listening ear to the voice forever sounding within him that he is immortal, eternal. Man lives within the narrow realm of the things that are near, and when he approaches the end, or things of the end, and imagines himself as passing out to some bourne whence no traveler returns, to some unknown state of being, he is filled with fear because of sin.

What, then, is sin? I pray you notice most carefully that this fear of death is not peculiar to men and women who have been guilty of what we sometimes term vulgar sins. Indeed, it is strange and yet true that the vulgar sensualist is often free from the fear of death, and that because of that he has so completely blunted the spiritual sense in his sensuality that he has no consciousness of it whatever. The fear of death comes to finer souls—using the expression in the common language of our everyday speech.

What, then, is sin? Sin is failure. I use the word almost with bated breath, because to say that seems to rob sin of its terror. Yet consider it carefully. If the Bible, by the language of which it makes use, means anything, it conveys that idea. Confining ourselves for the moment to the New Testament, with which we are all familiar, the commonest Greek word for sin, *hamartia*, means coming short, missing the mark. It is a Greek word which was used when a marksman shot an arrow at a target and failed to hit the center. Sin is failure. Sin is being less than I ought to be. Sin is failure to realize the meaning of my own life. Sin is failure to realize the forces that are within me. It is this sense of failure, this sense of limitation, this inner conviction that perchance never expresses itself in the language of a preacher, but, nevertheless, haunts the soul; this sense that the years are wasted, that the energies of life have not brought any true return to the personality—it is all this that overshadows man when he thinks of death. It is the true Divine instinct within the soul telling it that when it sloughs off this mortal coil, and passes in the nakedness of its personality into the light of the uncreated beam, it will be seen crippled, dwarfed, atrophied, having failed to realize the profound meaning of life. That is the sense of sin.

There is in that sense of sin, moreover, the sense of pollution; or—use the word that helps you most—guilt, defilement, uncleanness. It is that sense that fills the heart with fear when death is spoken of.

For the sake of illustration, imagine a man who has no sense of failure, a man who has not failed, a man whose life has been clean, pure, straight, noble, and infinitely more than all these virtues, which mark conditions rather than realizations, a man who has found out the secret of his own being and has adjusted his life to its true center, who has filled his own vocation—that man never trembles at the thought of death. To him death is entrance on life. To him death is the hour in which, crossing the border line, he shall find himself in the presence of the uncreated beam. That is the goal of life, the high ecstasy toward which life is forever moving, the final moment when he will be able to stand unafraid in the presence of God and see the beatific vision, and find the last solution of all the problems of his own life as he rests in the presence of God. When such a man thinks of death, he says, "O death, where is thy victory? O death, where is thy sting? The sting of death is sin; and the power of sin is the law; but thanks be to God, which giveth us the victory through our Lord Jesus Christ."

In those final words of the apostolic challenge and affirmation I have introduced the gospel of grace, and the real meaning of the Christian fact.

It is in the presence of such conceptions as these that the phrases of my text begin to have meaning. As a man shall say, I believe in God, and I believe that I am indeed in His likeness and image, of His very being, offspring of Deity, and I am approaching the bound of life where the burdens of time are laid down, coming to the hour in which I pass out into the nakedness of my essential life into the very presence of God, and I am unprepared. Then he inquires, Is there any way by which I can be prepared? Is there any way by which I can overtake the tragedy of lost years and expended strength? Is there any way by which I can be born anew? Nicodemus's difficulty was not a surface difficulty: "How can a man be born when he is old? Can he enter a second time into his mother's womb, and be born?" That is, can he force himself back through the years and undo the things that have been done, and change the set and tendency of his life? Can he begin again? That is the great cry of the human soul when the soul comes to consciousness of God, of its own spiritual nature, of the fact that this life is transient, probationary, and that the revolving wheels of time are bearing it ever closer to the moment when it stands alone in the presence of the God from Whom it came. The Christian evangel is the answer to that cry.

What, then, is the way of salvation? We may omit from our consideration from this moment forward the man who has no sense of sin. I would do it respectfully, reverently, but I would say earnestly to that man, From now on I have no message for you. I am here as the messenger of my Master, and He Himself said: "I came not to call the righteous, but sinners to repentance."

What, then, shall I do to be saved? some soul is asking. It may be that the soul that asks will never utter those words in my hearing, will never make application with this great spiritual inquiry to any prophet, priest, or teacher. It is a question of the inner life. What, then, shall I do to be saved? The great phrases of the Apostle are the perfect and final answer, "Repentance toward God, and faith toward our Lord Jesus Christ."

If we are to understand such simple phrases as these we must approach them in the simplest way. What is repentance? That is the first inquiry. Repentance is not self-reformation. Repentance is not sorrow for sin. Repentance is a change of mind, and a change of mind when it is true and deep necessarily and inevitably issues in change of attitude and change of conduct. The word of my text does not suggest sorrow—do not misunderstand me, I am not saying that repentance is unaccompanied by sorrow, but I want you to clearly understand that repentance is not sorrow. I have known men and women who have truly repented toward God, who at the moment had no deep sorrow for sin, but it came, and it grew and deepened with the passing years. I venture to affirm most solemnly, as a matter of profound conviction, that there are men who have been following the Lord Jesus Christ for half a century whose sorrow for sin is profounder now than when they commenced the Christian life. On the other hand, I have known men who have been genuinely sorry for sin but have not repented. There may be contrition, there may be lamenting over the thing done that cannot be undone, there may be the agony that cries out with Lady Macbeth,

> Out damned spot!
> Not all the perfumes of Araby will sweeten this little hand.

Yet there may be no repentance. Repentance is a change of mind. That is fundamental. The changed conception always expresses itself in change of attitude, and the change of attitude produces change of conduct. So that ultimately repentance is the turning of the back deliberately on everything that is out of harmony with the will of God. Fundamentally it is turning to God. This same Apostle, in one of the first, perhaps the very first, of his letters, that to the Thessalonians, gives a remarkable description of the commencement of the Christian life, "Ye turned to God from idols, to serve a living and true God, and to wait for His Son from heaven." In that description you have an exact account of what repentance is. It is turning to God.

But here is our difficulty. Let me say it with all the faithfulness of which I am capable: it is the peculiar difficulty of such a congregation as this. I have preached to congregations to whom the matter is understood in a moment, a congregation of men and women in the depths. It was quite easy to talk to them about repentance; such sinners understand that repentance means turning round and facing God. The difficulty in such an audience as this is that faces look up into the face of the preacher and say, Why emphasize this? We are not turned from God. But are we not turned from God? Godlessness has many manifestations. It is not the peculiar quality of the penitentiary. It is found in the university. It does not dwell alone in the slum. It is found in the suburb. It is not peculiar to vulgarized humanity. It is the more subtle wrong of cultured humanity. Godlessness! What is godlessness? Leaving God out of account in all the actualities of life. Intellectual search that does not take account of Him. Emotional outgoing that does not seek the purifying of His fire. Especially, the central volitional activity of choice that never thinks of Him until the choice is made. Life that lives as though there were no God and yet occasionally confesses God is godless. The man who conducts his business six days a week as though there were no God and comes here and worships, profanes the sanctuary and blasphemes. Repentance is turning round and facing God, recognizing the throne, submitting thereto, asking at the gates of the high place for the orders of every day and every hour. That is godly life. Repentance is toward God, the change of the mind back toward Him, that He may be taken into account; the change of the conduct so that it may square with that master conception of life that the will of God is supreme.

Let me say, further, that repentance is induced by the ministry of the Holy Spirit, but that repentance depends entirely on the choice of the human soul. It is induced by the Spirit. The Spirit of God induces repentance in the heart of a man by revealing to him the true nature of his sin, by revealing to him the attitude of God toward sin and toward himself. By the proclamation of the Evangel, by the enunciation of the Divine ethic, the Spirit induces man toward repentance. The Spirit reveals to man what sin is, showing him that sin mars the life, that no man can come to fulfilment of his own life who forgets God; that, because the very forces of life are God-created forces and life cannot come to highest realization or fullest meaning save within His will and under His law, sin therefore spoils the life. The Spirit reveals to man that such sin spreads insidiously. The forgetting of God which is casual becomes the forgetting of God which is habitual.

> Trailing clouds of glory do we come
> From God Who is our home,

and the little child, granted that its surroundings are what they ought to be, is familiar with God. How wonderfully familiar a little child is with God, but with the passing of the days there is, first, the casual forgetfulness, the failure to recognize God in the hour of volitional choice, then the forgetfulness that hardens into a habit until God is shut out of life, and the finest things of life are blunted, spoiled. The Spirit brings home to man this sense of failure.

I know the things whereof I speak; I know them in my experience, and I know them in this ministry of dealing with men and women personally that God has committed to me. Not many days ago a cultured, refined man, brilliant in scholarship, looked into my eyes, and I never shall forget the look of haunting fear on his face as he said, "Oh God, what a failure I am!" It was the sense of sin, of the spoiled life. I am inclined to think that this man might have said with the rich young ruler of old, in the presence of every commandment in the second table of the decalogue, I have broken none of them. It was the sense of failure that swept his soul. The Spirit of God thus brings a man—to use an old phrase, the phrase of our fathers, may it come to us with power—to conviction of sin.

The Spirit of God comes revealing to man not merely what sin is and that he is a sinner, but also revealing the attitude of God toward sin and the attitude of God toward the sinner. What has the Spirit to say concerning God's attitude toward sin? "Thou that art of purer eyes than to behold evil, and that canst not look on perverseness." What has the Spirit to say about God's attitude toward sinners? "God so loved the world, that He gave His only begotten Son, that whosoever believeth on Him should not perish, but have eternal life." The attitude of God toward sin is that of relentless hostility, because sin spoils man. God's attitude toward the sinner is that of love stronger than death, mightier than the grave, so infinite and wonderful and profound that it stoops to the level of the ruined man, and, gathering to itself all the pain and agony resulting from sin, cancels it in the passion of His own heart.

By this ministry of unveiling the Spirit induces repentance, but if repentance be induced by the work of the Spirit it must be a human act. Here is the realm of tragedy. Men come to this point, the Spirit revealing the fact of sin to them—not always in the hour of Christian worship, sometimes suddenly unexpectedly, right in the midst of daily business, sometimes in the presence of a great bereavement, sometimes when hope is springing within them and some new joy is coming to them—and, tragedy of all tragedies, there are men who do not respond to the Spirit and decline to repent, and turn back again to the beggarly elements of sin. For the advantage of the moment, for the supposed advantage of the moment, they shut out the vision of the infinite and bend themselves to the immediate. That is what some of you have done over and over again.

Yet we must go further. A man repenting is not a man saved. I may turn my back on sin and my face toward God, resolutely and with determination; but something more is needed. Change of attitude does not undo the past, neither can it alter the nature. Given a man repenting in answer to the Spirit's illumination, what does he really need? What he needs most of all is forgiveness, absolution. He cries for forgiveness for the past, does not believe it possible at first, cannot see how he can be forgiven; but he asks it, and I believe I interpret the deepest feeling of your heart as I speak out of my own experience and say, If you could persuade me that God simply says, We will say no more about the past—then I want more than that! I want loosing from the past, some cleansing from its defilement, I want something that shall purge me as hyssop cannot. I want some hand to blot out the past.

I need more. I want to be sure, when I turn my face to God, that He will receive me again. I who have rebelled against His throne, I want to know whether He will take me home again. I need more than that. And here is the profoundest thing of all, to me at least, I want to know how I shall be able to manage to-morrow, for, so help me God, I speak out of my own experience, if salvation means simply sin forgiven, and I am left paralyzed, it is hardly worth while. I have to face the same temptations, Can I be enabled? I have to go back from this quiet hour in the sanctuary to the city, to hear the thousand siren voices, to be lured by the glitter of the straw in the dust! Can I be made strong so that I shall stand erect? Whether I look back or within or on, while I repent I am still a needy soul.

This sense of need is met in the Apostle's second phrase: "Faith toward our Lord Jesus Christ." As he said the words

I venture to affirm that before his eyes there gleamed the glory of Christ Himself, and he saw how that Christ stands confronting the repentant soul, bringing to that soul everything for which it asks. What about this past? "Who His own self bare our sins in His body upon the tree." I had better leave it there. To try to explain that would but be to darken counsel with a multiplicity of words. To attempt to tell how in some infinite transaction in the darkness God has made possible the blotting out of sin is beyond me and increasingly beyond me. The longer I live, the less I can understand its mystery and the more I know its power. Christ confronts the soul and says He will put His hand, His pierced hand, across the page of the past and blot it out.

What about God's acceptance of me? Christ tells me that I need have no fear in this matter, that God never turned His face away from me, it was I who turned my face away from Him. In the one matchless picture that Jesus gives us of the Father in that old familiar parable in the fifteenth chapter of Luke's gospel that fact is revealed: "While he was yet afar off, his father saw him, and ran, and fell on his neck, and kissed him." That is God. That is what Christ came to show us. Christ did not come to persuade God to love us, but to show us that God never ceased to love us. He did not come to make God change His mind; He came to make me change my mind, and to tell me that when I turn back to God, God is far more than halfway to meet me. Even the parable of Jesus breaks down —I say it reverently—for God in Christ came all the way to the far country to find me, and now

> My God is reconciled,
> His pardoning voice I hear.
> He owns me for His child;
> I can no longer fear.
> With confidence I now draw nigh,
> And Father, Abba Father, cry.

What about to-morrow? How am I to stand erect who have so often fallen by the way? How am I to master the things that so long have mastered me? Again the Christ stands before me and says, I Who have blotted out thy sin, I Who have revealed the Father to thee so that thou mayest know His face is toward thee still in love, "lo, I am with thee all the days." A quaint yet beautiful story comes to my mind. To an old Scotsman his master said one day: "Donald, I am going to give you that little cottage and bit of land for your own." The Scotsman looked into the face of his master and said, "Master, I don't think I want it." "Why not?" "Well, I have saved nothing, and I can't stock it, and I can't work it." "Oh," said the master, "I think we can arrange that. I will invest a little capital, and give you the stock." The man looked up into his master's face and said, "If it's you and me together for it I think we can manage." Christ says, I give you back your birthright, I bring you back to God, blot out your sin, readmit you to the fellowship that you turned your back upon. I say, I am afraid, I am weak, I have failed! He says, "I am with you all the days." Then, reverently employing my parable, I say, With Christ I can. "I can do all things through Christ which strengtheneth me." If He will be with me in the coming days, then verily I can.

Faith is more than intellectual assent to the accuracy of a gospel. It is the venture of the soul on the gospel. Here is a check. I hold it in my hand signed. I believe in that check; but I really believe in it when I endorse it and cash it. Here is an enterprise. I believe in it. I really believe in it when I share in its processes. Then join it, and we shall know you believe in it.

> Venture on Him, venture wholly,
> Let no other trust intrude.

Look into the eyes of Christ and say, I repent, I turn to God, I come, oh, Christ, to Thee. I trust in Thy promise. I yield myself to Thy command. Lead on, and I will follow Thee. That is faith.

Wherever a man shall thus venture on the word of this Christ, having faith toward Him, having repented toward God, then life begins anew. If the vessel hath been marred in the hand of the Potter He will make it again another vessel.

CHAPTER X

THE PRIESTLY BENEDICTION

And the Lord spake unto Moses, saying, Speak unto Aaron and unto his sons, saying, On this wise shall ye bless the children of Israel; ye shall say unto them,
  The Lord bless thee, and keep thee;
  The Lord make His face to shine upon thee, and be gracious unto thee;
  The Lord lift up His countenance upon thee, and give thee peace.
  So shall they put My name upon the children of Israel; and I will bless them.
NUMBERS 6: 22-27.

The Lord bless thee, and keep thee;
The Lord make His face to shine upon thee, and be gracious unto thee;
The Lord lift up His countenance upon thee, and give thee peace.

THESE WORDS CONSTITUTED THE PRIESTLY BENEDICTION IN the Hebrew economy. They were included in the Divinely appointed liturgy of worship, and, in common with the whole of that pictorial system, were richer and fuller than the men who used them knew. It is only in the "grace and truth" which "came by Jesus Christ" that we can discover the full meaning of "the law" which was "given by Moses." Nevertheless, as the component colors of light are seen in the spectrum, so we may often be helped to an understanding of grace and truth by the ritual and formulas of the law.

The priestly office is mediatorial. Its function is twofold, intercessory and benedictory. Each of these functions has a double operation. The priest in intercession stands first in the presence of God pleading the cause of men, and then in the presence of men pleading the cause of God. The priest in benediction stands first in the presence of men pronouncing blessings from God, and then in the presence of God offering the praises of men.

Our present meditation is concerned with the first aspect of the benedictory functions, the pronouncement of the Divine blessing on men by the lips of the mediating priest. This solemn act was a distinct part of the worship of the Hebrew people, and its place in the order of our worship is indicated quite clearly in the twenty-second verse of the ninth chapter of Leviticus, where we read these words: "And Aaron lifted up his hands toward the people, and blessed them; and he came down from offering the sin offering, and the burnt offering, and the peace offerings." Thus it will be seen that in that liturgical service the pronouncement of the benediction followed the completion of the presentation of the offerings. The relation between the suggestiveness of these offerings and the pronunciation of the blessing is quite evident. Sin being dealt with, the priest may say: "Jehovah bless thee and keep thee." Dedication being now complete, he may say: "Jehovah make His face to shine upon thee, and be gracious unto thee." Peace being thus established, he may say: "Jehovah lift up His face upon thee, and give thee peace."

Without any discussion of the mediatorial ministry of our one and only Priest—the Daysman Who stands between us and God, laying His hand on God with the awful, holy familiarity of unity, and laying His hand on us with the equally surprising beneficent familiarity of unity—the work that makes the blessing possible, let us quietly meditate on this ancient formula of benediction as it reveals to us the inestimable advantages of our relation to God in Christ Jesus. In doing so we desire to observe that the whole fact of the advantage is included in the suggestiveness of the Name, while its component parts are revealed in the threefold form of pronouncement.

When this commandment was given to Moses it ended with this injunction: "So shall they put My Name upon the children of Israel." It was an instruction how the priest was to pronounce the Name of God in the hearing of the people, so that they might understand the advantages that came to them from God through priesthood as they were inclusively suggested in the name itself.

The Lord bless thee, and keep thee;
The Lord make His face to shine upon thee, and be gracious unto thee;
The Lord lift up His countenance upon thee, and give thee peace.
So shall they put My Name upon the children of Israel.

If I may fall back upon the figure already incidentally used, the Name is "light"; but, by the pronouncement of the Name in this fashion, light is analyzed and we see its component parts; and the colors that, merging into whiteness, become light are revealed for us in this ancient formula.

Thus let us consider first the revealing Name; and, second, the interpretative sentences.

Now may it be given to us by the guidance of the Spirit of God to approach this subject of the Name as here found, with all solemnity and with all reverence. We shall take time to remind ourselves of some things with which perhaps we are very familiar, but which are so vital to our subject that we must deal with them. We of the Christian age are at least in danger of losing something because of our holy familiarity with God through Christ Jesus. He has made it possible for us to talk with Him, all of us, as Moses did, face to face, as a man talks with his friend. By reason of this privilege I often feel that we use the holy Name somewhat carelessly. Reverence for that name characterized the Hebrew mental attitude. This reverence presently became pedantic obscurantism, and prevented these men from uttering it, and made them refuse to write it. At a later period, some translators substituted another title for the name in many passages, so that in our common reading of the Old Testament we are in danger of missing its revelations. To us the name is Jehovah, or, if some of you have been reading modern theological books, you have seen it spelt Yahweh, which is purely a piece of pedantry, because no one can prove that Yahweh is more correct than Jehovah. It never appeared on the Hebrew manuscript in one form or the other; but in the very appearance of the name was revealed that reverence to which I am making reference. To express it they used the tetragrammaton, YHVH. These four consonants stood on the page, the vowel points being omitted that the name might not be uttered, so great and sacred did it seem to be to these people. This particular name came to have greater sanctity to the Hebrew people than even the name Elohim, which is vaster and more wonderful than the former in its essential meaning.

It was used from patriarchal times without any clear apprehension of its meaning, but from the hour of the Exodus it was used with a new understanding of its meaning. Such I take to be the meaning of the word which I have already read to you in the book of Exodus, in which after communing with the great lawgiver, Jehovah is recorded as having said to him, "I appeared unto Abraham, unto Isaac, and unto Jacob, as El Shaddai, but by My name Jehovah I was not known to them." The Patriarchs had employed the Name, were familiar with it, but had not understood it. In the hour of ransom and redemption God began to explain the name by which they had named Him, but which they had never perfectly understood.

What, then, was the suggestiveness of the name? The name "Jehovah" does not stand as the symbol of essential being; the one name which stands as the symbol of essential being is that by which God revealed Himself to Moses in the presence of the burning bush. When fear and trembling possessed the soul of the man called to high enterprise, he inquired of God, Who shall I say has sent me? and the answer of God was this, "I AM THAT I AM." "I AM"—as though He were about to declare some truth concerning Himself, but suddenly limited Himself—"THAT I AM," in order that the listening man might understand that God was not giving him an interpretation of nature or character, but an affirmation of being. God is eternal "I AM." How often in the course of casual, necessary conversation I say, "I am," and yet, as a matter of fact, I have no sooner uttered the word than my tense has become a past. In some true sense, no finite being can say I am. It is the distinct word of essential life, abiding, timeless, dateless, infinite. That is essential being, but that is not the suggestion of the word Jehovah.

Neither does the word Jehovah declare all-completeness or sufficiency of essential being. That is found in the word "El Shaddai," God all-sufficient. In our versions it is translated God Almighty, but El Shaddai, God all-sufficient, is a word including not merely the thought of might, but the thought of wisdom, the thought of all resource; it describes God as the fount of all being and all manifestations, the last, final, ultimate fact out of which everything has proceeded, and of which everything in some form or fashion or sense, is an exhibition, a revelation. Jehovah does not mean that.

Jehovah is a part of the verb which is made use of when essential being is declared; but it suggests, not the being of God, but the adaptation of His being to some necessity, or—and I cannot find any better word, imperfect though it may be—the becoming of God, that He is One Who becomes; not the all-sufficiency of God, but that all-sufficiency is active on behalf of others; not that there is infinite fulness in the sea of Deity, but that the sea flows in and fills the gaps wherever they may be.

Already men had named the Name, already they had entered into the privilege of the fact, already the men of faith had found God becoming to them what they needed. Once the father of the faithful, in language of infinite suggestiveness, broke out into exposition of the word, perhaps hardly understanding the magnificance of his exclamation. In the supreme hour when he offered Isaac in sacrifice, the offering being complete in will, the ram was caught in the thicket, and Abraham said, "Jehovah Jireh," the Becoming One sees and provides, the Becoming One becomes that which necessity demands. But now, with ransom and redemption, the constitution of the nation, and the establishment of the prophetic and pictorial ritual, the name is to be interpreted, unveiled.

Then I take up my Bible, and my eye runs over the panoramic movement, and the story, through hours of faithfulness and hours of failure, is that of God becoming what His people need: fiery judgment in the hour of their unutterable folly, great compassion in the hour of repentance, a mighty fortress when the billows broke upon them; the land of magnificent distances when the heart was weary and tired; always becoming, until, at last, in the fulness of time the great truth sang itself out in the mystic wonder which can find no finer expression in human language than that of the seer of blue Galilee, who, when he would write the story of the central fact in human history, wrote it thus: "In the beginning was the Word, and the Word was with God, and the Word was God. . . . And the Word became flesh, and tabernacled among us (and we beheld His glory, glory as of the only begotten from the Father), full of grace and truth." That is, God becoming flesh, that through the veil of the flesh Divine might break forth the light that else were too bright for the feebleness of the sinner's sight. Not the I am of essential being, not El Shaddai of infinite, all-sufficient resource; but the I am that bends, bows, stoops and becomes, the infinite unapproachable glory as of a million suns, stooping as a sunbeam to kiss the face of a sick child, the becoming One, fulness of glory, fulness of grace.

We need no longer be afraid of the name. He took the infinite mystery of the name which Hebrew bards and prophets dared not write, and spelt it out in yet simpler speech, and the I am of God become flesh is Jesus. It was a commonplace name when He bore it. I have no hesitation in saying that even in Nazareth scores of boys were called Jesus, for it is but the Greek form of the familiar Hebrew Joshua. The great high priest in the day of restoration was named Joshua, the great successor of Moses, who led the people from the wilderness into the land, was named Joshua. For him the name was made. Hoshea was the name of the boy whose father's name was Nun; but when he entered on his work his name was changed to Joshua, the merging of the name of God with the fact of salvation, so that it means Jehovah, a Saviour. At last the angel said to Joseph, "Thou shalt call His name Jesus, for it is He that shall save His people from their sins."

When I turn to the other writings in the New Testament I find that, with reverence, He is named "the Lord Jesus Christ;" "Jesus Christ the Lord." Beyond the gospel narratives He was hardly ever called Jesus, except in two great writings, the epistle to the Hebrews, and the Apocalypse of the seer of Patmos. The writer of the letter perpetually called Him Jesus, and John, when writing of those wondrous visions, spoke of Him as Jesus. In these two writings we find, in some senses, the most resplendent revelations of His personality. The writer of the letter to the Hebrews introduced Him by declaring Him to be the very effulgence of the Divine glory. John gave us a matchless vision of Him.

Thus the name, suggestive, full of glory, was at last sounded in human history in the simplest of all names, Jesus, and the whole meaning of the name is that God incomprehensible makes Himself comprehensible, the Eternal and All-sufficient, bends and bows Himself into such form and fashion and method that humanity may be touched without being crushed, may be touched so as to be healed and helped.

> Salvation in His name there is;
> Salvation from sin, death and hell,
> Salvation into glorious bliss,
> How great salvation, who can tell?
> But all He hath for mine I claim,
> I dare believe in Jesu's name.

Reverently, let us turn from the inclusive suggestiveness of the Name to these interpretative sentences of the benediction:

The Lord bless thee, and keep thee;
The Lord make His face to shine upon thee, and be gracious unto thee;
The Lord lift up His countenance upon thee, and give thee peace.

It is one name, but pronounced in such a way as to suggest three aspects of the blessing for which it stands.

Take the first, "Jehovah bless thee, and keep thee." Here the thought is that of God as the Source of blessing; it is fixed, not so much on the blessing itself, which is not described, not so much on the keeping itself, which is not described, as on the fact that blessing and keeping alike are from God. The terms are general. "Bless thee," that is, quite literally, kneel to thee, in order to serve thee. The Lord kneel to thee, and kneel in the attitude of service! I know how daring the statement seems to be, how amazing it is. Once again, for illumination, the mind travels from the ancient mystery of the priestly formula of benediction to a simple picture of the New Testament. A group of men are gathered in an upper room, shadows are about them, darkness is already on them, and there is the One Who bears the name of Jesus, girding Himself with a towel as a servant and kneeling to wash the feet of these men. "Jehovah bless thee," kneel to thee in order to serve thee! "And keep thee," that is, hedge thee round about so as to protect thee.

If the terms are general, the ideas are of the fullest, suggesting the bestowment of all benefits, and the warding off of all opposing forces. When Paul came to writing the ultimate document of his system of teaching, the Ephesian letter, he opened it with a doxology, "Blessed be the God and the Father of our Lord Jesus Christ, Who hath blessed us with every spiritual blessing." When he approached the culmination of the same letter he introduced us to the realm of conflict, and makes us conscious of the opposing forces: "Our wrestling is not against flesh and blood, but against the principalities, against the powers, against the world rulers of this darkness." What now will he say to us? Stand "in the strength of His might." Thus the essential idea of the Name is expressed in these statements in certain respects. The Becoming One becomes all that is needed in order to reach His people in blessing, to hedge them round about, and protect them from their foes.

In that first movement of the great benediction I find the reason of my faith, the ground of my hope, and the inspiration of my love; for therein I am reminded that the source of all benefit that my soul most needs is Jehovah Himself.

Let us pass to the second phase of benediction. "Jehovah make His face to shine upon thee, and be gracious unto thee." Here the thought is still that of Jehovah Himself, not as the source of all blessing only, but also as the channel of blessing. The terms are now relative. "Jehovah make His face to shine upon thee." This is not the same idea as that expressed in the words, "Jehovah lift up His face upon thee." The Hebrew word translated "face" and "countenance" is exactly the same. The difference is not between "face" and "countenance," but between making the face shine, and lifting it up, upon. The thought here is of Jehovah as a channel of blessing. The terms, as we have said, are relative; the face luminous upon thee, Jehovah gracious unto thee. The ideas are the ideas of activity: Cause His face to be luminous; be gracious unto thee, that is, stoop in active kindness unto thee. "Jehovah bless thee, and keep thee" means that all benefit and protection come from God; but "Jehovah make His face to shine upon thee and be gracious unto thee" means that the blessing will come, not as a gift separated from Jehovah, but by and through the very coming of Jehovah. It is His face that is to be lifted; it is His grace that is to come to men in their need.

When I turn to the New Testament for the fulfilment of the suggestiveness I find it in another writing already referred to. How will He make His face shine upon men? The writer of the letter to the Hebrews declared that in Jesus was the effulgence of the Divine glory.

Then "Jehovah be gracious unto thee." How is this fulfilled? I turn to the close of the selfsame letter, and I find that the writer declared that the One Whose face was the effulgence of the Divine glory, that very One, passed beyond the camp to suffer and to die, in order to bring grace to men who are lepers, outcasts, failures. That is the supreme fact of Christianity. It is not merely that Jehovah is the source from Whom all benefits come, or that He keeps men who in themselves are what they ought to be, but who under some evil mastery would fail. It is also true that Jehovah lifts the light of His face upon men who have lost the sense of His nearness. Jehovah follows the man who has left communion and fellowship, and in some great mystery of suffering, cancels the leprosy and takes the man back to Himself. Thus Jehovah in His Son is revealed; His face became luminous through Jesus;

and in the graciousness of His stoop He redeems. In Jehovah the Son we have the clear shining of the face of God, and eyesight for eyes that were blind.

If in the first aspect I find the reason of faith, the ground of hope, and the great inspiration of love; in this I have the argument for the reason of my faith. The reason is that God Himself is the source of all my help; the argument that demonstrates the reason is that God became flesh, and so the glory of His face was seen, and the wonder of His grace became operative. In the same way, this is the proof of the ground of my hope, and this the whisper of the word that becomes the inspiration of my love.

So we move one stage further to the final unveiling. "Jehovah lift up His countenance upon thee, and give thee peace." Here the thought is no longer that of Jehovah as the resource of blessing, or as a channel of blessing; it is rather that of Jehovah as the experience of blessing in the soul of a man, of Jehovah Himself creating a new experience.

Here the terms are final. The luminous face of God is not luminous merely, but it is lifted, so that it shines upon the soul; not merely is He gracious toward me, but this with a grace that fills my heart with peace which He gives, which He conveys, by His own immediate presence.

The ideas are supremely pictorial. The uplifted face suggests perpetual day. The peace is that of abiding quietness and unruffled calm possessing the soul. If I would find the New Testament fulfilment of the suggestiveness of the ancient Hebrew benediction, I turn to the words of Jesus, in His last discourses to His own disciples. I find Him saying, I am going from you, but I will send you another Comforter, and then immediately explaining that statement as He adds, I come to you. God, by His Spirit, so comes as to create within the soul the experience of day. Yet again He says, I will send you the Comforter, and in connection with that declaration the gracious words pass His lips, "Peace I leave with you; My peace I give unto you," so that it becomes your peace, My peace is your peace. Our experience is that of perpetual day, for He, the Son of Effulgent Divine glory, is always with us; our experience is that of unruffled calm and peace, because His peace is ours. Thus Jehovah, by His Spirit, causes the shining of His face in Jesus, creating perfect day for man; and by His Spirit He causes His word, His revelation, His teaching, His message to become comfort to the soul so that it has abiding peace.

By the ministry of the Spirit blessing becomes more than a word spoken, more than argument in proof of the word spoken; it becomes experience, so that man living in the communion of the Holy Ghost lives in the daylight of the uplifted face of God, effulgent in the face of Jesus, and in the place of unruffled calm and perfect peace.

When these priestly words were committed to Aaron and his sons, they were to pronounce them in obedience, not understanding all their significance; yet within them, as the holy Name was thus placed on the separated people, there was the suggestiveness of the infinite mystery of the Trinity. Jehovah the Source of all blessing, bless thee and keep thee. That is the love of God. "Jehovah make His face to shine upon thee, and be gracious unto thee." That is the grace of the Lord Jesus Christ. "Jehovah lift up His countenance upon thee," so that the light becomes sunrise and day, and give thee peace. That is the communion of the Holy Ghost. These are the aspects of the one inclusive blessing that comes to humanity through the priesthood of our Lord and Saviour Jesus Christ.

This blessing and this keeping, this irradiating of the face of God and this gracious activity of God, this lifting of the face so that sunlight lights up the pathway, and this communication of peace, which makes panic impossible—these blessings come to men only through Jehovah, and the final test of priesthood is the ability to pronounce that benediction.

These blessings can be pronounced in their fulness and with authority and power only by the lips of Jesus. The ultimate wonder and amazement is that He has made us a kingdom of priests. Our business is to pronounce this benediction on men wherever we go. It is not the business of the preacher merely, but of all saints, so that from this hour of worship, if there be any value in it, we shall pass back to our homes, back to the city, back to the place of need and toil and sorrow and sin, saying as we go:

> "The Lord bless thee, and keep thee;
> The Lord make His face to shine upon thee, and be gracious unto thee;
> The Lord lift up His countenance upon thee, and give thee peace."

This is the function of the priesthood of the Church; and the words become dynamic in human history and human life when they are incarnate.

Let us, then, seek the holy shrine, let us worship at the altar, let us come to the place of mediation that He may speak to us the benediction, and that in order that we may pass out into the highways and the byways, amid the darkness and restlessness and bondage of humanity, fulfilling the high-priestly function as we bring to men this sense of God, this power of God, this gift of God, through Jesus Christ our Lord.

CHAPTER XI

THE RESPONSIBILITIES OF SALVATION

How shall we escape if we neglect so great salvation?
HEBREWS 2:3.

THERE ARE MOODS AND TENSES IN THE PRACTICAL CONJUGAtion of the verb to live in which this may be said to be the central and supreme question of the New Testament. They are the moods in which the soul is acute in its consciousness of spiritual things, and they are the times in which it stands between the appeal and aspiration of salvation on the one hand and the lure and lust of meaner things on the other.

Indeed, so incisively arresting is the question that to read it, or to hear it, is, for the moment at least, to be compelled to think of life in the imperative, and to apply to the present tense the values of the future.

There are three quantities in the question which combine to create this arresting power. Two of these are immediately recognized; the third is, I am inclined to think, not so obvious, but when it is once discovered it becomes the most potent of the three.

The two to which I refer are those of the salvation which is referred to, and the neglect which is suggested. The salvation is described as "so great salvation," and the term in its very simplicity is eloquent of the sublimity of the theme. It is smitten through and through with the glory of the grace of God. It is of the highest height, for it comes from the heaven of heavens. It is profound, for it descends to the lowest depths. It is so vast, so wonderful, that the only final adverb possible for the illumination of its greatness is "so," "so great salvation," the "so" which laughs at logic, defies mathematical exactness, and finds its own best explanation in the equally comprehensive declaration that "God so loved the world that He gave His only-begotten Son." When we can place our final measurement on the "so loved the world" we shall be able to express in final terms the greatness of the "so great salvation."

This conception of the greatness of the salvation gives urgency to the conception of neglect. To neglect is not to deny, it is hardly to ignore; it is rather to recognize, but to postpone; or to know, and to fail to do; or, yet again, to admit, and to fail to administer.

The third quantity is discovered by emphasizing the personal pronouns, "How shall we escape if we neglect so great salvation?" Without any doubt that was the mental emphasis of the writer, for he was comparing the responsibilities of Christian believers with those of the Hebrews under the Mosaic economy.

We may omit that particular comparison as irrelevant to our case, but we cannot escape the fact that the question in its first application is not asked of sinful men, but of Christian men.

That is the quantity in the text which is not obvious, but which being recognized gives startling, searching power to the question. If we, who are subsequently described as "holy brethren, partakers of a heavenly calling," neglect so great salvation, which is already ours in the provision of grace and through faith, then how shall we escape?

In considering the inquiry as addressed to Christian souls we shall first consider the implication of the question as to the responsibility of saved men in regard to their own salvation, and, second, the suggestion of the inquiry as to the peril of neglecting that responsibility.

First, then, as to this matter of the responsibility of such as are saved with regard to their own salvation, let us first of all inquire, What is the spiritual content of the word "salvation"? What does it represent? This word "salvation" is amongst the most familiar that pass the lips of Christian men and women. It is, indeed, central to Christianity. It has a dark background, its presupposition being that of peril, danger, lack of safety. It is a word which, save with reference to such a world as this, and to such men as I am, is without meaning; it would have no place in the language of the heavenly dwellings. The word "salvation" is rich in meaning in the presence of human sin and failure and degradation. Therefore it is the central word of the Church. The mission of Christ in the world was not that of presenting an ideal to perfect men, copying which they might maintain their perfection. If that may seem a dogmatic statement, it is but an attempted interpretation of the truth which found far more emphatic and dogmatic statement in the word of Jesus Himself, "I came not to call the righteous, but sinners to repentance." "The Son of Man came to seek and to save the lost." The presupposition of the word "salvation" is of a race of men and women who have failed, who have not realized the meaning of their own life, who have come short of their own glory. When once that presupposition is recognized, then we may pass to the inquiry, What does the word represent positively?

The New Testament is the literature of perfected salvation. It tells the story of the One through Whom salvation came. It reveals the conditions on which salvation may be obtained. It lays down instructions for such as having obtained salvation are now walking in its power until that salvation be completed, in the glory of the Advent.

This salvation originates in God. Its sources are the love

of God, and the wisdom of God, and the power of God. Therein at once is stated that which is peculiar to the Christian religion, that which differentiates it from all other religions. However high and noble they may be in certain respects, they stand distinct from it in this regard. All other religions, the highest and noblest of them, having in them light, walking in which men will surely be acceptable to God, all of them are attempts by man to find God, humanity climbing toward Him. The Christian religion declares that God has come to find man, that He bows and stoops toward man, offering him not an ideal of life to which if he shall conform he shall be admitted to the dwellings of light; but bringing to him salvation, recognizing his degradation and failure, from whatsoever cause arising, and offering him everything he needs in order that he may realize his own life. The teaching of the New Testament is that this salvation has its origin in the love of God, that it has been provided by the wisdom of God, that it is operative in the power of God. It was this conviction that made the great Apostle to the Gentiles, the pioneer missionary of the Cross, declare in his letter to the Romans, "I am not ashamed of the gospel; for it is the power of God unto salvation to every one that believeth." It was this that made him declare that the Cross is the wisdom of God and the power of God, these operating under the impulse of the love of God. It is, indeed, "so great salvation," for it is of God, proceeding from His love, conceived in His wisdom, and operating in His power.

In the experience of men this salvation has negative and positive values. The negative values are found in the fact that salvation comes to man in his sin, and deals with the whole fact and experience of sin. It brings man forgiveness of sin, cleansing from sin, and power over sin.

Salvation creates within the soul of man a consciousness of forgiveness, which expresses itself in a new passion against sin and a new endeavor to master that which hitherto has mastered. Forgiveness of sins in the Biblical sense of the word is not merely the passing over of sin, declaring that it shall be mentioned no more; it is loosing from sin, setting free from sin. The man who is forgiven, in the Biblical sense of the word, is the man who is set free from sin; he walks out from it, and escapes from it as to penalty and as to pollution and as to power. Not as to penalty alone, for I do affirm out of my own consciousness, and I believe I express the deep conviction of all who have pondered this subject, that if forgiveness is merely salvation from hell it is not enough; if it is merely that I am loosed from some penalty while I am still left polluted and in the power and grip of sin it does not meet my profoundest need. The more I ponder this question of the spiritual life in the light of Holy Scripture and in the light of my own experience, the more I come to this profound conviction, that the horror of all horrors to the human soul is the pollution of sin. Not the stroke caused by sin that falls on me, but the pollution that remains with me, contaminating me, that, when the spirit has once waked to the consciousness of it, is the final agony of sin. Conviction of sin is not fear that I am going to be punished. There are awful moments in the experience of the soul conscious of sin when the fires of perdition would be welcome if but the soul might hope that they were purgatorial fires, that so it might be cleansed from pollution. This salvation deals with the whole fact of the human consciousness of sin. It proclaims forgiveness, a loosing from the sin of the past; and in that forgiveness a cleansing from pollution and the communication of power in which sin is no longer dominant.

Yet these are but the negative values of salvation; they are but initial values. We pass, therefore, to the consideration of the positive values. These may be inclusively described as a spiritual rebirth, a new beginning of conscious spiritual life, new spiritual intellectual enlightenment, new spiritual emotional inspiration, new spiritual volitional freedom. Salvation brings to man a new birth of spirit, in which he comes to new intellectual apprehension of God, an intellectual apprehension which never comes to man but by this rebirth of his spirit. On the ordinary plane of our human life a man may be cultured, intellectual, and yet never know God; he may live and move and have his being in God; he may walk up and down in this world of ours, among its flowers and its fruits, its beauties and its glories, and never find God. It is the pure in heart who see God, discovering Him everywhere, in all the beauties of nature, and in all human life. In all the apparently chaotic movements of the time God is seen by men who come to new intellectual apprehension of Him by way of the spiritual rebirth that comes to them in this salvation.

There comes to them also a new spiritual emotional inspiration; a love never known before springs within the heart of the new-born man. The first evidence of new birth is the love that drives the soul out on some sacrificial service. The first movement of spiritual life in the soul of a man is a missionary movement. We should read out of the word "missionary" all ideas suggested by the word "foreign." There is no foreigner before the throne of God or to the true Christly soul. In salvation the love of God is shed abroad in the heart, not love for God, but the love of God. The soul new-born of the Spirit is immediately mastered by God's love; the very compassion of Deity touches it to new inspiration and new aspiration, and suggests the pathway of sacrificial service.

Salvation also brings volitional freedom. Is not a man volitionally free before he is born again? In certain senses, yes; in certain senses, no. In what senses no? Let the writer of the Roman letter answer the inquiry. "When I would do good," that is volition, "evil is present with me," that is volition hindered. That is the difference between the unregenerate man and the regenerate man. The unregenerate man admires goodness and even would be good, and makes the attempt but

THE RESPONSIBILITIES OF SALVATION 147

fails; his volitional power is not set free. He is free to choose, but he cannot do the thing he chooses, and so his choosing reacts on him and fills him with despair. When the soul is reborn from above through this great salvation, then not only is it present with that soul to will, but it is present with that soul to do. The thing I choose I can do in the power of the new life communicate.

If, then, we have received this "so great salvation" experimentally we have immediately entered upon grave responsibilities. If the sources of salvation are the love of God, the wisdom of God, the power of God, then we are responsible for the streams of the great river of salvation. They may thus be summarized: the fear born of love must become the law of the life of the man who is saved by love; the consciousness of folly that seeks for the Divine wisdom must be ever present in the man who realizes that he has been brought into salvation by the infinite wisdom of God; the consciousness of the frailty that depends entirely on God must always be present in the man who realizes that the great salvation has been brought to him by the energy of the might of the working of God.

Perfect love casteth out fear. That is true. But perfect love generates fear. That also is true. Perfect love casteth out the fear that is cowardly, but perfect love generates the fear that is in itself love. Until a man is brought into right relationship with God he is afraid lest God harm him; but when a man is brought into right relationship with God he is afraid lest he hurt the heart of God, lest he cause sorrow to the Holy Spirit. That is the true safeguard of life to the man who is saved, and we are responsible for the maintenance of that relationship with God in which fear abides with us as a sentinel, forever watching lest we sin against Him and grieve His heart.

The condition for the maintenance of right relationship

with God is the abiding consciousness of our own folly and consequent dependence for all things on the infinite wisdom which wrought for our salvation.

The condition of victory in life is ever dependence on God's might in the consciousness of our own weakness. "When I am weak then am I strong" is the apostolic word. As we become forgetful of our weakness and cease to depend on God we are in grave peril, for we are neglecting the responsibility of salvation.

To put the question of our responsibility in another form. In view of the negative values of salvation we have responsibilities. The first of these has to do with the forgiveness of sins. The responsibility of the Christian man toward that initial fact is abiding recollection thereof. Does that sound obscure? Let me illuminate it by quotation from the sacred writings. Peter, writing his second letter, grouped the graces which every man is responsible for developing in faith, and then said: "He that lacketh these things is blind, seeing only what is near, having forgotten the cleansing from the old sins." To make that more pertinent, practical, immediate, let me say that we are always in danger of forgetting that we are forgiven men and women. One sentence spoken at the Mundesley Bible Conference last year by my friend John Hutton burned itself into my own life. He said, "Christian men should never lose the look of forgiven men." We are always in grave peril when we allow our spiritual attainments to become the foundations of our confidence. We are in danger when we allow ourselves to imagine that because we have run well, and have rendered service to God, we are accepted. As at last, when the day's work is over, we shall expect to enter into light, saying,

> Nothing in our hands we bring,
> Simply to Thy Cross we cling,

so we are to live each day. That day is always lacking in some measure of strength that does not begin at the Cross and with the memory of the fact that we are forgiven men. He that lacketh Christian graces is blind, seeing only what is near, and one element of his failure is that he has forgotten that he has been cleansed from his old sins.

With regard to our cleansing from sin, our responsibility is that of perpetual appropriation of that selfsame cleansing. Here let me quote from the writings of John: "If we walk in the light, as He is in the light, we have fellowship one with another, and the blood of Jesus His Son cleanseth us from all sin." That Christian man is in grave peril who imagines he has arrived at such a state of sanctity that he needs no cleansing at nightfall, who in foolish arrogance declares that he no longer prays the Lord's prayer because he does not need to ask for forgiveness. Such a man has never really stood in the awful light of the Divine holiness. The man who stands there meekly assents to the word of Jesus concerning high Christian service, that all servants must say to Him, At best we are unprofitable servants. In the light of the holiness of God, that God Who chargeth the very angels with folly and in Whose sight the heavens are unclean, we are always conscious of the need of cleansing.

There is no breath of prayer that crosses my lips but that needs the intermediation of the Priest Who beareth the iniquity of our holy things. The doctrine of holiness that lifts Christian experience to a plane on which it has no need of cleansing is a doctrine that degrades the holiness of God and has no conception of its awful solemnity. We need perpetual appropriation of cleansing.

Again, if the negative value of salvation is that we have power over sin the perpetual responsibility is that we employ that power in unyielding, unflinching, unceasing conflict with sin. I am not safe for half an hour save as I put on the whole armor of God and take up the whole armor of God.

Let us pass from these negative values of salvation in

order to consider the responsibilities that arise from the positive. If the first positive value is intellectual enlightenment and consciousness our responsibility is to seek the light in all the things of life. If we know God and have become conscious of Him our perpetual business is to seek His face in order that we may know His will.

If the second positive value of salvation is new spiritual, emotional inspiration our responsibility is that we answer that inspiration. We begin our Christian life, and the propulsion of God's love suggests that we should go and seek someone and help someone. Such suggestions must not be refused. Judas will always be somewhere on hand and ready to say, Why this waste? Let us, then, solemnly remember that when we stifle the impulse of the Divine compassion within us we are stultifying our very own life. This is such a common failure. When you began your Christian life, how eager you were to serve! To-day you are content to attend one service, or perhaps two on Sunday, and you imagine therefore that you are religious. You are not! You have lost your religion if you have lost your love! That is the peril with all of us. The love of God is prodigal in its munificence. It pours itself out in service. When that love is in the human heart, the man possessed by it desires to spend and be spent for those who have not yet known the Saviour. But unless the call of love within the soul be answered the call becomes fainter and dies away. We are neglecting our salvation when we are indifferent and unresponsive to the love of God which suggests the pathway of sacrificial service.

If the third positive value is volitional freedom, the responsibility which that freedom creates is that we test our choices with God. Whenever we exercise that high function of human life, election, choosing, we must find our way into the Divine presence, that we may know whether our election is His election, whether our choosing is His choice; and that not merely in regard to those matters of Christian service which perhaps may be uppermost in our thinking now, but in all matters of life. If you are a Christian man you have no right to choose your profession without God, and if you are Christian men you have no business to elect to live in this or that neighborhood without God. The responsibility of volitional freedom, which is the benefit of salvation, is that all choices, all elections are remitted to God.

So it seems to me that, without very many words of mine, the second part of our meditation lies open and plain before us. If these are the responsibilities of the "so great salvation" the peril of neglect is perfectly patent. What is it to neglect? In hurried phrases in my introduction I attempted some definition. Let us come to closer quarters with the thought. This is a great word of ours, "neglect," meaning not to pick up, not to take hold of, not to gather, but just to let a matter lie, not to touch it. That is perfectly simple and most picturesque, but it is graphically arresting. The word of which it is a translation has in it, I think, even more of arresting power. It means without interest in, without concern. That is what it is to neglect. This is not a common word in the New Testament. It almost seems as though it were reserved for just such a solemn inquiry as this. If we are without concern about so great salvation, if our own salvation, that which is ours, that into which we have entered, no longer concerns us, how shall we escape? It is my very salvation, that which is mine in Christ, but does it concern me? It is there, it exists; but to treat it as something assured and positive which now may be relegated to some distance from the actuality of my life is to neglect it. The man who is so sure he is saved as to be careless whether he will be saved is in grave danger.

Again to attempt to illuminate the solemn word by the lines we have already followed. Neglect in the light of the positive values is indifference to the light that is granted, irresponsive to the call of love when it comes, inactivity in the presence of God in the matter of decisions, elections, choices.

It is being without concern! It is the attitude of appalling triviality toward his own salvation of the man who does not carry it with him into every hour and every transaction.

Negatively to neglect salvation is to neglect in practice remembering the cleansing from first sins. It is to travel to such a distance from the first ecstatic hour when the soul knew itself cleansed that the memory is not a present power. It is neglect of the ordinance of confession and absolution, given and received in quiet loneliness with God. It is neglect of the whole armor and of the fight.

How is it that we begin to neglect salvation, that we do not add to the supply of virtues and graces by diligence? What are the alluring forces that prevent our realization and demonstration of the salvation that comes to us by grace? Our attention to things instead of God, our listening to self with all its demands instead of listening to the cry of need outside ourselves, our giving ourselves to license instead of to liberty.

What is the issue of such neglect? "How shall we escape?" How shall we flee if we neglect? The answer is found in the twelfth chapter of this epistle. There is no escape, and the word there is slightly changed; There is no fleeing. In the word there is the thought of imprisonment. The man who neglects the responsibilities of his salvation becomes imprisoned by the things he chooses and is excluded from all the virtues and the victories of that great salvation.

In view of this meditation a passage from the writing of Paul comes back to us with new meaning and force:

> Work out your own salvation with fear and trembling; for it is God which worketh in you both to will and to work, for His good pleasure.

The working is mutual. Interdependent are these two things. I cannot work out anything save as He shall work in it; but if I fail to work out I stop the operation of His energy within.

Thus the final appeal of that passage from the Philippian letter, illuminating as it does the inquiry of the text, calls for caution on our part with regard to our salvation; we are to work it out with fear and trembling. But, thank God, it inspires with courage, "for it is God which worketh in."

Have we neglected our own salvation? Have we drifted away from these things in any measure? Then I thank God that in this same letter to the Hebrews there is one word capitalized; it is the word TO-DAY! It is a word that speaks of present salvation, and even though I have neglected, even though I have imprisoned myself, excluding myself from the very forces of life, and shutting myself up to the destructive things, yet even now a door is open, and I may turn back again to Him Who has brought so great salvation, and He will receive and restore me.

CHAPTER XII

BORN BLIND

THE DISCIPLES' PROBLEM   THE MASTER'S ANSWER

As He passed by, He saw a man blind from his birth. And His disciples asked Him, saying, Rabbi, who did sin, this man, or his parents, that he should be born blind? Jesus answered, Neither did this man sin, nor his parents: but that the works of God should be made manifest in him. We must work the works of Him that sent Me, while it is day: the night cometh, when no man can work.
                                              JOHN 9:1-5.

THE STORY OF THE HEALING OF THIS MAN IS IN ONE SENSE peculiar. It is the only case on record of Christ's healing of congenital disease. The Greek phrase which is translated "from his birth" occurs nowhere else in the New Testament. These things immediately fasten our attention on the healing of this blind man as being one of the singular and outstanding signs recorded by John.

It presents one particular phase of the complex problem of suffering, and this fact is made evident by this opening paragraph which is the subject of our meditation. The problem was stated in the inquiry of the disciples, "Rabbi, who did sin, this man, or his parents, that he should be born blind?" That was a surface inquiry, suggesting the problem, but not explicitly stating it. In that inquiry some solutions of the problem were referred to which evidently did not satisfy the disciples. In their question there is evidence of their assumption that there was some connection between sin and suffering. They were trying to account for the fact that a man was born blind, and attempting to square the fact with their assumption of the relationship between sin and suffering, "Who did sin, this man or his parents?"

To that problem we turn in order to consider Christ's dealing with it, and therefore in order that we may learn lessons of practical value to ourselves.

The problem is rendered concrete in the case of the man. Here was a man suffering the disability of blindness through no act of sin on his own part during his lifetime. If there were some connection between sin and suffering, why was that man suffering, seeing that he had not sinned?

The problem is a persistent one. We face it every day if we have eyes to see and hearts to feel, this problem of humanity handicapped from the beginning. I surely need not argue it. If some of you would have an illustration of it you may call here on Wednesday next at six o'clock and find your way into the Cripples' Parlor. There you will see little children crippled from birth. It is only the careless man who has never faced the problem in the presence of a little child twisted, deformed, from birth. In our national life we are attempting to face the problem of the mentally deficient. The profoundest manifestation of it, one, by the way, to which, perhaps, we give the least attention, is the fact that there are people who are born spiritually inefficient. Over against that, let us say in passing, the vast majority of people born into the world are not born handicapped. Sometimes it is well for us to remind ourselves of this when we are looking at a dark picture.

The same problem comes to us in another aspect: humanity not only handicapped, but humanity imprisoned. Vast multitudes are born into material surroundings which are against them from the very beginning. Naturally there comes to one's mind that strange, weird, terrific word of Bishop South, in which he declared that there are children in London who were damned at birth by the material environment into which they came, that thousands of children are born into a moral atmosphere into which had we been born we would have been other than we are. Save for a miracle of the Divine grace, such children as these are doomed from birth.

But why is this a problem? Why does that little twisted, crippled child create a problem in the mind? Why does that mentally deficient boy put your soul in revolt? Why does the spiritually inefficient girl or boy create within us a sense of protest? Our problem is created by our faith. The man without faith has no problem of this kind. Apart from faith—and by the word faith I now refer to that Christian faith which is conquering the world—apart from that faith, Marcus Aurelius will suffice us. Marcus Aurelius will tell us that in the workshop we are not to look at the shavings but at the perfected article. That will never do for the man whose eyes have seen the light and glory of the Christian revelation, even though he may not have been obedient thereto. Men who have faith in the God of the Scriptures, the God of our Christian faith, have come to another understanding of the dignity and glory of humanity. In their apprehension of the dignity and glory of humanity is created a protest against the physical, mental, spiritual cripples. The problem is a problem of faith. It challenges our conception of the goodness and justice of God. That is to state it with almost appalling frankness, but that is the problem. Here is this little cripple, deformed from birth, and the problem is, how are we to square that cripple with a good and just God? Whether those disciples meant that or not, that is what we mean when we speak of the problem of evil, the problem of suffering in any form.

Some attempts at solving the problem have been made. The disciples suggested that this man had sinned before his birth, or that his parents had sinned. It is an interesting fact that our Lord did not deal with the suggestion that this man may have had a previous existence, for it lurks in the question. He did not deny it, He did not affirm it, He did not correct it, He left it. There we must leave it. Their question suggested that the man was suffering in this life for some sin committed in a prior life, or else was suffering as the result of some sin of his parents.

Again, there is the suggested solution of the charge of injustice against God, formulated in the soul if never expressed by the lips; expressed by the lips only by men who will immediately correct their statement by denying their belief in the existence of God at all. That is in itself a significant fact. This is one of the untabulated triumphs of Christianity very seldom referred to. Wherever Christianity has come it has at least succeeded in making it impossible for men to think of any God other than a good God. This result is not produced by other religions. At the base of the majority of other religions is a slavish fear of God. The concept of a God who can be unkind, cruel, unjust, cannot live where Christianity has come. It is possible in the light of Christianity to deny the existence of God. It is never possible to believe in the existence of an evil God. Consequently, if we try to solve this problem by declaring that the child is crippled physically, mentally, spiritually, because God is unjust, we shall find ourselves unable to accept the solution. Another solution of the problem that has been attempted is denial of the existence of God. A man face to face with this problem eliminates God, and by doing so may end his problem; but there is one thing he does not do, he does not eliminate children crippled physically, mentally, spiritually. If you are in the presence of this problem in any form—the problem of suffering apparently undeserved, unmerited, out of place—and your soul is in revolt against the doctrine of a just God, and you deny His existence, do not forget that you have not escaped from the horror of the suffering, you have only attempted to find mental ease by denying the problem, and you are still face to face with the crippled child.

All attempted solutions are unsatisfactory. The disciples question proves it. The fact that they asked the question proves that they were not satisfied. The others, as I have said, ending the problem as faith is destroyed, leave the fact in all its horror, and there is no light on it. Blot God out of the universe and you retain human agony without light and without hope.

So let us at once say that from our standpoint the problem is unsolved because we do not possess all the data. If our Christian doctrine be true Christ does possess all the data. He does know the whole story. What, then, has He to say in the presence of the problem? What did He say to these disciples?

Following the story through, I shall ask you to observe three things:

When His disciples named the problem our Lord first replied to them by denying their suggestions. His denial was clear, explicit, definite, "Neither this man nor his parents." This denial of Christ admits the fact of suffering for which neither the sufferer nor the parents of the sufferer are to blame.

Then He made a statement, and here I am going to ask you to be patient, as I so often have to do, while we try to see what He really did say—to be patient, moreover, because I may run counter to a good many prejudices. I certainly shall run counter to almost universal interpretation of this passage. I am going to base a doctrine on punctuation. If you are inclined to object to that I pray you remember that it is already done, as you will see whenever you read this passage as it stands in the Bible.

The first matter is a simple one, and preliminary. The Authorized Version reads at the fourth verse, "*I* must work the works of Him that sent *Me*"; the Revised Version reads, "*We* must work the works of Him that sent *Me*." I draw attention to this simply to observe that the value of the teaching is not changed. I accept the scholarly consensus that the change is warranted. What Jesus really said was, "We must work the works of Him that sent Me." In the old rendering, the singular pronoun "I" agreed with the singular pronoun "Me," and emphasized the mission of Christ as the Son of God. In the new rendering, the plural pronoun "we" still recognizes the mission of Christ, but suggests the fellowship of His disciples in that mission. To that I shall return in conclusion. For the moment it is enough to observe that the superlative value is the revelation of the mission of Christianity as working the works of God.

Now we come to that which to my own mind is supremely important in an understanding of the statement of Jesus. Two readings of this text are made possible by a change in the punctuation, without the alteration of a single word.

"Jesus answered, Neither did this man sin, nor his parents: but that the works of God should be made manifest in him. We must work the works of Him that sent Me, while it is day: the night cometh, when no man can work." That is the punctuation as it stands in the Revised Version. That is in harmony with the punctuation of Westcott and Hort in the New Testament in the Greek. That reading places a period at the close of verse three. Let us now read it, changing that period into a comma:

> *Jesus answered, Neither did this man sin, nor his parents: but that the works of God should be made manifest in him, we must work the works of Him that sent Me, while it is day.*

We immediately recognize that this is a great change. While examining the problem, knowing my own incompetence in many ways, I submitted the passage with my suggestion to an eminent scholar. In his letter replying to my inquiries, he said:

> He would be an exceedingly bold scholar who would undertake to prove the punctuation to be one way or the other on the mere ground of the Greek itself. It seems as if the question would have finally to be decided on doctrinal grounds, for it is plain that the difference in punctuation of the verse would change the meaning altogether. If one reading would be more in spirit with the tenor of Christ's teachings, as seems quite probable, that would be quite naturally preferable.

I accept that dictum and on the basis of it have come to the position of personal assurance in this matter. If we leave the period where it is in our version, the whole statement is: "Neither did this man sin nor his parents; but *he was born blind* that the works of God should be manifest in him." As an elliptical sentence it demands the insertion of the words, "he was born blind." That means that suffering is caused or permitted as an opportunity for the display of the works of God; it means that a little child comes into the world twisted in order that God may have a chance of showing how He can heal it. That I do not believe.

Read the passage as I have suggested, and Jesus simply denied the suggested solutions, and gave none; but over against the problem He stated the central fact of Christianity, and gave the man sight. The problem was not solved but the disability was removed; the mystery of evil and pain was not unveiled, but the fact that Christ had come into the world to deal with evil and to banish pain was made manifest.

What, then, are the values for us of such a meditation as this, for it is quite conceivable to me that it may be said that

I have raised a great question which I am not answering. I have not raised a question, I have voiced one. It is my question as well as yours, yours as well as mine. I have attempted to voice it in this narrative as did the disciples, who were my representatives long ago, and I have done so in order to see how Jesus dealt with it. He said to His disciples: Your suggested solutions are not solutions; you are all wrong. Come with Me, and you and I together will remove the disability which creates the problem. That is the inclusive teaching of the story.

Let us now attempt to gather up some of the values. The first value is that the fact that the Son of God is sent to remove disability demonstrates another fact, that such disability is not the will of God for men. Said Jesus, He hath sent Me to do His works. What are they? To open those blind eyes! Therefore those blind eyes are not the will of God for a man. I think this discovery is a gain, for even in Christian circles we hear a great deal—I was going to say blasphemy, I will amend my word and say nonsense—about suffering being the will of God. Every crippled child is contrary to the will of God; every mentally deficient man or woman is contrary to the will of God; every spiritually inefficient being is contrary to the will of God. There may be a sense in which it is in the will of God that they should continue to suffer disability. That is not a contradiction. I go into the room where my little child is in bed tossing with fever. It is entirely against my will that my child should be in bed tossing with fever. My little child says to me, Take me out! I answer, No, darling, you must stay here! Am I contradicting my original intention? God's will is not human suffering and disability, but human perfection, glory, and beauty. Yet, in that larger discipline of life the meaning of which will break upon us from the other side, He allows us to remain in circumstances of affliction, the meaning of which is postponed. The deepest fact in the story is that when Jesus opened the blind eyes He said in the midst of the world's history, God is against all human blindness.

Because God is against all human disability, disability is part of sin. We must not narrow the meaning of sin at this point. Sin is failure, missing the mark; sin is coming short of the glory of God. Sin does not necessarily include the idea of human responsibility and guilt, but it is always failure. Thus we are bound to face the problem of sin.

Involved in that conception of sin as failure is the Christian doctrine that the possibility of such failure resulted from the volitional element in the spiritual nature of angels and of man. We are compelled to recognize in this and in other ways the fact of the self-imposed limitations of God. It is inconceivable that God could create beings with the grandeur and greatness of volitional power without also creating the possibility of sin—not the necessity for it, but the possibility of it. So that if a man in his heart rebel against God for permitting sin, he rebels against God for creating man, or any intelligent being having the gift of volition. God can create no being with volition without creating the possibility for sin. Therefore, the man who is in rebellion against God for permitting sin in his life can rectify God's blunder only by destroying himself. Only let him remember, this is what he cannot do. Thus we are shut out of this infinite mystery; it is impossible of final solution by finite minds, and God has given us no solution of it. Christ did not attempt to explain it. From beginning to end the Bible offers no solution. Over against this fact of sin, however, God has placed the fact of ransom, redemption, a mystery profounder than that of sin, and yet so beneficent and mighty in its working that I am compelled to believe, "That cannot end worst which began best," and that "though a wide compass first be fetched," there must ultimately be the infinite triumph of the God Who created.

If still there be in the heart of the thinking man a sense of protest, then I shall say to him that the vindication of God is twofold. Our theology is our theodicy; or, in other words, our doctrine of God is in itself a vindication of God. Our doctrine of God is that He is love, and that, consequently, He is righteous and true and just. Therefore, whatever there may be of mystery or of problem in the things on which these eyes are looking, I rest assured as the years run on, and I suffer pain and watch the suffering of others, that the Judge of all the earth must do right. Oftentimes I cannot understand the meaning of the things on which my eyes may look; but hear me patiently, not clearly, not finally, but actually, Mine eyes have seen the glory of God, and there I rest.

But there is another line of vindication. The redeeming activity of God, in all its manifold applications, is a vindication of God. I came across some striking words the other day in a sermon by Baldwin Brown:

> The preacher will best help that consummation by letting the light of the gospel shine clearly, and troubling himself for the present little with theodicies. We are not God's advocates, we are His witnesses. We have no case to establish for Him or for His truth. We have simply to bear witness to the truth.

It was a great word, and I affirm that the light of that gospel of redemption in Christ Jesus is God's vindication.

Without any reservation, I say, If this great God had created man with this volitional capacity, knowing that he might use it to entail on himself limitation and misery, and had made no provision for such catastrophe, then I could not have loved Him, I could not have believed in His goodness. But oftentimes perplexed by this mystery of evil, I stand in the presence of the dignity and majesty and glory of humanity and watch its achievement, its struggles, its failures, its risings and pressings forward; and, watching, I see not only the crippled child, the mentally deficient, the spiritually inefficient; I see also the cripple healed, the mentally deficient enabled to understand, and the spiritually inefficient born into new realization of the true, and so I find, operating in the midst of humanity, a redemptive force that remakes; and I hear Jesus saying: Your solutions are wrong, but in order that God's work may be manifest let us go to His work, open blind eyes, unstop deaf ears, open the prison houses and make possible the reconstruction of the humanity that is limited and spoiled by sin. That is my ultimate resting place.

There are men to-day who deny our faith and so escape our problem. They are not troubled to-day about the problem in this form, because they have denied this God. And yet as I watch them I see them striving to remove the disabilities, and I say to them, Remember, my brothers, remember, this work also is Christian work. You may have denied my faith intellectually, you may have tried to find rest for your troubled heart by denying the government of God, but you still look with pity on the cripple and try to heal him. That is the unconscious, but very definite, result of the very faith you are denying. Sometimes I have said that England is not Christian. There is a sense in which that is perfectly true. Christian England, no! And yet, yes! England is far more Christian than pagan, thank God. There are thousands of men in this land of ours flinging themselves against disability in its material and mental forms. That also is Christian. I am not now dealing with their individual responsibilities and relationship to God, but with the passion and activity of their lives. There was a day when the disciples would fain have called down fire from heaven to destroy men who were casting out devils. Jesus said, "Ye know not what Spirit ye are of." "He that is not with Me is against Me; and he that gathereth not with Me scattereth." He that gathereth, even though he name not My name, is with Me. Do not forget that.

Now I come to a narrower circle as I conclude. I would do it with carefulness. I may be speaking even in this audience to those who are sufferers, perchance from birth, and who suffer still. It may be that I am speaking to some who, with personal pain of heart, have thought of some loved one in their home. I would like to say some word to them about the light that comes from this story on all such suffering. I would remind them, first of all, that their disability is retained within the realm of the Divine activity by redemption.

I would remind them therefore that they may be—who can tell?—foreordained workers together with God in the very fact of their disability. Not that such disability was foreordained by God or caused by God, but that because they would suffer this disability and limitation, they were foreordained to afford opportunities for the manifestation of the works of God.

At times His purpose is served by the removal of the disability, at other times by the temper in which the disability is endured. It is a long stretch of time and of country from the days of His flesh to the year of our Lord nineteen hundred and thirteen, and from Palestine to the United States. Yet let us not separate these places; let us keep them together! Here in Palestine was a man born blind, suffering disability through no sin of his own; the work of God in him was the immediate opening of his eyes. We have all read the almost matchless story of Helen Keller. Have we really read that story? I read yesterday, for my own spirit's help as I thought of this passage, *The Chant of the Stone Wall.* Helen Keller was blind, deaf, dumb; yet to-day, through Christly ministrations, she positively speaks. She cannot see, she cannot hear; yet, refined, Christian, beautiful, she has felt her way by the rough stone wall, and interpreted its music for the world. Not all her disabilities have been removed; but the glory of God is manifested in the temper in which she has endured and won her victory through the ministry of Christly souls on her behalf.

These are superlative illustrations, I grant you, and for

that reason I like them. They constitute the boundaries of illustration, and somewhere between you comes, my brother, my sister, with your persistent weakness, a glorious opportunity for the display of the tone and temper of the Master. Or perchance there may be, even in this house, someone from whom disability has been removed by the ministry of medicine, for I decline to have medicine and surgery put outside the government and Kingdom of God. All activity that makes toward the removal of disability is Christian. Christ did not come to solve mental problems immediately, because He knows I am unequal to grasping the meaning of the things He could say. That is Christ's own teaching. He stood and looked at the group of His disciples—and do not minimize His words, take them in their fulness—and He said, "I have many things to say unto you, but ye cannot bear them now." He has them to say. We shall know the meaning of these things. Light will flash from the heart of Deity on the last dark problem that perplexes the soul, but we could not bear it yet. Therefore Christ says to us, That man did not sin, neither did his parents; postpone your discussion of the problem and come with Me and help to open the blind eyes and heal ruined humanity. That is My mission in the world.

Finally, accepting this reading of our text, "We must work the works of Him that sent Me," let us observe that according to the interpretation of this matchless story His works are those of ending disability, physical, mental, spiritual, and bringing individual men and women, and all the race, to the full realization of the meaning of their own lives.

Let us remember, therefore, that we are workers together with God in all such endeavor.

When into the Cripples' Parlor you pass, to make glad the life of a little child, or perchance by deft fingers so minister to its pain as to ease it, you are a worker together with Him!

When, teacher in the day school, you take extra time

and patience with the boy or girl somewhat mentally deficient to enlarge that child's outlook, you are a worker together with God.

When you take time and prayer and patience to lead dead spiritual souls toward the light of eternal truth, you are a worker together with God.

CHAPTER XIII

SANCTIFICATION

In sanctification of the Spirit.
     II THESSALONIANS 2:13; I PETER 1:2.

THE TWO OUTSTANDING FIGURES IN THE BOOK OF THE ACTS of the Apostles are Peter and Paul. Each in his respective sphere was a pioneer in the great Christian campaign springing from the Pentecostal effusion. The phrase which suggests the line of our evening meditation is found in the writings of each of these men. Peter employed it in writing to Christian Jews of the dispersion in Pontus, Galatia, Cappadocia, Asia, and Bithynia. Paul made use of it writing to Gentile Christians of Thessalonica. The phrase refers to a great purpose of God in the life of men, sanctification. Moreover, the phrase reveals to us the fact that this purpose is possible of fulfilment in the life of men through the ministry of the Holy Spirit: "in sanctification of the Spirit."

I am perfectly well aware that this is not a sentence; it is not a statement. I am equally well aware that I take it from its context, but I trust that in our meditation on the things that it suggests we shall do no violence to that context. When, perchance, at your leisure you turn again to the paragraph read in your hearing by way of lesson, you will discover that the great theme of Peter and of Paul was salvation, and in this connection, dealing with the subject in different ways and from different standpoints, but with one purpose, each of these outstanding figures in the book of the Acts of the Apostles makes use of the phrase, "in sanctification of the Spirit."

There are two phases, then, of consideration that I propose to you. First, sanctification in regeneration; second, sanctification in experience. Let me immediately say that these must not be separated from each other as though they were distinct. They may be separated, however, for the purpose of teaching. There is a sense in which they cannot be separated from each other, for that sanctification which is provided for us in regeneration is potentially what we need for the final perfecting of our lives according to the great and gracious will of God. Apart from that regeneration, there can be no final sanctification. On the other hand, I think we may grant immediately that to which I shall refer again, that there are multitudes of men and women who without any hesitation would claim to have received the gift of life, who can rejoice in the fact that they have been born from above, who, nevertheless, would hardly claim to know the experience of sanctification. Consequently, I think I am justified in dividing our meditation into these two parts: sanctification in regeneration, and sanctification in experience.

In dealing with the first of these, let me immediately say that this word "sanctification" is undoubtedly one of the great words of the New Testament, and, at the same time, it is a word singularly feared by Christian men and women to-day. Indeed, not only is this particular word feared by Christian men and women, but all its cognate words, terms which have relationship to the idea that it presents, are feared. Its equivalent *holiness*, or the phrase, *Christian perfection*, are avoided by thousands of Christian men and women in our churches to-day; they are afraid of the terms. I am not at all surprised that multitudes of Christian people are afraid of these terms. So many insane things have been done in the name of sanctification, so many unrighteous things have been practiced by people who profess holiness, and so much appalling imperfection has been witness in the lives of those claiming Christian perfection, that one is not surprised that many Christian people are afraid of the terminology. I believe that often the fear is born of true sanctity of life; in many cases it is a protest against an altogether unwarranted narrowness of interpretation, against a mechanical, ritualistic ideal of sanctification which excludes from the experience of Christian men and women whole areas of life which they ought to capture and consecrate rather than abandon. But it is not fair to abandon a great New Testament word or a great New Testament doctrine because the word has had evil associations and because the doctrine has been misinterpreted. It is surely rather the duty of those who desire to enter into the real meaning of their life in Christ to inquire what God means by sanctification. He has left us in no doubt; in this New Testament the teaching is quite clear as to what His purpose is. "This is the will of God, even your sanctification." If that be true, then it is my business to find out what that will is. I ought not to be satisfied with anything in my life that falls short of that will. Moreover, I ought to set myself resolutely to enter into that will, even if in so doing I have to act in opposition to a great many who are speaking to me of sanctification in terms other than those of the New Testament, or calling me to something to which the New Testament never calls me.

I trust these preliminary words do not suggest an air of controversy. Nothing is further from my purpose. I have spoken them that I may capture those who are afraid of this great theme.

What, then, is sanctification? The root idea of the word so translated in the New Testament signifies something which is awful, that which fills the soul with awe, not necessarily with dread, for there is a vital difference between dread and awe. Dread is of the nature of slavish fear; awe is of the nature of reverence. There should be no dread in the soul of man when he draws near to God. No man ought to draw near to

God save with a sense of awe. The thought of the word is that of something awful, filling the soul with awe. Its use in the New Testament is always of separation to God, and therefore of holiness. The vessels of the sanctuary in the old economy were holy, they were sanctified; they were set apart to sacred uses, and, consequently, they were necessarily maintained in cleanliness by ceremonial ablutions, and that because they were dedicated and consecrated to the service of God alone. In the word "sanctification," then, both as to its root intention and its common use in the New Testament, we have these simple ideas. Sanctification is entire separation of the life to God; consequently, it is the cleansing of the life to the condition of holiness or spiritual health.

Every new-born soul is sanctified. Every believer is a saint. Christian people will often say, the sincerest of them, those who are most truly and really attempting to follow their Lord: We do not profess to be saints. That saying is born of that fear of the doctrine of sanctification to which I have made reference. Let me repeat, therefore, that which I have already said, but in another form. If you are a Christian man you are a saint. If you are a believer in Christ Jesus you are already sanctified. Perhaps the speediest way in which to emphasize the truth is to remember that Paul, writing to the Corinthian church, commenced his first letter—almost wholly a letter of correction—by describing those to whom he wrote as "saints," and yet, within a few paragraphs, after having so described them, he said, "I, brethren, could not speak unto you as unto spiritual, but as unto carnal." Yet they were saints, they were sanctified. It is quite evident that the apostolic reference in the opening of that letter was to the Divine purpose, and not to the perfected experience of these people. They were saints, they were sanctified; but they were not living as became saints, they had not entered into the full experience of sanctification. In that we have at once a distinction and a difference which it is important that we should recognize. To call men to sanctification who are already Christians as though they were not sanctified is to lose the most powerful argument for sanctification possible. It is when we realize that the man who had yielded himself to God by one volitional act of faith has become a saint that we have the right to appeal to him to enter into the experience of sanctification, because by failing to do so he is robbing God of that which is God's by sovereign and redeeming right. Sanctification is not a privilege offered to the few within the Christian economy. It is a privilege, but it is also a responsibility devolving on every soul who has yielded to Christ. Saints within the Christian Church are not an aristocracy of spiritual souls; they are the whole commonwealth of the new-born. We owe a persistent and pernicious misinterpretation of the great doctrine of sanctification to the Roman Church, with its calendar of saints. We all are familiar with the phrase, *counsel of perfection;* men in business use it, men in the ordinary life of every day use it; the meaning of the phrase is that the idea referred to is a fine one but that it cannot be realized. This phrase comes from the Roman Church. Counsels of perfection are laws and instructions for those who desire to enter into the life of saintship. They teach that no man can live the saintly life unless he withdraw himself, not from actual sin alone, but from all the ordinary activities of every day life. They declare that no man can be a saint save as he retires from the highway to the cloister, and to seclusion and the loneliness of meditation and prayer, and by these methods perfect himself into saintship. The New Testament teaches that men can be saints in fishing boats, in varying places in the midst of travail and toil, in all the turmoil of life, or else they can be saints nowhere. Sanctification is a condition of life enabling men to enter into the common vocations of all the days and irradiate them so that they themselves shall become God's means of revealing Himself to others on the dusty highway of life.

Sanctification, I repeat, is not the privilege of the few; it is the birthright and responsibility of the whole commonwealth of Christian men and women.

In what sense, then, can we affirm that sanctification comes to men in regeneration? Regeneration is that act of the Holy Spirit in which He supplies the life necessary to carrying out a covenant with God. The first word of the message of Jesus to the world in the days of His preaching, and until this hour, is, "Repent." When a man hears that word, and in obedience thereto thinks again and changes his conception of life, he will immediately become conscious of his own shortcoming, not merely of his past sin, but of his present incapacity for godliness; and to that new-born sense of incapacity Christ will present Himself with the second word of His message, which is, Believe on the Son of God and thou shalt have life. When a man obeys the word, "repent," and yields himself in confidence to the Saviour Christ, he is entering into a new covenant with God. All that is but the human side of the great transaction that makes a man a Christian, and it is immediately responded to on the Divine side by the birth from above, the communication of new life, the filling of the life with the Spirit, changing the outlook, changing the desires, changing the whole set of the life, as it is placed in living, vital, actual relationship with God Himself. This covenant between God and man is the covenant of restoration.

It is a covenant of will. God wills the good of man and man wills the glory of God, and they enter into a sacred covenant, God to secure man's good, and man to seek for God's glory.

It is a covenant of emotion. God loves man, and enters into a covenant to work on his behalf and seek for him the highest and the best; and man finds his heart responsive to the love of God, for "we love Him because He first loved us," and enters into a covenant to love and serve Him. God covenants in love, to care for man; and man covenants in love that he will endeavor so to live as to give no sorrow to the heart of God.

It is, moreover, a covenant of intelligence. God, as God perfectly knowing man, covenants with man to place all His infinite wisdom at the disposal of man; on his part, man, knowing something of God, gives himself to ever-increasing study of God that he may know Him perfectly.

Let any man make that covenant with God; let me make it with Him as though I had never made it before. Conscious of my past of sin, and conscious of my need for repentance and of my own incapacity for all high and holy things, and yet earnestly desiring those things by His illumination, I desire to enter into a covenant with God through Christ—a covenant of will, a covenant of love, a covenant of knowledge. Therefore I stand, turned to God with a strong and true desire, but utterly unable to fulfil my desire. Men will never get beyond that unless there be for them some supernatural bestowment of power from on high.

This, then, is the Christian evangel, that now the Spirit is given through that Lord and Saviour Jesus Christ Who in the past eternity emptied Himself in order that He might fill men with the Spirit. With the incoming of that Spirit there is bestowed on the man who makes his covenant with God the life that shall enable him to fulfil that covenant; new strength of will, new passion of love, new illumination of knowledge, that in the power of that life communicated, he may keep his covenant with God. That takes place in the hour when a man yields himself to God to obey, and by that covenant, ratified and rendered dynamic by the Holy Spirit of God, a man becomes separated to God, holy to God, a saint of God. Whether in the sight of men I know not and care little, but in the sight of angels that man becomes an awful being. Suppose—and why not?—that even already, while I have been trying to speak by way of teaching, some man, all unknown to friend or neighbor, has made his covenant with God, even though no tongue of fire has appeared to these eyes of sense, no sound as of a mighty rushing wind has been heard, yet the Spirit of God has baptized that man into life, and he has become a saint of God, and immediately all orders of angels view him as an awful being in the universe of God, a man separated to God, for "are they not all ministering spirits, sent forth to do service for the sake of them that shall inherit salvation?"

Speaking from my own conviction, it is when I have seen this thing that I have discovered the profoundest argument for a life of true sanctification. Let me therefore now speak of sanctification in experience. We may be sanctified ideally, potentially, but not empirically, or experientially. That is the story of thousands of us. We were perfectly sincere as we turned our back on sin and our faces to God, perfectly sincere as we cried out for salvation and yielded ourselves in faith to the perfect Saviour. In that hour of our sincerity we were made children of God, sons of God, we were sanctified; but we have never entered into the experience of sanctification. The experience of sanctification is a positive event, it is a progressive exercise, and, finally, it will be a perfecting excellence.

I speak of it first as a positive event. When may a man enter into sanctification experientially, positively? That experience may be coincident with regeneration. I am compelled to say, speaking now from experience, my own and that of those whom I have known in the Christian life, that it is not often coincident with regeneration. The fact is always coincident with regeneration, ideally, potentially, but not experientially. It was so in the case of Paul. I cannot find anywhere that Paul had a second blessing, and I cannot find any warrant for the doctrine of a second blessing as absolutely necessary in the teaching of the New Testament.

What, then, is this experience which I describe as a positive event? On the human side it is comprehension of the real meaning of the relationship which I entered into with Christ when I gave myself to Him. That is the first thing. I remember a generation ago hearing Dwight Lyman Moody say, "Christ is as great a Saviour as you make Him. What you ask He gives. If in your first coming you ask forgiveness, you receive it." That is quite true within limitations. He always gives me more than I ask, but I can appropriate only that which I ask or understand. I think one reason why a great many Christian people do not enter into the experience of sanctification in the hour of conscious regeneration is that we have not preached sanctification as we ought to have preached it, we have not presented to men all the truth concerning their relationship to Christ. There comes to the child of God, if not in the first hour of yielding, or of regeneration, yet sooner or later, by this ministry or that, this method or that, the comprehension of the real meaning of the relationship into which they entered with God. "Who gave Himself for us, that He might redeem us from all iniquity, and purify unto Himself a people for His own possession, zealous of good works." That is the program of the Christ-life. That is the full meaning of the covenant we make with God in Christ. When there breaks on the soul of the truly Christian man, the man truly born again and hitherto not having fully apprehended the meaning of his relationship to Christ, the meaning of that covenant, that God saved him, not from hell alone, but in order that he might be in himself a vessel meet for the Master's use, a vessel clean and pure and strong, an instrument of righteousness in the world, then he comes to the hour in which the event of santification is possible.

But the event on the human side is more than comprehension of the real meaning of the covenant; it is consent thereto. That is the point of struggle, if struggle there be; and I think there is always struggle. Oh, the spiritual tragedy of some men and women, who at some moment—it may be under the preaching of the Word, it may be in the quietness of their own meditation thereupon, it may be in a thousand ways to which I cannot refer—come to see what God really means, and then turn their backs on it, refusing to consent to the terms of the covenant, and withholding themselves from that abandonment to the will of God which is the secret of all sanctified life. Such men and women still gather in the sanctuary of God, still utter the shibboleths of the Kingdom. That is the tragedy of the Christian Church. We waste our time discussing statistics and attempting to galvanize dead men into activity, when what we supremely need is revival within the Church in order that there may be revival within the nation. Revival within the Church means going back to the point of disobedience in order that there may be obedience, a going back of saints to saintship, a going back that there may be confession, contrition, and that life may be given to God in all its fulness.

Wherever, on the human side, there is comprehension of the meaning of the covenant and true consent thereto, then immediately on the Divine side there is cleansing of the nature and the consecration of the soul of man to God. If in this hour—and let me speak with you rather than to you on such a theme as this—there shall come to me some fuller meaning of the covenant and I dare to consent, then in that moment the answer to my consent will be the cleansing of my nature by His Spirit and the consecration of my personality to Him. Then His Spirit will possess it to illuminate it, empower it, fill it with new and tender emotion.

Sanctification, experientially, is a progressive relation, for not by an event of light and conscious cleansing and consecration does any man come to maturity in the Christian character. All that is the condition for growth, not its ultimate perfection. Consequently, sanctification is a progressive exercise, it is gradual as well as sudden, that which is gradual resulting from that which is sudden; that which is sudden being the adjustment of the life to God and the immediate reception of the power; that which is gradual being the administration of the territory yielded, and appropriation of the blessings bestowed. So we go from strength to strength, from height to height, from light to light, from experience to experience. This is the work of the Spirit also, and that in two ways. First, the Christ revelation to the soul of the saint is a progressive revelation. The Spirit is always bringing the child of God some new vision of Christ. Then, whenever a new vision is presented to the trusting soul a new crisis is created for that soul, and the soul will either obey and march into larger life, or disobey and turn backward. The man or woman who has the largest, fullest knowledge of Christ is the man or woman who is most conscious that he or she has hardly yet begun to see His glory. The Spirit of God, line upon line, precept upon precept, here a little and there a little, with infinite patience, is forevermore unveiling to the eyes of faithful, watching souls the glory of the Christ; and as each new glory is revealed it calls the soul to some new adventure, to some new exercise, to some new sacrifice; and wherever there is response to the revelation, realization follows. So by this process of illumination and instruction we grow up in all things into Him Who is the Head, even Christ Jesus.

Every response to light means fuller understanding and enlarged capacity for further revelation. The true Christian life is a growth, which finds no maturity in this world; the ultimate is never reached in this land of shadows. There is no exhausting of the light and glory and beauty of Christ, and if He has not startled and shamed me recently it is because somewhere in the past I disobeyed and have lost my power to see. Sanctification is progressive, the Spirit of God patiently leading us from point to point in the life of faith and light and love, and forevermore astonishing us with new unveilings of the glory of our Master.

SANCTIFICATION

At last sanctification will prove itself to be a perfecting excellence. There will come to those who follow on to know the Lord an hour of full and final realization. John said, "Behold what manner of love the Father hath bestowed upon us, that we should be called children of God: and such we are . . . and it is not yet made manifest what we shall be. We know that, if He shall be manifested, we shall be like Him; for we shall see Him as He is." That is the final fact of sanctification, the perfect, absolute, and ultimate surrender of the life to Him and His surrender of Himself to the surrendered life. The God Who said of Him, "This is My beloved Son, in Whom I am well pleased," will ultimately say of all the saints He brings to glory, These are My beloved children, in whom also I am well pleased. The last fact in the new creation is like the last fact in the first creation. When God had made man He rested from His labors, finding His rest in man in the perfection of his manhood. Jesus said amid the weariness and woes and wounds of humanity, "My Father worketh hitherto, and I work." God and Christ together will find their eternal rest in the sanctified sons of men, perfectly conformed to the image of Christ.

What is our present position if we are Christian men and women? We are "called saints" "in sanctification of the Spirit." What, then, is our present responsibility? That we should walk "as becometh saints" "in santification of the Spirit." That we should avail ourselves of the resources at our disposal. That we should refuse to be content with anything less than that which brings satisfaction to the heart of God our Father. That we should have done forever with comparing ourselves among ourselves. That we should have done forever with being at rest because men are satisfied with our Christian attainment. That we should press ever resolutely with new determination into the light of the Divine thought and the Divine requirement of our Father's will and purpose, always remembering that He has no high purpose for the soul of man but that He has provided power sufficient for the realization of that high purpose.

Let us make our covenant with God, and the Holy Spirit will give us life sufficient to enable us to fulfil it; or if we have already done so, then let us say, to no man but to our own hearts, as in the presence of God, We will be satisfied with nothing less than the comprehension of His meaning. In the measure in which we know that meaning, let us consent thereto, and that with perfect confidence that "He will perfect that which concerneth us."

CHAPTER XIV

THE FILLING OF THE SPIRIT

They were all filled with the Holy Spirit.
ACTS 2:4.

THAT IS THE CENTRAL AND SUPREME WORD ABOUT THE DAY of Pentecost. The sound of the wind and the sign of the fire were symbolic, and not essential. The ecstatic speech in tongues was an outcome, temporary, transient, and of no permanent value for the purpose of the propagation of the Gospel; for they did not preach in tongues, they offered praises, through the very gladness of their hearts. The supreme fact of which both wind and fire were signs, and of which speech was an immediate outcome, was that recorded in the text; "They were all filled with the Holy Spirit." The verb here is a simple one, meaning exactly to fill, but it was used figuratively in the sense of imbuing, supplying, furnishing; and whereas none of these words would convey the full meaning, yet they may help us to an understanding of that meaning. They were all imbued with the Spirit, they were all supplied with the Spirit, they were all furnished with the Spirit.

The emphasis of our text is on the act rather than on the condition of repleteness which resulted. What Luke has chronicled for us here, to which he draws special attention, is that then and there, under the conditions described, this wonder took place. Suddenly these waiting people, the eleven apostles, with the women and the Virgin Mother, and our Lord's brethren in the flesh, those who had been waiting for ten days since last they looked on the glory of the risen face of Jesus, these people were suddenly caught up by the Spirit, penetrated through and through by the Spirit, brought completely under the power of the Spirit. They were now born of the Spirit into a new consciousness of their Master, of themselves, and of all things. Suddenly, and without being able to explain the how of the infinite mystery, they found themselves in a closer companionship with Jesus than they had ever known during the days of His flesh. Suddenly there began to break on them understanding of mysterious things which He had uttered in earlier days; there came to them unveilings of the meaning of things they had watched Him do, but which they had not understood. In that hour the enigma of His own Personality was in a measure solved.

In that hour, moreover, they came to new consciousness of themselves, saw their own weakness as they had never seen it, understood their own foolishness as they had never understood it, mourned over their past blunders, discovered how narrow and incomplete had been their highest understanding of their Lord's ministry as it had expressed itself ten days before, when they asked Him if He was about to restore the Kingdom to Israel. There broke on their astonished souls the vastness of His enterprise, the glory of His mission; they found their hearts stormed by the whole wide world, and Jerusalem was but the center of the concentric circles of Judea and Samaria and the uttermost part of the world to which they found themselves the appointed messengers of their Lord and Master.

In this hour all things became new. God was new, the world was new, and life was new. This little company had been walking in a wonderful light for three years, and yet, in this moment of Pentecostal effusion and spiritual illumination, they looked back, and, lo, the whole landscape was bathed in a glory they had never dreamed of and never before looked on. Life became a rapture, a delight, an infinite possibility; and they were conscious of a power driving them out in the Name and nature of their Lord and Master to begin the great work of proclaiming Him.

That was the daybreak of Christianity. In all the full meaning of our great word "Christianity" there had been none in the world until that moment, apart from Christ Himself. These men had never understood Him, they had never been brought into very close fellowship with Him, and, more than once, as we follow the story of His teaching of them, we are conscious of the sighs that escaped Him, and of His sense of limitation and inability.

Let us reverently attempt to meditate this morning on this experience; first, in its relation to the work of Christ, and, second, in its relation to the experience of the disciples.

Inclusively we may at once say that Pentecost in its relation to the work of Christ was the culmination of the earthly mission of the Son of God and the commencement of the heavenly mission consequent thereupon. An intelligent study of these Gospel narratives and of the fact of Christianity demands that we recognize the difference between the Gospel narratives and this brief story of the book of the Acts. We may remind ourselves that that difference is marked by the very way in which the beloved physician commenced this second treatise to his friend Theophilus. As Luke said to him, "The former treatise I made, O Theophilus, concerning all that Jesus began to do and teach," he suggested the incompleteness and imperfection of all that had gone before. It was complete and perfect in so far as it was within the will and economy of God, but the past had not reached completion. We may say, superlative as the declaration appears to be, that the Lord Jesus Christ, the Son of God and Saviour of the World, began His work on the Day of Pentecost. Everything else was primary, preparatory, while necessary and fundamental. All through the public ministry, and even in the hour of the Cross, and beyond the Cross until He ascended on high, His own word will accurately describe His experience: "How am I straitened!" This is not for a moment to undervalue all that had preceded. Apart from that which had preceded, this Pentecostal effusion would have been impossible; apart from all that of which we have the narratives in our Gospels, we never could have had the wondrous apostolic service, or the early history of the Christian Church, of which the first fragment is written in this book of the Acts. So while this Pentecostal hour was the culmination of the earthly mission of Jesus, it was the commencement of the heavenly. From that moment in which the Spirit came and filled these men, may I reverently point out, the Lord Jesus could no longer say, "I am straitened." The bonds were broken, the barriers swept away, the limitations at an end, and Christianity began.

Let us trace the work of our Lord rapidly, as it is recorded for us in the New Testament. In order to do so we pass back into the heavenly places and the heavenly ages, recognizing that these are utterly beyond our final apprehension. We cannot express them, we cannot perfectly understand them, but for the illumination of our present life the veil has been drawn aside, and things have been revealed about that past. The very word "past" is a revelation of our human limitation, but we must employ it. Christ's ministry began, not on earth, but in heaven, began in that mysterious and wonderful self-emptying to which Paul referred when in his Philippian letter he spoke of Christ as being in the form of God, and yet not counting this equality with God a prize to be snatched at or held for His own enrichment. He emptied Himself.

I think it is well that we should immediately say that this is a declaration in the presence of which we must wonder and worship, and confess our inability finally to explain. Much has been said, especially in recent years, concerning that great kenosis, that great self-emptying of the Son of God, and much harm has been done by some interpretations thereof. We are warranted in saying of it so much as Holy Scripture says, that whatever functional relationship Jesus held with essential Deity He laid aside in the interest of humanity. He did not count His right of equality with God something to be held for His own enrichment, but laid it aside. Stooping from sovereignty to submission, from some form of manifestation suited to heavenly beings to a form of manifestation suited to man in the time of limitation, He took upon Him the form of man. As we thus see the work of the Son of God at its commencement as a self-emptying that laid aside all the rights of equality with God and laid aside all co-operation with the Spirit on the basis of equality, consenting in some infinite mystery to be born of the Spirit, and in its continuation consenting throughout the whole period of a life to be an instrument of the Spirit, we touch the profound and infinite things that lie behind the Pentecostal effusion.

The first fact in the ministry of the Son of God for human redemption was that self-emptying, and the final fact was that "they were all filled with the Holy Spirit." He first emptied Himself, and finally He filled these men with all the pleroma of Deity. This was a new activity in co-operation with the Spirit wherein, according to His own word, He did receive from the Father and pour forth on these men that infinitely mysterious and yet wonderful gift of the Spirit. Then the new day broke, the new life began, and the Christian fact was established in the world.

Between that first fact of self-emptying and that final fact of the filling of these men lay all the processes with which we are most familiar. First, the Incarnation, whereby God, veiled in flesh, manifested Himself to the sons of men; the patient ministry of word and work through which the will of God was revealed to men who had lost their understanding of it, and the glory and the grace of God, which were made to shine again, so that men, seeing these things, found Him. Centrally there was the infinite mystery of the Cross, and beyond it the Day of Resurrection, whereby the bonds of death were broken and the perfection of the atoning work was sealed. Finally there was the Ascension to the right hand of power.

Our Lord emptied Himself, He was made flesh, He went about doing and teaching, He bore our sins in His own Body on the tree, He broke the power of death and arose from among the dead, He ascended to the right hand of the Father, receiving gifts, yea, for the rebellious also; He poured out the Spirit, and "they were all filled with the Holy Spirit."

The blessing thus bestowed is suggestively described to us by certain phrases of the New Testament. The work of the Spirit is described as a baptism, as an anointing, and as a sealing. Men are baptized in the Spirit, men are anointed of the Spirit, men are sealed by the Spirit, and these three phrases describe different phases of the one great and inclusive fact. The filling is the supreme matter: the filling is baptizing, the filling is anointing, the filling is sealing.

The filling of the Spirit was, first of all, a baptism, by which phrase is suggested the death into life, which is the peculiar and fundamental fact of all personal Christian experience, a dying to the false life and rising to the true, a dying to sin and rising to holiness, a dying to the world so far as the world is separated from God, and a rising into the life of the ages which is the life of dominion over all the cosmos. Baptism stands as the sign and symbol of that passing from death unto life which is the fundamental fact in all

Christian experience. In that moment when these men and women were filled with the Spirit they were baptized of the Spirit into life.

The anointing of the Spirit ever signifies the preparation of those who are baptized of the Spirit for service. It is the peculiar word of the old economy, made use of in the new, reminding us of that anointing for priestly function and all holy service which men in the old dispensation passed through. The Spirit anoints for service all whom He baptizes into life to the service of God.

The filling is also a sealing. The seal is the sign of a covenant. As the Spirit of God came to these men He came as the seal of a covenant between themselves and Him, a covenant by which they belonged entirely to God and God belonged wholly to them, placing Himself in all His wisdom and all His might entirely and absolutely at their disposal, lifting them to the height of interest in His purpose, descending to the level of interest in their enterprises. In that moment when they were filled with the Spirit, filled with the Spirit as the result of the perfecting of the work of their Lord and Master Christ, they were baptized from death into life, they were anointed for all enterprise and service, and the covenant made between God and themselves was sealed.

So we pass to consider the fact in the experience of the disciples. Here again we may inclusively declare that in this filling of the Spirit men on earth were joined to the Man at God's right hand. Paul writing to the Corinthian Christians said, "He that is joined unto the Lord is one Spirit." We do no violence to the declaration if we state the selfsame truth from another standpoint, and say, He that is of one Spirit with the Lord is thereby joined to the Lord. This is the mystic side of Christianity which we must not lose. If by the use of the word mystic I suggest something unreal, then I fain would change it. This is the actual essential central fact of Christianity. Who is the Christian man? That man who is living one life with the Lord of glory, not the man who has merely seen a vision of Christ and admires it, not the man who is sentimentally in agreement with the purposes of Jesus of Nazareth, but the man who, in an infinite mystery that is always beyond final explanation, does live one life with the Lord of glory.

"They were filled with the Spirit." The Spirit proceeding from the Father, from the Son, came to them, and in that moment they lived one life with Him, and that is the explanation of the things we referred to at the commencement; a new vision of themselves, His vision of them; a new vision of the world, His vision of the world; a new vision of God, His vision of God. Their eyes were strangely and wonderfully and actually illuminated by the light of His mind and outlook. They had the mind of Christ by the baptism of the Spirit of Christ. Not only is it true that they saw as He saw; it is also true that now through their eyes He was able to look at men, through their hands He was able to touch men, and by the cession of their feet to Him He was able to travel anew through Judea and Samaria, and to the uttermost parts of the earth. They were joined to the Lord, and the limited and localized Body of Jesus of Nazareth was thereby immediately multiplied a hundredfold, and the multiplication has continued through the centuries. Every new man, woman, boy, girl won from the territory of the world into relation with Him has become a new Body for Jesus, in which He lives, through which He looks, in which He speaks, in which He travels, and through which He comes nearer and yet nearer to the wounds and weariness of humanity, healing the wounds and resting the weariness.

If this be true, we may pass with great solemnity and reverence over the pathway of this Man as we surveyed it, and declare that now in these men these essential things of

His limited ministry are realized anew. These men were filled with the Spirit and lived one life with the Son of God. Then the first principle of their life is that of self-emptying. He emptied Himself; He did not consider that which was His by eternal right something that He must hold for His own enrichment, but laid it aside. That is the story of the Spirit-filled life, that is the fundamental fact in all true Christian life. If I affirm that in any hour, or by any experience, I have been filled with the Spirit and still live a self-centred life, I blaspheme against the Holy Ghost. He emptied Himself. He that is joined to the Lord is of one Spirit; he also empties himself.

Therefore these men filled with the Spirit of God became God—manifesting men. Said Paul to the Corinthians, "Your body is a temple of the Holy Ghost!" That is the meaning of Pentecost. It resulted in such capture of the bodies of men and women that through them in all their habits and all their ways, through all their lives, God shall be manifest to men. I know there is a lonely and unique meaning in the incarnation of God in Christ Jesus, but the great principle is continued through all the Christian era, and every Christian man and woman in their day and opportunity is an incarnation of Christ, Who is the incarnation of God. It was this which Peter meant when describing the Church of God he said, "Ye are an elect race, a royal priesthood, a holy nation, a people for God's own possession, that ye may show forth the excellencies of Him Who called you out of darkness into His marvellous light."

To be filled with the Spirit is to be an instrument for the manifestation of God to the sons of men.

To be filled with the Spirit is to live the life of love and service, in word and in work.

To be filled with the Spirit is to share the suffering that saves. There are lonely and mysterious and infinite elements in the passion of the Son of God that are always beyond us and from which we receive the benefits of the eternal grace. But we can share in His saving work only as we share in His sacrificial love. The fulness of the Spirit is ability to suffer with Christ on behalf of men. The fulness of the Spirit is the unlocking of the gates of life, that the life may be poured out in work and weariness and toil and travail, through which, and through which alone, the Kingdom of God can come.

To be joined to the Lord is to be one spirit with Him, and therefore it is also to have fellowship in the deathless life, to be ready to say with Paul, As dying, but behold we live, as always bearing about in the body the stigmata of Jesus, and yet always being led in triumph in Jesus Christ, so that no forces can destroy. The fulness of the Spirit is the fulness of resurrection life in Jesus.

To be filled with the Spirit is not merely to share in the suffering of the Cross and the power of the Resurrection. It is to reign with Him as the ascended One, to sit with Him in the places of authority in the heavenlies, to wait patiently with Him for the ultimate victory, and all the while with Him to reign over circumstances and happenings and forces.

Again, to be filled with the Spirit is to be able to communicate the Spirit to others. Do you challenge that affirmation? Then I pray you think of our Lord's figurative teaching as given at the Feast in Jerusalem and recorded for us in the seventh chapter of John: "If any man thirst, let him come unto Me and drink. He that believeth on Me, as the Scripture hath said, out of his inner life shall flow rivers of living water." And John adds, "Thus spake He of the Spirit." There is no power for Christian service that does not consist in the communication of the Spirit of God to other people, and only as we are suffused in the power of the Holy Spirit can we become the media which communicate this Spirit of God to others. He that ascended on high and received the Spirit and poured it forth on others links us to Himself in this holy life so that we also receive the Spirit in order that we may pour it forth on others.

This Pentecostal effusion is not an event of two millenniums ago, but the perpetual rushing forth of the river of life proceeding from the throne of God by the way of the altar; and whithersoever the river comes, there is life. These rivers of living water are to flow from the saints, who themselves being filled to fulness and to overflowing communicate the gift to others.

All this great ministry of the Spirit is suggestively set forth in the symbolic language of the New Testament. The symbols of the Spirit in the New Testament are those of wind, springs and rivers of water, and fire—the great elemental forces. Each has its distinctive features. The wind is in itself the very element of life. The rivers of water are always those that bring satisfaction and renewal to everyday life. The fire is always the emblem of searching purification and of perpetual energy. These are the peculiar symbols that the New Testament employs to give us some understanding of the work of the Spirit. Let us note the ideas common to all these figures of speech, the wind, the water, and the fire. They are forces mighty and mysterious. They are forces capable of destroying life. We are familiar with the hurricane that sweeps the sea, the devastating flood that destroys everything in its path, the conflagration that leaves desolation behind it. Yet all these forces are necessary to life. They demand obedience in order to render service. Obey the law of any of these forces, and the force becomes your servant. Disobey the law of wind or water or fire, and you will be destroyed.

When these men and women were filled with the Spirit they entered not only into a realm of privilege, but also into the place of responsibility. What is our responsibility to the

Spirit as suggested by the symbol of wind? That we live on the heights and inhale the breath of God. What is our responsibility in view of the filling of the Spirit as suggested by the symbol of the waters? That we live in the stream and drink. What is our responsibility in view of the filling of the Spirit as suggested by the symbol of the fire? That we dwell in fire, knowing that fire destroys nothing but that which cannot be permeated and filled with its own nature, and that we quench not the Spirit.

We have no responsibility in this Pentecostal age to seek or ask for the Spirit. Our responsibility is to discover the laws of the Spirit and obey them. In proportion as we are careless of the laws of the life of the Spirit the experience fades and the power recedes. In proportion as we obey, the experience grows and the power increases.

To some it may be that all this is an unknown tongue. To them, therefore, I bring the words of Jesus, words spoken to men who had not then received the gift of the Spirit: "If ye being evil know how to give good gifts unto your children, how much more shall your heavenly Father give the Holy Spirit to them that ask Him." That word is not for those who have received the Spirit, it is for those who never yet have received the gift. If you have never received the gift of the Spirit you may receive it by asking for it now. The Pentecostal effusion is not to be put back two thousand years as something dim and distant and far away. The river of God is moving, the winds of God are blowing, the fire of God is burning. Then, without sign or sound or confession made to men, ask the gift and receive.

Or it may be that having received, the vision has become dim and the forces weak. Then open again the eastern windows and yield the life once more to that Spirit Who needs no asking to enter but only the unlocking of the doors and the opening of the avenues of life. For those who thus yield there shall be repeated the experience of the first Pentecost, the baptism of fire that destroys the impure and energizes the life, the wind of God

> that bloweth lustily
> Our sicknesses to heal;

the flowing of the river that quenches our thirst, and then becomes the means of blessing through us to other men.

CHAPTER XV

NEHUSHTAN

He brake in pieces the brasen serpent that Moses had made; for unto those days the children of Israel did burn incense to it; and he called it Nehushtan.

II KINGS 18:4.

WE AT ONCE REALIZE WHAT AN ASTONISHING STATEMENT the Chronicler makes here concerning king Hezekiah. Hezekiah ascended the throne of Judah in the third year of the reign of Hoshea, king of Israel, a young man twenty-five years of age; and immediately—undoubtedly acting under the influence of Isaiah, the great evangelical prophet of the old economy—he commenced a work of reformation. One of the first acts of the reign of the new king was that of smashing to fragments one of the most valuable and historic relics in his kingdom.

So strange an action is in itself worthy of our closest attention, and I think we shall find in our meditation a revelation of some of the great facts of human nature and of some perils threatening men in the region of the most sacred things of their lives; and, consequently, a revelation of principles of perpetual value and of immediate application.

Let us first attempt to put ourselves back into the days when, with what must have appeared to be the strangest disregard of cherished prejudices, Hezekiah commenced his reformation by this act of iconoclasm. I need hardly tarry to remind you of the facts concerning this brazen serpent. In order that we may have our memory refreshed we read the simple story as it is contained in the book of Numbers. However, it may be well to notice one fact. According to the story as there told, it is not suggested, neither was it suggested to the people at the time, if we follow and accept the words as here recorded as being correct, that there was any healing virtue in the brazen serpent. No suggestion was made to the people of Israel that the serpent itself could produce any mystic effect. To read the story simply is to see to its very heart. The sin of the people had been their departure from the attitude of absolute submission to the government of God. In the midst of this rebellious people now punished by God, the brazen serpent was erected, and the word of God which Moses was commanded to speak to them was a declaration that if any man, bitten and in peril, would look at the uplifted serpent he would be healed. That was God's word. No explanation of the relation between the looking and the life was given. We sing, "There is life for a look at the Crucified One," and in so doing we may be singing what is perfectly true, or we may be singing that which is entirely false. What brought these men back to life was the fact that they returned to submission to the government of God, as, for the moment, that government was focused in that wonderful and yet simple provision. The healing virtue came from God, and was operative in answer to that act of submission in which men, no longer arguing as to the wisdom of the method, submitted to the Divine command. Because men in rebellion must be dealt with as children— there must always be a picture, something that appeals to the eye—God in infinite grace said to these men, Take a serpent of brass and set it on a standard, and let the word of My government for the moment be My command to look. Men looked because God commanded, and looking because God commanded, they turned by that act to the Divine government and were healed. This is the history.

It was in itself a remarkable thing that the serpent of brass should have been so long preserved. Between that event in the wilderness and this iconoclasm of Hezekiah at least seven hundred years had elapsed. Think how carefully it had been preserved—by Moses during all the years he remained with these people, all through those tedious and perilous journeys through the great and terrible wilderness; by Joshua through all his forty years of campaign and settlement as he led the people into the land; during the strange and troubled period when the judges as dictators were raised up to govern the people according to immediate necessities; during the splendor of the reigns of Saul, David, and Solomon; and through all the troublous and turbulent times of the kings succeeding to Solomon on both sides of the border, in the Northern and Southern Kingdoms. Somewhere this brazen serpent had been preserved. I repeat that for over seven hundred years it had been a relic, historic, interesting, and essentially valuable, in that to illuminated eyes and waiting souls it was forevermore a reminder of their own sin in the past, of the judgment which fell on them in consequence of that sin, and of the deliverance which God had provided for them.

In process of time interest grew into veneration, until this very symbol was set up in the midst of the people as an object of worship. At last they actually burnt incense to this brazen serpent. This was the deification of a symbol, the turning from the veneration of a relic for the sake of its essential values to the veneration of that relic on the supposition that it had some virtue resident in itself.

We immediately see that this story is not old, as at first it appears to be. Indeed, almost absurd as it seems, this very idea persists to this hour under the shadow of what is named after Christ. In the Church of St. Ambrose, in Milan, they will show you this brazen serpent. In the year 971 a Milanese envoy in Constantinople was asked to take some treasure of the city as a gift, and he chose a brazen serpent which the Greeks assured him was made out of the very pieces of the serpent which Hezekiah broke into fragments. That certainly is in a country still enslaved by Roman superstitions, but the same things are practiced among us, if in more subtle forms.

Looking back to the ancient story, I ask you to notice that this deification of the brazen serpent, this setting it up as an object of worship, and this burning of incense to it, was in itself a most significant sign of the condition of the people at that time. It was, first, a revelation of their loss of consciousness of God. These people never could have burned incense to the serpent if the presence of God had been recognized and realized. One goes back in memory to the solemn days in the history of these people in the wilderness, when it was necessary to erect this serpent, days when they had before them the outward symbols of the presence of God in the Tabernacle, with all its suggestiveness, and when they had no right to sin. Yet they had sinned, and had been punished by God, and had turned back to Him. We call to mind also the whole history of these Hebrew people, not to dwell on any single detail, but to make this general statement: in hours when they were supremely conscious of God setting up such an object for worship would have been absolutely impossible. It is patent that the sight of these people gathered together around the brazen serpent for the purpose of burning incense to it, making this particular relic of their past history an object of worship, demonstrated the fact that they had lost the consciousness of God.

Yet their action proved more than that. I see a people hungering after what they have lost. An idol always means this. An idol created by the fingers of men, or chosen by men and appointed to the place of a god, is forevermore a revelation of the sense of need, the sense of lack. It is an evidence that the deepest thing in the human heart is its cry after God. This is not to defend idolatry, not to defend the action of these people in the deification of the brazen serpent, but to say that when people lose their consciousness of God they do not lose their sense of need for God. Whereas I look back on these people in this hour and say they have lost their vision of God, have lost the sense of His nearness, have wandered far away from that spiritual communion with Him which is in itself a fire and a force, I say also that having lost the vision and having lost the sense, they are restless. When the one true and living God, having been revealed and known, is lost to consciousness the heart will clamantly cry for that which is lost. This worship of the serpent was certainly a revelation of the hunger of the people after God.

There is one other matter which I think this event reveals. Having lost their vision of God, and still being conscious of the necessity for some object of worship around which their spiritual life could gather, their deification of the serpent was a revelation of the utmost confusion. It was history misinterpreted. A blessing of the olden days was made a curse in the present moment by that misinterpretation of their own history. Setting up the brazen serpent as an object of worship suggested that the serpent itself had been the means of their healing on the past occasion. Their vision of God lost, and the cry of their souls after such a God, and the blundering confusion of a people who, looking back at their own history, emphasized it wrongly, interpreted it falsely, and treated the serpent as though it had been the means of their healing in the past—such was the abuse of the brazen serpent.

When Hezekiah came to the throne he did two things. First of all, he named the serpent "Nehushtan," a piece of brass, or, with fine contempt, a thing of brass. Then he broke it in pieces.

The naming of the serpent thus was intended to be a

revelation to the people of their unutterable folly: they were burning incense to a thing of brass! It was intended to be a revelation to the people of their unutterable sin: These people whose worship had been of the unseen and eternal God, Who had demonstrated Himself to them by all the wonder of their history, were actually worshiping a thing of brass! There was a fine contempt in this naming of the brazen serpent, undoubtedly intended by the king to reveal to men their unutterable folly and the absolute wickedness of their idolatry.

Now, what will this king do with this thing of brass? No blame can be attached to the people for having preserved it; there was no sin in their preservation of the serpent; it was something which, coming up out of their past history, ought to have reminded them of God and the spiritual lessons they had learned in that hour of sin and of judgment and wondrous deliverance.

Hezekiah took this sacred relic and broke it in pieces, its associations notwithstanding. This he did because, with true insight, he understood that it was a source of danger to the people and therefore he could make no compromise with it. It was an act of true reform. It was the act of a man who would make no peace with that most sacred thing, a thing which in itself was not an evil thing, which in itself had no virtue and no vice, but which had become a source of danger to the people. It must therefore be destroyed. That is the story. Now let us make certain applications of it to our own day.

The first I suggest is this: God's very gifts to men may be so abused as to become positively injurious. Anything to which we are burning incense merely because of the sacredness of its past associations is a peril to our spiritual life, and ought to be destroyed. Let me be pertinent and practical. What are some of the things to which we are in danger of burning incense to-day?

I have known Christian congregations burn incense to the very building in which they assembled for worship, as though it were sacred in itself, as though to pass its threshold and be under its roof were to be in the very house of God and at the gate of heaven. That in itself is idolatry. We may so revere a building as to make a true worship of God impossible inside it. This is a strange paradox, and I shall ask you to bear quite patiently with me as I give you a very simple illustration out of my own past experience. I remember twenty-five years ago it had been arranged that I was to go to a certain church—of what denomination and in what town is of no matter—to conduct special mission services for fifteen days. As the time drew near I had a letter from the officers of the church saying that while they still felt the need of such services, the church had been recently renovated, and they had decided to abandon the mission in case the paint should be injured by strangers coming in! That is cold history. We may say that we should not do such a foolish thing as that; but we need to remember that the attitude of mind which made such an action possible is a perpetual peril. We call bricks and mortar a church. There is a sense in which that is true; but there is a sense in which a material building may become a grave and a terrible menace to the spiritual life of a church. We burn incense to our buildings and imagine that when we have passed into them we are separated to the worship of God. It is possible for a man to sit in this building from beginning to end of the service and never draw near to the true place of worship.

Then there are the exercises of public worship; we may burn incense to them, and make our form of service so ornate, so regular, so beautiful, that the very Spirit of God Who, like a breath of wind, would pass over the congregation, would not be able to find room to enter. We may burn incense to order, and so create the gravest disorder.

We may burn incense to the ministry considered as a

caste. It may be that here we are in no danger of doing that. It may be that those of us who belong to the Free Church are in no danger of that particular form of idolatry, yet the peril lingers even among us. I know men who do not care to take the sacrament unless some ordained man preside. That is priestcraft. I would be quite content to take the bread and wine from the hands of some godly mother in Israel.

We still burn incense to the individual man, and though we have never used the word nor do we think of using it, our attitude is that of the deification of the individual. We have an idea that the whole Kingdom of God will fall if a certain man fails us, or moves to some other sphere of work. A subtle idolatry threatens us in spiritual things, sacred things. The danger that threatens us is that we may worship that which is the means rather than the God Who reaches us through those means.

It is possible to burn incense to a creed, to systematized theology. It is possible to crib, cabin and confine spiritual growth by loyalty to some dead hand of orthodoxy. I venture to say with all boldness that I am the right man to say that kind of thing. This Divine Library is final in authority; but not your interpretation of it, nor mine, nor that of any man. No creeds that have been drawn up by honest souls in the past are final interpretations of the literature of the heavens. This Bible is as wonderful as the Spirit of God, forevermore breaking, annulling, destroying human interpretations, and blossoming into new beauty, singing itself out into new poetry, making poor the finest utterances of past interpretation. Yet there are men who ask me to sign a creed, and subscribe to a dogma, and contribute to systematized theology. They are burning incense to a creed. They are making a creed, which is a thing of men's hands, devout and sincere in itself, an object of worship.

I have even known men to burn incense to a trust deed

and allow the work of God to be interfered with and spoiled because of the terms that lie within some such deed, drawn up amid some conditions that long since have passed away. There was a need for a certain wording of the trust deed at the time; but that is no warrant for saying that a trust deed must hold men to-day and prevent them from going forward and doing the work to which God is calling them, work which the age demands and which the mental mood of the hour is calling them to do. In many ways we are doing what these Hebrews did, lifting a serpent of brass and burning incense to it.

It is possible to be idolatrous in the matter of prayer, and in the matter of the sacraments of the Lord's Supper and baptism. It is possible to treat all these things which are means of grace as though they were grace. It is possible to treat these things which are Divinely appointed ordinances, symbols, signs, sacraments, outward and visible signs of the inward and invisible grace, as though they in themselves were channels of the invisible grace. That is sacerdotalism. Not merely the claim of the priest of Greek, Roman, or Anglican ordination, but the worship of the sacrament by men who profess to have escaped from all such bondage. That is burning incense to an idol.

I have known men who were worshipers of the day of their conversion. I know men who tell me that ten, twenty, or thirty years ago, here or there, they were born again; and to-day they are dead in trespasses and sins, but still burn incense to the old experience, imagining that to be true worship. The memory of an hour of illumination, of clear shining, may change the volition and transfigure the life, I admit it; but such a memory has no value to-day unless to-day the light is shining, the soul is poised toward God, and the attitude of the life is what it ought to be toward our fellow men. Yet we burn incense to these dead things. They were living things at the moment, they had their place and their value, they were God's own means of blessing to us; but to-day we gather about them and worship them and have no dealing with God.

Of all such action, looking back at the ancient story, I will say that such abuse of things in themselves sacred and right and God-appointed can come only out of spiritual degeneracy. Loyalty to God will maintain all these in their true place and true proportion. The serpent was never the depository of virtue, nor is any one of these I have mentioned.

The only way of virtue, using the word in its broadest and best sense as meaning strength and sanctity—the only way of virtue is the way of immediate dealing with God. So surely as men are burning incense to the brazen serpent, to creeds, to human instrumentalities, to ordinances, even God-appointed ordinances, so surely it is because they have lost the power of commerce with heaven and communion with God. No man will ever burn incense to any of these things who lives and works in the light and hears the voice of God within his own soul. The man who hears the voice of God within his own soul can find Bethel in the railway train, on the highway. It is loss of the vision of God that is demonstrated by the deification of anything less than God.

Yet, blessed be God, this deification of the little is demonstration of the fact that man cannot find rest except in God Himself. If you have lost the vision and the true spiritual communion, then you must worship something, you must put something back in its place. That, as I said before, is not to defend idolatry, it is not to say the final word concerning the activity, for if it be true that idolatry demonstrates capacity for God, it is equally true that idolatry ultimately destroys the capacity for God. If it be true that having lost God, I put this idol in His place, so surely as I do I shall presently become like the idol I make, and having eyes I shall see not, and having ears I shall hear not, and having hands I also like my idol shall not be able to feel, I shall become insensate. Deification of anything less than God demonstrates the capacity for worship and is a revelation of hunger; but it issues in the destruction of the very capacity it demonstrates.

What is the right attitude toward all such things? I suggest that our right attitude is first to name the things rightly. Look and see that this cunning artifice of brass is not a serpent, it is brass. Then name it Nehushtan, a thing of brass. Call the church a building of bricks and mortar. Call the minister a man, and remember that he is none other, and if he is other he ought not to be in the ministry. Call the exercises of worship forms, remembering that form without power is in itself a curse. Call creeds and systematized theology human opinion, and respect it as human opinion and in no other way. Call the trust deed paper or parchment, as the case may be. Call prayer words. Call the day of your conversion past.

If any or all of these things are coming between your soul and God Himself break them in pieces. Not merely the idols which your fathers had before the flood, not merely the idols which you found in the land, but the idol which is one of your sacred things which in a past hour of need was God's provision for your well-being. If it has become an idol, then must it be broken in pieces.

Let us bring our most sacred things to the test, and let us remember that to whatever we burn incense we must destroy if the burning of the incense has resulted in the loss of the vision of God and issued in inability to commune with God. Infinitely better to be stripped of every means of grace, and to come to worship as a naked spirit with God alone, than to allow these things which He has instituted to help us to such worship, to stand between us and Himself. That is the teaching.

Yet a final word is this; the true attitude of the soul is

that of the retention of all these things in their true place and in their true proportion. The true attitude of the soul is that in which it looks back to the day when life began in Christ and rejoices in it, but immediately brings that past experience into expression in the living present. The great autobiographical passage of the Apostle Paul in the Philippian letter has often been quoted; let us hear it once again. Writing to his Philippian children from prison and reviewing the process of his Christian life, looking back to the hour on the Damascus road when he was apprehended by his Master, he said, "Howbeit what things were gain to me, these have I counted loss for Christ." That counting was at least thirty years before, but there was no virtue in that. A little further on he added, "Yea verily, and *I count* all things to be loss." The "I counted" of yesterday is of no value unless it be carried into the "I count" of to-day. If to-day I count all things but loss, then I shall never undervalue that past experience on the way to Damascus; but the light that shone on me on the way to Damascus, or in the midst of that revival of thirty years ago, is of no value to-day unless there shines on my soul this morning the light of God, and I answer it.

So with prayer. Savonarola declared on one occasion that when prayer reaches its ultimate height words are impossible, that when the soul has come to terms of communion with God words are left behind. I think every Christian man and woman who knows anything of the secret place knows how true that is. There is another application of the great truth concerning prayer that we often lose sight of. In my experience the prayers that have most profoundly touched my soul and moved me, the prayers that I have felt have most perfectly taken hold of God, were prayers that broke down in the middle, that could not be continued, but ended in blundering articulation and half-finished sentences, and then a sob and silence. That is prayer. If the sense of God that produces such an attitude in the soul of man is absent, then elegance of diction is blasphemy, and beauty of phrasing is impertinence, and we are burning incense to a thing of brass rather than worshiping God. The true attitude of the soul is that which—to use the word of the old economy—brings with it words, and pours out thought in speech before the throne of God, setting no value on the form of the words, but all value on the grip of the soul on God, and the touch of God on the soul.

Not to proceed further with these things already referred to, the final thing is this; let us keep this serpent of brass, let us learn to keep it by making the necessity for its destruction unnecessary. Let us retain it and let it speak to our hearts its true lesson. Let it say to us forevermore: I remind you of the hour of sin; beware of sin; I remind you of the hour of swift judgment which must come again if you sin; I remind you of the hour of deliverance. If we so keep it, and let it thus speak to us, we shall never burn incense to it, but when it has thus spoken we shall forget it as we worship God.

CHAPTER XVI

THE POSSIBILITY OF RESTORATION

If from thence ye shall seek the Lord thy God, thou shalt find Him, if thou search after Him with all thy heart and with all thy soul.

DEUTERONOMY 4:29.

THE BOOK OF DEUTERONOMY IS A SINGULARLY BEAUTIFUL one. It is not a history. It is more than a code of morals. It consists of the last messages Moses gave to the people of his heart. It is a prophecy in the fullest sense of the word. It is a book full of light and full of fire. Here the words of law are indeed uttered and the importance of law insisted upon, but as we read it we are not so much conscious of the binding nature of law's requirements as of the driving power of love's great reason. Not that in this book the moral standards are lowered, but that there seem to be wonderful revelations of the secrets by which men may realize these standards.

Sometimes I have been inclined to call this book an evangel of the law. It is evidently that, as this man spoke for the last time to these people whom he had led through forty years his heart was full of tenderness. These are the words of a man who had come into close association with God Himself, a man who had stood in the awful light in which there is no darkness at all, but who in that light had found that infinite love which goes far beyond our dreams.

In this text we have a beautiful illustration of this consciousness of the man of law of the tenderness of the heart of God. He had been supposing the possibility of the backsliding of these people in spite of the revelation they had received. In the light of subsequent history that supposition proved to be prophecy, for, just as he suggested, they forgot God and wandered from Him, and the very calamities which he described fell on them. After describing in detail the process of such possible backsliding until the ultimate issue of it was revealed, suddenly, and apparently with a sense of relief and gladness, he turned from the fierce denunciations and said: "If from thence"—the uttermost and ultimate place of backsliding—"if from thence ye shall seek the Lord, ye shall find Him, if thou search after Him with all thy heart and with all thy soul."

My message has to do with this possibility of backsliding, this possibility of turning from the higher to the lower, until, perchance, at last the lowest is reached. I am especially anxious to speak to those who may be addressed in the words of the great Apostle: "Ye did run well. What did hinder you?" Or perhaps to those of whom Christ would say in the language of His message to the church at Ephesus: "I have this against thee, that thou didst leave thy first love."

I want to speak to men and women who, in the consciousness of their own secret hearts, know full well that the running is not what it was, who have lost the joy of first love, the love of their espousals to the Lord Christ, and who are lamenting the loss. I am going to ask you, first of all, as you follow me reverently and patiently, as I am sure you will, to let, not what I say about my text, but the text itself, the living Word of God, appeal to you. I am going to ask you resolutely to submit yourselves to its light and its suggestion and its teaching, remembering your splendid isolation, that you are quite alone in the crowd, that no man, not even the preacher, can know what transpires between your soul and

God. If you find that the running has slackened, or the love has grown cool, or that there is something of distance between you and the Master, I ask that you will listen to the word of hope. Or if, perchance, by the grace of God, you pass uncondemned from the process of examination, I appeal to you to pray for the man who may be sitting next to you who has fallen somewhat from the high estate. It may be that some man in this crowd is in the depths of degradation because he has turned his back on his Lord and Master. The message is especially for him.

The measure of backsliding matters nothing. The tragedy is not in the ultimate corruption, but in the first cooling of passion. It is the loss of first love that is fatal. Everything else is a necessary sequence, and sometimes the latter stages are almost more full of hope than the earlier ones. I pray that as we come to the consideration of so solemn and important a theme we may be kept by the brooding Spirit of God face to face with the unseen and the eternal things.

The text itself suggests the lines of our consideration. First, the process and issue of backsliding: "From thence," the word "thence" illuminated by the context; in the second place, the conditions on which there may be restoration: "*If*—if thou shalt seek the Lord thy God; *if* thou shalt search after Him with all thy heart and with all thy soul"; and, finally, the great word of the text, "Thou shalt find Him."

First, for a few moments let us quietly and earnestly consider this matter of backsliding. This ancient message contains a very living revelation of it, and although the local setting is not this setting, and the coloring of the details has faded from the canvas, the outline stands clear and plain, a revelation for all time of how men, in backsliding, turn away from high things and descend to low things. Hear these words again from the context: "When ye shall corrupt yourselves, and make a graven image in the form of anything, and shall do that which is evil in the sight of the Lord . . ." In them we have a revelation of the whole process by which men backslide. *When* they shall corrupt themselves, *when* they shall make a graven image, *when* they shall do that which is evil in the sight of the Lord . . .

The first step in backsliding is self-corruption; the second is always making a graven image; the ultimate is the habitual and persistent doing of evil in the sight of the Lord. The first is inward, and consequently unknown to friend or neighbor: the corruption of self. The second is more manifest, and yet not always clearly so to other people: making a graven image, the substitution of the false for the true in worship. The last is the stage in which the inner corruption of self becomes manifest, not only in the sight of God, but in the sight of men.

Self-corruption is devotion of life to any thing lower than the highest. What is the highest? That depends entirely on you. The highest to you is what you have seen to be the highest. I shall presuppose in this presence, and speaking to such a congregation as this, that you have seen the highest in the Lord Christ. That which appealed to you may not have been that which appealed to your neighbor, but you saw in Him something that spoke to the deeps within your life; some vision of His loveliness broke on you, you came to some conception of Him that appealed to you, that lured you. You knew perfectly well when the vision came that it was a vision of something high and noble and pure and good. It may have been that in His severe and noble ethic, His strong ideal of life, His fine conception of morality, you saw the height and set your face toward it. That was the highest for you. It may have been that the highest to you was the revelation of His supreme and matchless tenderness, that greatness of heart wherewith He ever traveled forth across the desert to find the lost, that superb compassion that ever made Him willing to sit by the side of sinful men, despising the shame of the Pharisee, while in comradeship with the defiled He communicated first compassion and then purity.

There came a moment when you changed your life to something a little lower than the highest, under swift, sudden, subtle temptation, it may be. You lowered the ethical standard that He had revealed, and for the sake of some advantage offered to you on the plane of the material you denied His call to your soul. In that moment you began the corruption of your life.

It may be that you refused to answer the cry of His compassion to your soul. You did not break your bread with the hungry. You declined to bear the scorn of men while you served the cause of such as were defiled. Remember, this happens to preachers as well as to others! In that moment, when we descended from the highest and refused to answer His call, we began the corruption of self, we were already on a declined plane. In the moment in which a man lowers himself he begins spoiling himself. It is the first stage.

Backsliding always begins there. Take up your newspaper, and you read of some man who held high position in the Christian Church, who is now in the depths. He did not begin with that outward act. There was first a hidden refusal to answer the call of the highest. Almost unknown, perchance, to himself at the moment, he began the descent.

So backsliding begins, begins over and over again in the midst of the Holiness Convention, at the center of a Bible Conference, because there the call comes to the highest; and if we refuse to obey we corrupt ourselves.

What is the next step? Someone will say that my figure of speech will now break down. Men do not now make graven images. I beseech you not to take refuge in subterfuges of that kind. A graven image is a thing that a man creates for himself when he has lost close fellowship with the one true and only God. All idolatry is the revelation of man's capacity for God. In these days men are not making to themselves graven images, as did these men of the olden time; but the moment a man turns from allegiance to God as revealed in Christ he puts something else in the place of God. It may be knowledge, it may be wealth, it may be that which is infinitely more mean and trivial, pleasure; but something steps in so insidiously that a man hardly knows, and it takes the place of God.

How may I know that anything has taken the place of God in my life? To whatever I am devoting my real thinking, my real energy. Whatever is the supreme and most important thing in my life, that is God to me. I may sing the songs of the sanctuary, the liturgy of the Church may still pass my lips, I may recite with intellectual conviction the creeds; but the God I worship is that to which I am giving the force and energy of my life. Ere a man knows it, when he has turned, be it ever so little, from the highest, he puts something else in the place of that from which he has turned and makes a god to suit the level on which he chooses to live.

Presently—mark the tragedy of it—he will turn even from that to something a little lower, and so, slowly but surely, corrupt the life, until the last step of backsliding is the habitually doing evil things in the sight of men. Then the man laughs at faith, sneers at the very things of religion which once were the supreme things, and mocks at high ideals. This is the ultimate in corruption; this is the stage of definite and open and avowed sin.

And what is the issue of it all? The issue of it all is clearly stated: "I call heaven and earth to witness against you this day that ye shall utterly perish from off the land whereunto ye go over Jordan to possess it; ye shall not prolong your days upon it, but shall utterly be destroyed. And the Lord shall scatter you among the peoples, and ye shall be left few in number among the nations. Ye shall serve gods, the work of men's hands, wood and stone, which neither see, nor hear, nor eat, nor smell."

These are the issues of backsliding; loss of possession, loss of power and influence, servitude which is in itself degradation.

When a man loses fellowship with God he loses power to possess anything that God gives him. I suppose the most flaming illustration of the thing in all the Bible is the story of Judas, the story of Judas in those last and awful hours. He turned from the highest, and he sold the Highest for thirty pieces of silver. There was no purchasing power in that silver. Judas had it, but he never possessed it, he never changed a single coin. Through the centuries I hear the clamor and the clangor of the silver flung on the halls of the sacred place, teaching this awful lesson, that the money a man gets when he sells the highest will never purchase him anything.

Do not lose this. You own broad acres. You cannot possess them without God. Oh, you may shoot over them two weeks in the year, but you do not possess them! I will come to something far simpler. You cannot possess a flower if you have turned your back on God. You can botanize, but you have no dealing with the flowers if you are away from the God of the flowers. To turn your back on God, Who gives you land, is to lose that land; and to fail to have dealings with God Who has revealed Himself to you and lured you to the highest is to lose the very earth for the possession of which you have sacrificed the highest and the noblest. I call heaven and earth to witness against you this day that the very things into which you have come, all of them by the goodness of God, you cannot possess if you turn your back on the highest, which, at least, you saw, and toward which you set your affection.

Moses went on to tell the people that they would be scattered through the nations, be held in contempt by the world. I am one of those who never feel that they have any right to speak disrespectfully of the Jew. I believe the Jew is still God's man. But I cannot escape from this tremendous truth, and I had better express it in the language of one of the prophets, Jeremiah, who said: "Refuse silver shall men call them, because Jehovah hath rejected them." Never forget this: deeper than the Nonconformist conscience, deeper than the Christian conscience, is a human conscience which is in perfect accord with God, Who is the unwarped Conscience of the universe. When a man turns his back on God men despise him. The most worldly man holds in supreme contempt the Christian man who once set his face toward the highest and then turned back to the beggarly elements in which the worldly man is always living. Do you not know that there is something profound and searching in the thing the man of the world says to Christian men in surprise: "I did not expect to see you here"? When a man turns from God he loses not only his power of possession, but also his influence. He is despised, held in contempt.

The last descriptive word concerning the issue is the most terrible. The people of Jehovah, the people of the eternities, the people of vision, the people delivered by the high hand and outstretched arm of God, the people who came through the sea, and have been fed in the wilderness, and in all material things have had traffic with the spiritual; the people whom God has been teaching that man cannot live by bread alone, but by every word that proceedeth out of the mouth of God, they are to serve gods without eyes, or ears, or hands, or smell, insensate deities, gods having no answer in the hour when the heart is wrung with anguish and cries out for succor; gods, the supreme helplessness of whom is revealed in one prophetic word: "There is no breath in them."

If we turn from the high to the low, then also will

come the hour when we shall serve as slaves the god to whom we have given ourselves; and when our hearts are lonely and we cry for help, there will be no answer. No eye will pity, no ear will hear; we shall stretch out lame hands, and our gods will not be able to put underneath us the everlasting arms. It is not when the sun is shining that humanity becomes most conscious of itself. It is out of the bruising of life that men utter their supreme cries. The last stage of turning from God is the appalling loneliness of the darkling void in which God is not, and from which no answer comes back to the soul in its agony. Is there someone listening to me in that ultimate place of loneliness? I beseech you to remember that you are not alone. "Closer is He than breathing, and nearer than hands and feet." He and you meet in the depths! Listen! "If from thence thou shalt seek the Lord thy God, thou shalt find Him." That is the message of the text.

On what conditions? Notice most carefully these words. The search is not geographical, it is not circumstantial. A man is to seek for God, and not for the lost condition. Moses did not say to these people, If in that day of ultimate backsliding you shall seek for the land you will find it. Nay, verily! Nor, If ye seek for the lost influence you will recover it. He said, If ye seek for God you will find Him. The search must be for God. Let us solemnly consider this. If, indeed, you have descended from the heights and given yourself to the lower things, and have reached the ultimate, or if you are on the way to the ultimate, it is useless to making up your mind that you are going back to the heights. You won't do it that way. It is useless to determine that you will get back your lost influence. You will never get it that way. What, then, is the soul to do? Search for God, turn back again to God.

Moses repeated his "if" in order that there might be no

misunderstanding of his meaning. He not only said, "If thou shalt seek for Him"; he added, "If thou search with all thy heart, and with all thy soul."

I am not going to suggest that if you are at a distance from God the pathway back is necessarily an easy one. I am going rather to say to you: In the Name of God and your own humanity, be done with your fooling, and put blood and passion into the business of getting back. With all your heart, and with all your soul, means bringing resolutely yourself together in your endeavor to seek after God. That is the condition of getting back. It is of no use to sigh for the lost heights, it is of no use to resolve that you will so live as to win back the lost influence and the lost power. Never, never, never! You had better become for a little while—do not misunderstand me when I say it—you had better become for a little while careless about the heights, you had better come down into an appalling loneliness in which you say, O God, if there never be a height again for me, if there never again be influence for me, let me find Thee, let me get into real, living, vital, first-hand relationship with Thyself. That is the true attitude of a seeking soul.

Now, let it be granted that somewhere in this crowd that cry has gone up to God. No human ear has heard it. No human eye has been keen enough to detect a soul's turning back to God; but God has seen it. Now, then, I may come to the last word of the text, "Thou shalt find Him." This is certain, because it is you who changed, and not He; it is you who wandered, and not He; it is you who turned your back on Him, and not He His back on you. The Bible never speaks of God being reconciled to man; it speaks of man being reconciled to God. Oh, if you are going into dialectics, you can prove that one involves the other; but I am going to stand by the language of Scripture, for there is supreme value in it. I affirm to you, and I say it for the comfort of my soul—for I also have known backsliding—God never turned His face from man. Thou shalt find him. Where? Right there, where you are. Oh, but I am out of the land, I am in a foreign country, I am far away from the center of things! Nay, for thou art not far away from God, and He is the center of all things. But I am in the desert! And God is in the desert, and when your face turns back to Him resolutely, He will make the desert blossom as the rose. I have wandered far from the fountain of living waters, and I am on the sandy wastes, dying of thirst! God is there, and in the desert He shall make the springs of water to flow. He has never turned His back on you. I wish I could reach that man to-night who feels he is far off, and that nobody cares, and that even the Christian Church is prepared to give him another push downward in order to be rid of him. Man, God is with you where you are. Turn thy face toward His face, and He will lift on you the light of His countenance!

Thou shalt find Him, and to find God is to find everything. Suppose, for the sake of argument—I shall not end there—but suppose, for the sake of argument, you never win back your influence, you never reach the old heights of experience and ecstatic joy, to have found Him is to find everything. Ah, but that was only a supposition. To find Him is to find all in another sense. Go back over the process of your backsliding. How did it begin? You corrupted yourself. To find Him is to find yourself redeemed in all the full, vital sense of the word; to find Him is to find the One Who heals the life. Old Jacob coming back from Jabbok said a great thing: "I have seen God face to face, and my life is healed"—in our modern sense of the word, infinitely more than "preserved." "Preserved," in our modern sense, suggests to us that Jacob meant, Behold the wonder! I have seen God, and I have not been destroyed! It means infinitely more. I have seen Him, and I am healed. When he finds God, the man who has corrupted himself knows that he is redeemed.

To find God is to be able to use the language of Ephraim, "What have I to do any more with idols?" What, indeed, have I to do any more with idols after I have found God? Dagon falls and is broken into a thousand fragments when the soul has found God.

Evil ceases to be dominant in the life, the outward habits and activities of evil end; and goodness becomes dominant. There will yet be conflict. That will never end until we pass into the life that lies beyond. But the victorious element will be goodness, and the fall and blunder by the way will be the accident and not the habit of the life. To find God is to find not merely the ideal goodness, but the dynamic for goodness. The paralyzed, powerless, beaten soul that has been for years the sport of lusts and passions and evil things will be able to say, "I can do all things through Christ which strengtheneth me."

The issues of backsliding also will be changed. The land will be repossessed. To find God is to find the flowers, and to find the birds; to find the things which you thought were yours, but from which you were excluded by sin.

My mind travels back over forty years. I am a boy again in my father's garden. There comes into that garden a young man who has been brought to Christ in some services that my father has been conducting. I was only a boy. In that garden that young man walked round with me, and his arm was round me, and suddenly he stooped—I see him now—to pluck a nasturtium leaf. He showed it to me, and said, Look at it, look at it! I looked at it. He said, Is it not wonderful? Look at the glory of it. And to think I have lived thirty years and never saw one till recently. I have never forgotten that. I know now what he meant. To get back to God is to get the key of everything, to enter into the land and to possess.

It is also to find a restoration of power and influence.

You need not trouble about the Pharisee who will not receive you. Live your life with God and your influence is going to tell.

And, yet again, instead of being the bond slave of gods having no eyes or ears or hands or feet, insensate deities, the bond slave of dead things, after restoration to God you will find yourself reigning in life, realizing all the meaning that was in the heart of God when He gave you your first breath and your original being.

Are you away from God? Was it only yesterday that you turned from the highest? Oh, back to Him, back to Him! You traveled further than you knew when you said, "No," to the high and the noble thing. Back to Him to-night! Where are you? In the far country? You have lost your reputation, nobody really wants you? Back to God, back to Him now! See Him in the face of Jesus, find Him by answering the call that comes to you when the very Name of Christ is named. Answer Him! After Him! And do it now! Put into the business all your heart and all your soul. Gather yourself up, and now, with all the passion and principle of your life, in the silence, in the quietness, without sign or signal, without human eyes or ear detecting, resolutely break with the past and turn your face to God. In the sight of heaven and of hell act, and act now.

"Thou shalt find Him." Will He come in a flaming glory? Oh, perchance not. Will He come with some trumpet tone that I cannot mistake, a supernatural voice? Almost assuredly no. How, then, shall I find Him? Perhaps your first consciousness of nearness will be the new passion for the high, reborn within you, and the first thrill of power by which you begin to move on toward Him. It may be that your first consciousness of the answer of God will be the sense that you are not alone in the darkness.

So we will end, not with words of exposition, but

with this great word of Holy Scripture—and let the "thence" apply to the place where we are if we are at any distance from God: "If from thence ye shall seek the Lord, thou shalt find Him, if thou search after Him with all thy heart and with all thy soul."

CHAPTER XVII

DANIEL, A MAN OF EXCELLENT SPIRIT

Then this Daniel was distinguished above the presidents and satraps, because an excellent spirit was in him, and the king thought to set him over the whole realm.
DANIEL 6:3.

THE STORY OF DANIEL IS VERY OLD AND FASCINATING. ALL who had the advantage of godly training, and that supremest advantage in the life of a child, a mother who told Bible stories in the early days, remember how they loved the story of Daniel. I believe that as I read it for our lesson, in the heart of every hearer, there came again the consciousness of the old fascination and the old interest. The story of Daniel is fascinating because it reveals the possibilities of godliness in the midst of the circumstances of ungodliness. Daniel and his friends in that age long ago, were loyal to God even in the land of their captors, and amid all the enticements of the court. In such circumstances perhaps the subtlest of all temptations assail the man of faith. It is so much easier to float with the stream than to stem it. The principle of accommodation appeals so strongly to that lurking desire for ease which is one of the sure evidences of the fall of the human race that it needs very definite courage to resist, to be godly amid ungodliness, to take a definite and positive stand for principle where everything seems to be against principle.

The key to Daniel's splendid fidelity may be found in

the statement of my text, repeated in other parts of the book, "an excellent spirit was in him." This statement literally means that in Daniel spirit predominated, was uppermost, was enthroned. We are accustomed to use the word "excellent" with other values and intentions, all of which may be right in certain connections. For instance, we say that "excellent" means fine, noble, admirable; and we are justified in thus defining it; but the etymology of the word has another signification. Excellent is something that excels, goes beyond, predominates, and the word translated "excellent" in our text carries exactly that meaning. We may with perfect accuracy read our text thus—it would not be rhythmic or admirable as a translation, but at least it would be accurate—"A spirit that excelled was in him," a spirit that projected was in him. Not flesh, but spirit was the chief thing. This is evident at the very beginning of the story of Daniel. To him, it was not the king's dainties or wine from the king's table that were the principal things, but rectitude, which means life harmonizing with the infinite, the true, the eternal. The principal thing in Daniel was not the physical, though he was fair, ruddy and splendid; spirit was the dominant factor in the personality of this man. Daniel was not a man who thought of himself within the physical as possessing a spirit; he thought of himself within the spiritual as possessing a body. "An excellent spirit was in him." He was a man who began life in the spiritual, and from that center governed the material. He was not a man who began life in the material, and from that circumference crushed and bruised and killed the spiritual. In other words, Daniel was a man proportioned after the pattern and ideal of God. In himself, and in all his relationships, he recognized that the supreme quantity, the supreme quality, was spirit. He was "a man of an excellent spirit."

Let us, then, examine the qualities of spirit manifested

in the life story of the man in whom spirit excelled and was the principal thing. I want to say four things about Daniel as revealing what life is, where spirit excels, is dominant, is enthroned. This man of excellent spirit, in whom spirit excels, was, first, a man of purpose; second, a man of prayer; third, a man of perception; and, finally, a man of power. The first two things tell the cause; the second two describe the effect. The cause, or inspiration, of all this man's life story is found in the fact that he was a man of purpose and a man of prayer, and the effect is seen in the fact that he was a man of perception and a man of power. Purpose and prayer, these are the words that indicate our responsibility. Perception and power, these are the words which indicate what will follow in some way in the life of every man in whom spirit is dominant, and who, therefore, is a man of purpose and a man of prayer.

Daniel was a man of purpose. "Daniel purposed in his heart that he would not defile himself with the king's meat." Notice carefully what this means. Purpose is at the beginning of every thing. Directly after finding himself in a place of peril "he purposed in his heart." This is the matter of supreme importance. Thousands of men drift into evil courses for lack of a definite and positive committal of themselves to some position, for lack of having purpose, something settled in their hearts. To delay in the moment of the first consciousness of perilous surroundings is to compromise presently, and, unless we are very careful, it is finally to apostatize. Daniel speaks to us to-day in no uncertain tone, and the message he utters at the very beginning is:

> Dare to be a Daniel,
> Dare to stand alone,
> Dare to have a purpose firm,
> Dare to make it known!

That may be doggerel, but it is philosophy—the deepest secret of life for every young man or woman. I would to God that I could impress that thought on all young people! Purpose in a man's life is all-important. It affords him anchorage in the time of storm, creates for him a base in the day of battle. To have committed oneself to some definite thing is always of value in every walk of life. When a man has formed his purpose he is halfway to victory. That is so with a boy who is looking forward to his life work. When he knows what his purpose is, he is halfway to victory. He is not all the way to victory. It is quite possible to have formed that purpose, yet never to reach the goal; but it is equally certain that the goal cannot be reached without purpose. The first thing for a man to do is to define the inner and deepest thing in his life. Underlying his life somewhere, every man has a purpose in the Divine economy. Daniel found it, named it, announced it, stood by it. It is quite impossible for a man to live without a purpose of some sort. Purpose lies at the back of will, and purpose operates through all activity. Some men have a score of purposes, but never one named, defined, announced, to which they are committed. In matters political, social, in all departments of human life, it is the man who has some definite purpose who is likely to arrive somewhere. I am sorely tempted to use an Americanism. I will. It is the man who has a purpose who *gets there!* As in the smaller, weaker, lower things of life, it is true a man needs a purpose definite and announced; so also it is true supremely in matters of the spirit, in things of Christian life and service.

Daniel's purpose was a very simple one, and yet it was sublime: simple in its expression, sublime in its great underlying principle. What was the simple purpose announced as he came down into the midst of the Chaldean court and its corruption? I will not touch the king's dainties; I will not drink the king's wine! That is the simplicity of the purpose, but not the sublimity of it. What underlay it? "He purposed in his heart that he would not defile himself with the king's dainties nor with the wine which he drank." He purposed in his heart that his spirit was the supreme thing. He would not permit fleshly indulgence of any sort to rub the bloom from spiritual life, to weaken the nerve of spiritual endeavor, to dim the vision of spiritual outlook. He purposed that he would not defile *himself;* he was a man of excellent spirit, offspring of God, kin of the eternal, child and heir of the infinite; and he said, "My purpose is not to defile myself." Purpose found expression in his case in refusing the things that were likely to weaken the tabernacle of his flesh, and so defile the indwelling spirit which was himself. Daniel's deepest purpose was loyalty to God, expressed in separation from the corrupting influences of his position. Because he stood there at the beginning, he was strong and victorious through all the coming days.

My brothers, I urge on you the importance of having a purpose and declaring it, of committing yourselves absolutely and positively, not merely in the sanctuary, but everywhere and always, to some clearly defined position. To-day, amid the allurements and enticements of a godless age, let every man purpose in his heart that he will be loyal to Jesus Christ. That is the sufficient purpose for all life to-day. You and I live in a much easier age than Daniel lived in, with forces at our disposal far more potent than had Daniel. This age may be more complex in its temptations, more subtle and insidious in the way it is likely to spoil men, but it is also an age in which true life is become possible because of the simplification of the purpose. The simplicity of the purpose for each of us is that we commit ourselves to Christ. I am His avowedly; His confessedly; I will follow Him. That is the first and the simple purpose to which I invite every man. Remember that this purpose of loyalty to Christ, formed in the heart, confessed with the lips, is simply the center from which a man is to correct everything else in his life. For Daniel the deepest purpose of all was loyalty to the God of his fathers, and the expressed purpose was his refusal to touch the things that were likely to corrupt that loyalty to God—likely, therefore, to defile him. That was but the beginning of things—the king's wine and the king's meat. There would hardly be a day that Daniel would not have to defend his position and declare his loyalty to God. Some of the youths had to affirm their purpose when Nebuchadnezzar set up his image. The purpose was the same in every case.

I am a little afraid lest I make this thing look complex when I want to make it simple. Purpose loyalty to Christ, affirm it; and then from that center you may begin to construct your circumference and set the externalities of your life right. I meet scores of men who say, I try, but I fail. I want to be a Christian, but this or the other thing stands in my way. I reply, You are not to do these things in order to become Christian; you are to become Christian in order to be able to do these things. Do not attempt to construct your circumference in order to be in right relationship with your center. Find your center in order to correct your circumference. We have not forgotten how impossible it is to form a circumference until we have found the center. It is said that Giotto could make a perfectly round O. Well, he was the only man who could ever do it, and (forgive the skepticism of this) I have never seen one he made. But I am perfectly sure in the moral realm, in the life you and I have to live, we shall never make the circumference of life true and beautiful until we have found the center. The first thing is that the man has a purpose in his heart, and that purpose, to crown Jesus Christ. I will begin there, and then, if the king's meat and the king's wine are likely to interfere with my loyalty, I am to refuse and stand upon this central purpose of life.

Daniel was also a man of prayer. Nothing stands out more clearly than this fact. When the interpretation of the king's dream was asked, Daniel called his friends together into a compact of prayer, asked them to pray with him, that he might have the necessary light for interpretation. As the story moves on, it reveals the truth that he was a man who had regular habits of prayer, who three times a day turned his face toward old Jerusalem, thought on God, spoke to God. Here we touch the secret that underlay his fulfilment of purpose. Strong purpose is powerful in execution only as we are dependent on God. The heart may be firmly determined on loyalty, but unless we know how to lean hard on God the forces against us will prove too much for us. A man meaning to do right and depending on God is absolutely invincible. If the purpose has been formed in the heart, what next? Be men of prayer. What lies beyond the fact of a man's praying? First, his sense of personal limitation; second, his profound conviction of Divine sufficiency. What is prayer with these things lying in the background? It is the use of the means of communication between a man's weakness and God's power, between man's limitation and God's sufficiency.

If we desire to live this life in which spirit excels, the life of victory and of power, it is not enough to have purpose. You and I must recognize our limitations, frailties, weaknesses. In the days of our young manhood we feel so self-sufficient. When the eye is bright, the step elastic, the will buoyant, we think we can do the high thing, the noble thing, in our own strength. Oh that God may reveal to us at once that this is not so, that sooner or later, the godless life is always a failure and a wreck! Was there ever a man of stronger personality or individuality, apart from Christ, than Saul of Tarsus? Yet he confessed, "When I would do good, evil is present with me." He declared that though he willed, purposed, the high and the true, in execution he stooped to the low and the false. That is not the story of his high Christian experience, but the story of what he was apart from Jesus Christ. It is the story of every man who has not learned the deep secret of prayer. His own limitation, the fact that the forces of evil about him are too many for him, is one of the deepest and most important lessons any man can learn. "Let him that thinketh he standeth take heed lest he fall."

Side by side with this there needs to be the set conviction of the strength and the sufficiency of God in every human life. Let me put this in the very simplest way so that it may be helpful to some of you. The lot is cast in this great city. Centered in London is every pernicious thing that is likely to blast young life. You have come up to this city, some of you with the great advantages of godly parentage and home training, and some of you have the greater advantage of having been born in the city and so of being familiar from childhood with its allurements and its vices. Be that as it may, sooner or later, unless you learn the secret of dependence on God, you will be wrecked and ruined on one side or other of your nature. I shall never tell you that all you have to do is to realize your own manhood, and fight the battle and conquer. I am here to tell you that evil is too strong for you, that the forces that lure are the forces that ruin. In your own strength you cannot overcome. If that were all I would be silent. But there is another truth, the truth that Daniel knew, the truth that God and Daniel were stronger in combination than all Chaldean corruption and idolatrous evil, the truth that you and God in London are invincible against all the forces that will sweep against you.

Doubtless I speak to some who have fallen, who have sinned, and they know it. I take you back to the point of your fall, and tell you that your fall was due to your independence. Had you been a dependent soul, trusting in God, recognizing His power, communicating with Him by prayer, always leaning hard on Him, you would have won where you failed. Yet how often young men say, I have failed and I could not help it. That is partly true and largely untrue. Even if you have purposed solemnly in your heart you will be loyal to Christ, you cannot help failure if you are attempting to fight the battle in your own strength. But if you and I know what it is to trust in God's sufficiency, and to pray, there is no temptation we may not overcome, no advance of the evil one that we may not repulse. Man dependent on God is absolutely invincible. Evil cannot master me if I have attached myself to the infinite resources of God, and if that attachment is maintained by the prayer life. Form habits of prayer. Daniel prayed with his face toward Jerusalem every day. I urge you to have special times, special seasons; I urge you to continue in prayer.

But there is another word about prayer. When Jesus swept away the Temple at Jerusalem, He made all the earth a temple for the true worshiper, and not merely in this house or in your own private Bethel, not merely at the appointed moment, but wherever you are, with the eye unclosed and the word unuttered, you can pray. The Puritan fathers talked very much about ejaculatory prayer. I pray God that we may form the habit of it. Realize that when peril confronts you, without waiting for time or place, in the midst of your daily vocation, you can pray; and in the moment of such praying the answer of prayer is with you. The great word of the Hebrew epistle is, "We may find grace to help us in time of need." At the back of that phrase we have a Greek phrase, which we can safely translate by an English phrase with which we are all familiar: "Find grace to help *in the nick of time.*" Right there, when peril threatens, there I may have grace to help. The strong man in London is not the man who says to Jesus in the morning, I will not forsake Thee to-day, and then goes out to fight his battle alone; he is the strong man who says to his Master in the morning, Lord, lead me to-day lest I fall, and then prays in the city, in the office, in the warehouse, in the most subtle place of peril, that of loneliness. Everywhere grace to help awaits the cry of the praying soul. Purpose first, and prayer perpetually.

Then follow the two results I have mentioned. First is a spirit of perception. There is no doubt that the gift of interpretation which Daniel received was especially bestowed by God for special purposes. The immediate application to us is that to the man who has made his purpose and prays will be given a clarity of vision which will enable him to accomplish the Divine work allotted to him. It may be, as in the case of Daniel, that of interpretation, or it may be in some other form. The thing of importance is that the man who has purpose and prays will be of quick understanding in the fear of the Lord. Have you not felt that you need spiritual perception to discern between right and wrong, and that quickly? How often a man says, "I did it before I knew it; I fell before I was conscious of the temptation." But to the man of purpose and prayer come a growing keenness of insight, sensitiveness of soul, quickness of perception in the commonplaces, and a keen vision in the crises of life. Special illumination from God flashing on the pathway saves him in the moment of his peril. Habits have to be formed, whether they are good or evil, and on the basis of purpose and of prayer a habit of quick understanding of the will of God in matters of life and conduct and a keen insight in the subtleties of temptation come to a man.

Finally, Daniel was a man of power, first, as we have seen, in small things, but also in great things. I am not suggesting that if you take this position of purpose and maintain it, take this life of prayer and follow it, that if you have this quick, keen perception of God by the Holy Spirit, you will come to a place of wordly power. It certainly is remarkable that this man held office in three kingdoms—Babylon, Media, and Persia. The man of purpose, the man of prayer, the man of perception, was recognized by the men of his age and trusted, and put into places of power, and, as the text says, "the king thought to set him over the whole realm." I am not saying that this kind of promotion will necessarily follow in every case; but I am saying that the man of purpose, of prayer, of perception, becomes the man of power—power that enables him to say no. It is a very old story (some of you are tired of hearing it—it was told you in Sunday school) the story which says that the man who can say no is the strong man. It is still true. Sometimes it takes more courage to say no than to lead an army. The highest courage is not the courage of the battlefield; it is moral courage, the power to say no. I am not giving you an ethical lecture and advising you to say no. I am here to say to you: Be a man of purpose, of prayer, and you will be able to say no. What nerves a man to say no in the presence of temptation is the fact that he has taken his stand and is a man of purpose, is a man of perpetual prayer, and, therefore, a man of perception, seeing the issues, understanding the virtues, and able to say no when the moment comes. Our age wants men who are superior to it, not men who are driven by it. Men who are superior to the age are men in whom spirit excels, men in whom spirit has its anchorage in purpose, its source of strength in prayer, its ability to lead in perception, its consequent power in all departments of life.

My last word shall be as my first. For the Christian man the principle has been focused in a Person, so that true purpose is loyalty to Christ, true prayer is communion with Christ along the pathway of life, true perception is submission to Christ and the answering illumination of the Holy Spirit, true power is co-operation with Christ in the commonplaces and crises of all the days. I pray for you, my brothers, as I pray for myself, that we may be men of excellent spirit, men in whom spirit is crowned, enthroned; and that we may cultivate purpose and prayer so that we may find what it is to be men of perception and power. The age waits for such men, and wherever they are to be found the result will be that others also will be led into true life.

CHAPTER XVIII

THE TOUCH OF FAITH

Who is it that touched Me?

LUKE 8:45.

IN THIS NARRATIVE WE HAVE AN ILLUSTRATION IN THE CONcrete of Christ's relation to the crowds, and in the particular question which constitutes the text a revelation of that principle of discrimination which was always manifest in His attitude toward the multitudes that gathered round about Him.

It was a strange question from the standpoint of the disciples who were close to Him on that memorable occasion, and from the standpoint of the multitudes who observed. It was not only a strange question, to them it must have seemed absurd. "Who touched Me?" Peter, spokesman of the rest, said to Him in effect, Lord, how sayest Thou, Who touched Me? Everyone is touching Thee who can get near enough to do so. The multitudes press Thee and crowd upon Thee. In the last half an hour it may be that a hundred people have touched Thee! But He said, Nay, someone touched Me differently, for I perceive—and I like the Authorized Version, although the Revised may be more literal—virtue has gone out of Me. I perceive that virtue—in the old and gracious sense of the word in our English language—has gone out of Me. Who did it? Who touched Me? A hundred men have touched Me within half an hour, but someone has touched Me differently!

Let us look at the picture. I do not know among the pictures of the New Testament another that makes a more powerful appeal to me than does this. At this time Our Lord was conducting an itinerant ministry, passing from place to place, consenting to receive the necessaries of His physical life by the ministration of a company of women of substance who loved Him and followed Him. Luke tells us in this chapter that Jesus went about through cities and villages preaching and bringing the good tidings of the Kingdom of God, and with Him were the twelve and certain women who had been healed of evil spirits and infirmities, "Mary of Magdala, Joanna the wife of Chuza Herod's steward, and Susanna, and many others, which ministered unto them of their substance." This is the only account we have of that fact; it is the only place where some of the women are named. A little company of women, whom He had healed and helped physically, mentally, and spiritually, were now responding to His ministry by supplying His daily needs. So He was passing from place to place, exercising His great ministry of teaching, preaching, and healing, these accompanying Him as He went.

Among other places, He had just been to the country of the Gerasenes, and on the very shores of their country had given an evidence of the meaning of His ministry by casting out the evil spirits from a man who had been the pest of the entire neighborhood, and at the same moment had rebuked their unholy traffic by destroying their swine. They had made a protest, and had besought Him to leave them. There is infinite pathos in the declaration that He entered into a ship, and crossed the sea. Now on the other side of the waters He took up His work again, and that wonderful declaration is made: "And as Jesus returned, the multitude welcomed Him; for they were all waiting for Him." As he proceeded on His way two wonderful things happened, the stories of which are so interwoven that we cannot deal with the one without considering the other, for there are values in the one which belong to the other. These two things were the healing of the child of Jairus and the healing of this woman, the woman who touched Him.

Let us see the picture. Our Lord was passing on His way. The multitudes were following Him. Sometimes, while reading this story and others, I like to sit down and allow myself to attempt to picture the actual scene. I attempt to look into the faces of the crowd, to watch the different expressions on their faces. Strong men jostle each other to get near the Teacher, to get one glance into His eyes. In all probability, mothers lift their children that the little ones may look just once at Him Whose fame has gone so far afield. For the most part reverently, men and women following after Him, interested men and women, attracted multitudes, were prepared to welcome Him, not merely from the standpoint of idle curiosity, but because of their real interest in Him. They went after Him as He traveled, eager that if He should say something they might hear it, desiring supremely to see Him work some wonder, that they might observe it. He Himself was the center of attraction.

Then I see approaching Him a man, a ruler of the synagogue. If I had the artistic sense I would like to paint the picture of Jairus. On his face sits a terrible shadow. Back in his home is a child, his little daughter, twelve years old; and she lies dying. To that nothing can be added, nothing need be added in the case of those who have ever known anything of the experience in their own lives. Look at Jairus; notice the agony, and anxiety and earnestness in his face. He has asked the Lord to come and heal the child ere it be too late. With an immediate response the Master walked along the highway toward the house of Jairus. If I could paint that picture I would. It is one of the great pictures of the New Testament. If I were painting it as a picture, this procession toward the house of Jairus, I would place Jairus a little ahead of Jesus, walking with eagerness, desiring by any means to hurry Christ to his house. At the center of all the thronging crowd we see the one figure, regal, beautiful, dignified, full of tenderness, the Christ Himself.

Suddenly the procession was arrested because the Master stood and said: "Who touched Me?" Then the protest of the disciples was heard, "Master, the multitudes press Thee and crush Thee." But, said Jesus, someone has touched Me, for I perceive that power has gone out of me. So far, no one knew what had happened except the Master and one other. Then in the hush and the constraint, and amid the almost amused glances of the people who thought it was a foolish question, a woman was seen moving round, until she knelt in front of Him, and there she told Him all the truth. Bending over her, and looking straight into that woman's eyes, He used to her the only particularly tender epithet that He is ever recorded as having addressed to a woman, "Daughter, thy faith hath made thee whole; go in peace."

And where was Jairus while this was taking place? Waiting, eager, anxious, if I know him, and I think I do. I think I know him by actual sympathy with his breaking heart. I think he was almost rebellious because the Lord had halted. Yet I think that when that woman had told her story of how by touching she had been healed, there was a song in the heart of Jairus, new light on the shadowed pathway, a new hope breaking in his soul, for that was a new evidence of the power of the One Whose aid he had come to seek.

Then they moved a little farther forward, and there come messengers from the house of Jairus, who said: Do not worry the Rabbi, the child is dead. In a moment another voice sounded in his ears, the voice of Jesus, saying: "Fear not, believe only; thy child shall be made whole." Arrived at the house, He said: "She is not dead but sleepeth"; and they laughed Him to scorn. He put them all out. It is the only proper treatment for such people! Besides Himself, He kept in that room three disciples, the father and the mother, six of them; and the dead child made seven. Then bending over her, He said—and I am going to take liberty with the translation, and try to express some of the poetry of the Aramaic in our English tongue, not "Maiden, arise"—that is altogether too formal a translation—but "*Talitha cumi*," that is, "Little lamb, arise." The beautiful eyelids quivered, and the eyes surely looked first at His face. Then He gave her back to her father and mother, and went on His way.

Now, in the atmosphere created by these stories I ask you to fasten your attention on this question of Jesus, so startling, strange, uncalled for, absurd in the hearing of the men who listened to it, "Who touched Me?" There are three things I want to suggest concerning that question. First, it was selective; it separated. Second, it was a revealing question, one that resulted in a revelation, and ultimately in a confession. Finally, in the case of the woman it was causative; it brought her to a new relationship with Christ, in advance of that which had been established when she touched Him.

I say in the first place that the question was selective. It revealed the fact that in that crowd all the multitudes were not on the same footing, that someone had reached Him in a way that others had not reached Him. It was a question revealing, on the part of Our Lord, discernment, discrimination, division. "Who touched Me?" A hundred men have touched Thee! Nay, one soul has touched Me! Everyone is jostling Thee! But someone has got near to Me! But surely they were all near. No, they were far away, though brushing by Him; removed to infinite distances, though looking right into His eyes. Someone has touched Me! It was a selective question, dividing the crowd, and putting some one person in separation from the crowd, revealing the fact that some one person in that curious, jostling, interested, reverently kindly multitude stood on an entirely different footing from the rest. "Who touched me?"

The question, therefore, was revealing in the sense that it

reveals the fact that there is a contact which makes demands on Christ, and there is a contact which makes no demands on Him. It reveals that men may come very near to Him, and yet never be near to Him; that men may look into His eyes, and never see Him; catch all the accents of His voice, but never hear Him; jostle His garments, be familiar with the sacraments of His house, observe all the externalities of worship, and yet never make contact with Himself. It reveals the fact, therefore, on the other hand, that there is a contact which, if once made, He must answer. Without the uttering of a word, virtue will pass from Him to the person who makes that contact. I had nearly said—and I will say it, though I have to amend it—without volition on His part. I amend it by saying without apparent volition on His part; not without volition, for did He not know she was near Him, did He not know, was He not prepared for her approach? Surely, yes. He needed not that any man should tell Him what was in man, for He knew all men. He knew the crowds intimately and particularly, and knew every individual life in the crowds. A crowd was never a mob to Jesus. It was always a company of individual souls. There was no need for Him to turn to find her. He knew she was there. His question was not a question asked that he might discover who it was, but that He might bring her yet nearer to Himself; and that He might create a value for another breaking heart, the heart of Jairus. He knew, He knew she was coming; and in that moment when she made contact with Him, far more quickly than the lightning's flash, virtue, power, health, healing, strength passed from Him to her, and all that canceled her limitation and restored to her everything that she had lost.

What, then, was the contact? This question is answered best by a little careful examination of the story, and a little careful observation of the woman. Mark her condition. The story, as Luke tells it in medical terms, reveals a fact, which expressed in the terms of the Hebrew economy, may thus be stated: On account of the peculiar form of physical disease from which she was suffering she was excommunicated from the temple, not allowed to mingle with the worshipers. By that selfsame law she was divorced from her husband, not allowed to live with him. By that same law she was ostracized from society, and in appalling loneliness she had lived for twelve years. It is quite easy to say all this; but let imagination help us to understand it. Twelve years of a disease that had weakened her day by day, until all her physical powers were feeble. Twelve years shut out from the fellowship of the saints as they went up to the house of God. Twelve years shut away from the comradeships of home and the fellowship of her husband. Twelve years shut out from all the circle of her friends and acquaintances. Twelve years of suffering and weakness. Twelve years in which she had done all she knew for healing; for Luke tells us she "had spent all her living upon physicians, and could not be healed of any," or, as writes Mark, who held no brief for doctors, "She had suffered many things of many physicians, and had spent all that she had, and was nothing bettered, but rather grew worse."

Now look at this woman again, thin, emaciated, worn, weary! She heard that Jesus was coming her way. What did she know of Him? Ah, I cannot tell. All I can surmise from the story is that she had heard of Him, that the news of Him had reached her in her weakness and in her suffering; that she had heard how He had healed the sick and given back strength to those weak and infirm. Now the moment had come when He was actually coming by her, coming her way. I never can quite understand how she reached Him at all. It is very difficult even for a strong man to get through a crowd. Yet, somehow, that woman made her way through the crowd.

Now, I pray you, observe her. Was this faith which moved her firm, strong, absolute, settled? I do not think so. What, then, was it? It was a profound sense of need, an acquaintance with a testimony that told of His power; it was hope springing in her heart that perhaps He could help even her. Then it was faith, the outcome of hope, hope based on testimony; but principally it was faith expressing itself in a venture. She found her way through the crowd, and there hung the tassel on His garment, that cord of blue, according to the ancient economy. I see her struggling to reach Him; at last she is near enough to stretch out her hand; and it was not a passing touch she gave; she clutched it, grasped it!

This was an act growing out of need; it was an act inspired by testimony heard; it was the result of hope springing anew within the heart; it was an act of faith inspired by testimony, hope; it was faith venturing to make an appeal, the appeal of a touch. Call it superstition if you will; and the answer of the Lord in power, and the words spoken to her presently, are of infinite value, and become more impressive, the more we see that the act of the woman was not the act of a reasoned and argumentative and logical faith. It was a venture in an hour of great need.

That is the contact that Christ always answers. I have of set purpose attempted to put the event in the light of its simplicity. I do not think that woman came to Him with profound and strong conviction. Hers was a great agony, a great need, a simple willingness to believe a testimony spoken by others, expressed in a determination to make the final venture. So surreptitiously, hidden away, she clutched at His garment. That is the contact that He answers, that is the attitude to which He is compelled, by virtue of what He is in Himself, to make an immediate response. Need, agony, without logic and without reason, but in answer to testimony and to hope, making a venture—to that He responds, and the virtue passes from Him to the seeker, and heals.

Writing of this story, and contrasting the crowds that pressed Jesus with the woman who touched Him, Augustine said, "Flesh presses, faith touches." How true the words still are. Flesh presses; that which is merely of human interest and human curiosity, presses Him; but faith reaches Him, touches Him; and, believe me, this Lord of hope and glory still knows the difference between the jostle of a curious crowd and the touch of a weak and frail and appealing soul. Not the healthy, robust, self-complacent, satisfied, curious jostle of a crowd draws anything out of Him; but the weak, frail, agonized, almost hopeless and yet venturing, touch of a hidden woman is answered by a flow of virtue and a rush of power, and the healing and the health for which the soul is waiting.

But the question in itself was not only selective, and revelatory to us of the difference between the press of the flesh and the touch of faith. The question in the case of the woman was causative. She hoped to get her healing and quietly depart. She hoped to touch, and get her blessing, and quietly to slip away, with no one knowing. How many people hope to do that! But this woman was not permitted to do so. She must come from behind and stand in front. She must come from that attitude of hiding into the open. It was necessary that if she had received a benefit she should confess the Lord, not in order that He might find out who touched Him, not in order ultimately that the crowd might discover why He halted, but that she might come in front and confess Him.

Now notice carefully what happened. First, that confession brought to the woman a yet deeper blessing. She told Him in the hearing of the crowds, and I think there was a great hush over them as she spoke, how she had come, and how she was healed. Then He looked at her, and He said, "Daughter." Oh, after all, what a faulty thing preaching is! I cannot say that as it ought to be said, and I am almost afraid to try. Put yourself in her place—not weak any longer, but strong, for when He heals He heals. He never plays at healing, this Lord of ours. But though healed, she was still excommunicate, with no right of entry to synagogue or temple; still divorced, for even if there would be restoration presently to home and husband, it was not yet accomplished. Still ostracized from society, and likely to remain ostracized, because she had lost all her property. But He said, "Daughter." Then what do you think she cared about anything else? What did it matter now? She was excommunicate from temple, shut out from home, ostracized from friends; but He said, "Daughter"; He had adopted her, and by the sweet word of ineffable tenderness had brought her to His heart and had given her His own heart. "Daughter!" There is an old Roman legend—very foolish many of them are, and very beautiful some of them —that this was Veronica, the woman who, by the by, in the hour of His dying, was the only one who ministered to Him. It is only a legend, but if it is not true, it might be. He said, "Daughter;" and heaven dawned, all the shadows melted, and new life began. Not merely had He adopted her as His daughter in order that she might be benefited, but He had admitted her to fellowship with Himself in fullest grace. Just before this, acording to Luke, He had said, Who is My mother, and who are My brethren and My sisters? They that do the will of My Father in heaven: "My mother and My brethren are these which hear the word of God, and do it." Now He added another word, "Daughter." Do you observe the profounder, more glorious blessing that came to the woman when she ceased her attempt to remain in hiding and confessed Him? For her own sake it was necessary that she should no longer be content with gaining the blessing which the fringe of His garments diffused, but should pass to the front, look into His eyes, and come into personal and eternal fellowship with Him as He said to her, "Daughter . . . go in peace."

But there was another reason why she should make her confession. I hinted at it just now, and will do no more than return to the matter in a brief word. Look again at Jairus. I think I know something of what was passing through his mind. He was surely saying within himself, Why does He wait? My girlie is dying! He will be too late! My girlie is twelve years of age; my home has been full of sunshine for twelve years. Her laughter and tears have made rainbow radiance in my home for twelve years; and she is dying! What is that woman saying? Twelve years of shadow, why that woman has been ill just as long as my child has been with me! She has been under the shadows all the time I have been in the sunshine. What is this the woman says? Her shadows have gone and the sunshine has come back to her! Then if He could heal her, and help her when she does but touch the border of His garment, let us get Him on, and home. For the strengthening of Jairus' faith she must confess.

Yet is not the final word the highest? Not only for deeper blessing she must confess, not only for the strengthening of Jairus' faith; but surely also, and supremely, for the honor and glory of the Lord Himself. It was fit that she should confess Him. In that jostling, curious crowd were men lurking, already planning and plotting for His murder. It was surely fit that the voice of one who had been healed should be raised to confess Him. For His sake then. And so the question caused deeper blessing for the sufferer, strengthened the faith of Jairus, and ultimately glorified the Lord Himself.

So the story itself preaches if the preacher fails. You say, That is a very old story. No, not so very old. It is as new as this wonderful morning. Ere I pronounce the benediction it is all being repeated. We here are interested in Jesus Christ. I think I am safe in saying that. We all feel we would like to be near to Him, for there is something in the very name that calls us to higher things. There is always a beauty in the story of Jesus, even though it be told for envy; it is ever a victorious story; even though Christ be preached for very strife, Paul must rejoice. We have gathered this morning, a part of the great crowd around Christ, reverent, interested. But His question is this: "Who touched Me?" I cannot answer it. He knows who touched Him. We may have been in His immediate presence, and never near Him, even this morning. But someone has touched Him. Some broken heart, some weary soul, some bruised man or tired woman has touched Him, has ventured, and already is feeling the force of the virtue that heals. You were in entire despair half an hour ago. You are going to make another venture. You had almost given up the strife after righteousness when you entered this building, but now you are going to begin again. I cannot interfere, only to say to you that the Lord asks that if you have received the benefit you will confess Him.

"Who touched Me?" Did you? Did you touch Him, brother mine, sister mine, hidden away in the crowd? Do you feel the thrill of the virtue? Has the glory of a new vision broken upon you? Then, in the name of the Lord and Master, confess Him. Or to gather the philosophy of the New Testament story and utter it in the splendid language of the old psalmist, "Let the redeemed of the Lord say so, whom He hath redeemed from the hand of the adversary." I call you who have received the virtue to confess Him for your own sake. Do not be satisfied with the blessing so received. Confess Him; looking into His own face, avow yourself His own and His follower and listen for the voice that speaks some word more beautiful in its music, more powerful in its values, than any other blessing you have ever received. I call you to confess because of some Jairus hiding in the crowd, anxious, stricken, and smitten. Do you know how you can prove Christ to him and save him? By telling what Christ has done for you.

Finally, and this is the last argument, not for your sake alone, not principally for the sake of helping other men, but for His own glory and honor, and that you may stand by His side, one committed to Him, confess Him.

THE TOUCH OF FAITH

Brethren, of the things I have spoken this is the sum:

No fable old, nor mythic lore,
  No dream of bards and seers,
No dead fact stranded on the shore
  Of the oblivious years.

But warm, sweet, tender, even yet
  A present help is He;
And faith has still its Olivet,
  And love its Galilee.

The healing of His seamless dress
  Is by our beds of pain;
We touch Him in life's throng and press,
  And we are whole again.

CHAPTER XIX

OUR ALTAR

We have an altar.

HEBREWS 13:10.

THE MAJORITY OF DAYS IN THE LIVES OF THE MAJORITY OF men are ordinary days. Nevertheless, all men have extraordinary days, red-letter days; and whatever may be the nature of the experience which makes them stand out from all the rest, these are the days that give character to all the rest. Men mark or celebrate such days in different ways. We very often reveal ourselves quite unexpectedly by the manner in which we celebrate them, and we reveal our God almost unknowingly. This fact may be illustrated in very many ways. There are men, quite irrespective of their educational advantages or social position, who celebrate any day that stands out from the rest by a drink or a feast. They are revealing themselves, and in the biting, scorching satire of the great Apostle we may say of them, "whose god is their belly." There are men of a much higher type who will celebrate the day of emotion, whether it be of joy or of sorrow, by a great song, a treatise, some expression of the inward life that others may know it. There are men who celebrate a day of tragic sorrow, a day of ecstatic joy, by a bequest, or by raising a memorial.

The men of the Old Testament turned all such days into opportunities for raising altars. It is very interesting to run through the Old Testament and see in what varied circumstances these men raised altars. According to the record, when Noah found himself in possession of the world he raised an altar. When Abraham, after some tarrying, found himself at last in the land to which God had directed him he raised an altar. In that ultimate and final experience of his soul, when after long processes and much fellowship with God, groping after Him and finding Him and coming ever nearer to Him, he at last reached the spiritual experience which was higher than that of desiring privilege, namely fellowship in suffering, Abraham erected an altar on which to offer his son. And in after years that son, a man of quietness and peace who stands out on the pages of the Old Testament as celebrated for digging wells and living by them, when at last he was left in peace after a commonplace quarrel between herdsmen concerning wells, he too raised an altar. When Moses had prayed all day with uplifted hands, and Amalek was defeated, he built his altar and called it Jehovah-nissi, the Lord our Banner. When at last Ai was reduced, after the defeat of the hosts of God as the result of the sin of a man, Joshua built his altar. When Gideon was going through the process of preparation for delivering his people from the oppression of Midian, he built an altar. When God had wondrously appeared on behalf of His people, and through a thunderstorm had discomfited the foe, Samuel built an altar and called it Ebenezer. When David sinned, and the people were visited by plague, and when the plague was stayed, right there, where it halted at the threshing floor of Araunah the Jebusite, David built an altar.

These men were always building altars. At a time of great joy they built an altar, in the time of sorrow they built an altar, if they were defeated they built an altar, if they were victorious they built an altar, if they sinned they built an altar, if they triumphed over temptation they built an altar. This rearing of altars by the old patriarchs was revealing.

When the Mosaic economy came, careful instructions were given for the private raising of altars. Such was the instruction we read in the book of Exodus. In the ceremonial system the altar had its place, its central place; but the idea that was suggested by the altar was larger than the ceremonial system. For what we see in it is God accommodating Himself to, and answering, the human heart in its great need; and that which thus sprang out of the human heart came originally from God. So deep answered deep in the provision of the law.

The writer of this letter to the Hebrews took up the sacred things of their religion in order to show how all found fulfilment in Christ. In all this letter there is a theoretical value; it is a defense of the faith; there is also a practical value, for it is a revelation of the conduct resulting from that faith. From beginning to end the writer sees in the Son of God the effulgence of the glory of God, and in all the ministry and mission of the Son he sees the fulfilment of those things which humanity had been groping after. Almost at the end of the letter he said, "We have an altar."

Our meditation is intended to deal with the idea suggested by the altar rather than with the particular ritual to which the writer was referring. When he said, "We have an altar, whereof they have no right to eat which serve the tabernacle," he was dealing with the putting aside of all ritual method of the past; but he retained the altar, and thus retained the idea of the altar, and claimed that while the veil of the tabernacle had been rent in twain and all the Mosaic ritual had been superseded, the essential thing which the altar always symbolized remained, "We have an altar."

I have made this somewhat lengthy reference to the place of the altar in the Old Testament in order to say that in proportion as we are finding our way back into the habit of these men, the habit itself being cleansed, purified, fulfilled, made glorious in the light of the Christian fact, we are finding the true attitude to the day of crisis, to the day that stands out, to the day that casts its light or its shadow on all other days. Just such a day came to some of us last week, when all the light of life went out, or when suddenly there broke on a pathway that long had been shadowed a new and glorious light in which we rejoiced. There was that one hour last week in which, in spite of all professions and protestations, and sincere they were, we fell into sin, and the dark horror of it is on our soul, and all the days are threatened by the shadow of it. What are we to do in these days? These men of the olden days built an altar, and laid on it a sacrifice, and watched the material fire devour it, and forced their souls into the spiritual conception suggested by the fire, and so got back to God. There are days when we feel we would like to do exactly the same thing, get away to some quiet desert place and slay something and see it burn for the readjustment of spiritual things. But we do not do these things to-day. Nevertheless, as this writer says, "We have an altar."

Keeping in that atmosphere of the past, I want this morning to find out for my own soul's sake what these men meant, in order to discover what my attitude ought to be to the day which stands out, black or radiant, in order that neither the darkness nor the light may affect the other days in such a way as to spoil them. "We have an altar." Let us get back to these great men of the past. When they built their altars, what did they mean? Fundamentally the action was one of worship; actively, it was sacrifice; experimentally, it was readjustment and new beginning.

First it was worship. The erection of an altar was an expression of belief in God. The erection of an altar was the expression of the sense of need of God. The erection of an altar was the expression of desire for God. The erection of an altar was the expression of submission to God. If that analysis seems almost unnecessary, as though having said "worship" we have said all; yet these are elements that we have to remember. When that man is building his altar, watch him at his work; forget all that surrounds him, forget the immediate occasion of the building, and inquire quietly while he builds his altar what he is doing and why he is doing it. Building an altar means that a man believes in God, not that he knows God perfectly, not that he understands God adequately, not that he has anything like final fellowship with God, but that he believes in God. It means more; it means that the man not only believes in God, but is conscious within his soul that what he needs is that very God in Whom he believes. Whether for his joy or his sorrow, his darkness or his light, he needs that God. Not only does it mean that he believes in God and feels his need of God; it also means that he desires God. If one could listen to the deepest thing in the life of any man who is seen building his altar we should hear him say, One thing I desire, it is that I may find God and order my way before Him! There are occasional singers who actually utter words, words which became the inspiration of pilgrims through all the ages; but for the one man who sings the actual words there are a thousand men who are acting in harmony with the song which they cannot express.

The altar means more than belief, more than confession of need, more than desire. Whenever a man builds an altar he is expressing, imperfectly, inadequately, but nevertheless sincerely, his desire to submit himself to the God to Whom he thus builds. As I find my way through these pages of the past, with all their magnificent revelation of contradictory things in human life—passion, prejudice, pride, lust, love—and I see these primitive men, rough, unhewn men, building altars in all sorts of circumstances, making every new occasion in life the opportunity for building an altar, I see men worshiping.

But observe carefully that it is an altar each man builds, and that the meaning of the altar is always sacrifice. An altar built by a man who believes in God, needs God, desires God, and submits to God, is a confession of his consciousness of distance from God, and a confession, moreover, of something within him that speaks of the possibility of restoration to nearness, which must be based on some mystery of sacrifice and pain. Every altar means sacrifice.

Experientially, the altar as these men of the past raised it, meant as I have said, readjustment in all circumstances. The events giving rise to the altar were set in the light of the altar. The joy that fills the life and makes man raise his altar is now to be conditioned by all that the altar stands for. The sorrow that has overwhelmed him, out of the agony of which he has built his altar, is now to be put in the light of these essential things which the altar suggests to him. The altar forever speaks of the readjustment of life in the presence of God through the mystery of sacrifice.

The altar always meant more than that experientially in those Old Testament narratives. After the altar, there was the move forward, according to the things of the altar. I will not stay to illustrate it. Take your Bible and spend an hour or two going through the story of individual altars, and you will find in every case that after the altar there was a move forward, a line of progress; and everywhere the forward movement was the result of the readjustment of the life in the presence of the altar. The men who moved forward from the altar which they had raised in the hour of their solemn, sacrificial approach to God carried with them in the forward move the things which gave occasion to the altar. Joy, sorrow, light, darkness, defeat, victory—the values were wrested from all these in that hour of the altar's worship; and the men marched forward, stronger for these very experiences as they were found and sanctified in the hour of worship in the presence of the altar.

"We have an altar." I need not stay to remind you that the whole subject of the letter to the Hebrews is that in the Lord Christ we have found all that men were seeking after, and seeing dimly by the altar and the priest and the sacrifice.

In the Lord Christ we have that coming near to us of God, which means the discovery of the meaning of defeat, the answer of the desire of our heart after God, and the removal of all those things which prevented our realization of fellowship with Him. The writer of the letter to the Hebrews says, "We have an altar," that is, an abiding altar, which in some senses we have not to erect, for it is always erected; yet an altar which in some senses we must ever erect, erect again and again, and bring to its measurement and its correction every crisis in life that appals the soul with fear or joy, with trembling or with a sense of triumph.

Let us go back again for a moment to the old story. Not without profound significance were the instructions which Moses gave concerning the erection of these altars. We have no means of knowing the form or fashion of them in those patriarchal days before these instructions. Moreover, we must not confuse the instructions of Moses here concerning the altar with those instructions on the great altars of the ritual which he received in the Mount. The instructions here were quite clear and simple, and, indeed, most astonishing, for they were for the man who desired to erect an altar for himself. It must be of earth, or if perchance it should be of stone, then it must be of unhewn stone; and, further, no steps were to help him in his ascent to the altar.

The altar was to be of earth; that was the first simple command. If some man should desire to raise his altar amid rocky fastnesses where perchance no earth could be found, then let him build it of stone; but he must not grave or polish his stone, or set any tool on it; he must erect quite simply a heap of rough stones, and he must not under any circumstances approach it by steps. Without any interpretation, we all realize the wonderful significance and suggestiveness of these simple requirements.

The altar is to be of earth, it is to be of the commonest, it is to be of that which every man or woman could find close at hand, earth, common earth. Build your altar of that; just make a heap of earth, that is all! Is that all? No! There is more. Listen: "In every place where I record My name I will come unto thee and I will bless thee." Wherever a man shall thus erect his altar of earth God will come to him, and from that moment of revelation, man would understand the meaning of the altar he had erected in the twilight. Wherever a man gets earth together and erects an altar, God comes there, heaven touches earth, God is nigh at hand. His approach to the human soul is dependent on that desire of the human soul for Him which expresses itself in the sacramental symbol of the heap of earth. There, says God, I will come to him.

If the altar be of stone, then let it be of unhewn stone. No tool must be lifted on it; there must be nothing of artifice in the symbol of approach to God, nothing to create self-consciousness in the worshiper, no human workmanship. Note the appalling severity of the word. Who can doubt the accuracy of it: "If thou lift up thy tool upon it, thou hast polluted it"? No steps to the altar, no approach by climbing, "that thy nakedness be not discovered thereon." How appallingly human nakedness is discovered when by its ornate ritual it attempts to get near to God. This man says—nay verily, let me be true to the context—this Church says, "I am rich, and have gotten riches, and have need of nothing," and the Watcher with eyes of fire says, "Thou art the wretched one, and miserable and poor and blind and naked." That is a Church climbing to the altar by steps carved and beautiful, by a ritual which is self-conscious and self-assertive. In these ultimate matters of the dealing of the soul with God, the altar must be of the earth or of unhewn stones, of such things that man can find in them nothing that ministers to his own pride. There will I meet with thee, says God.

"We have an altar." If the altar shall be seen to be the Lord Christ, then let me say the things that are in my own heart. The wonder of God's revelation of Himself in Christ is the simplicity of Christ, the humanness of Christ, the fact that in all the brief period of His revelation in human history He walked the plane—I hardly like the word, but let me use it—of the commonplace. If some of us had lived with Him as He then lived, we would not have spoken to Him. He had no social position. He was of the earth, the lowest of all the low, and the lowliest of all the lowly! That is the marvel. There are some of us to whom others will not speak, and we are angry. He was not angry. It is not only true that in that human life of His He was beneath the notice of some people; it is also true that He was perfectly happy there. If in His presence those who hold their fellows in contempt are rebuked, those who in turn hold in contempt those who hold them in contempt are also rebuked. Do not forget this. Again forgive the phrase—there is no meaning in it in this connection in Ruskin's sense—but here we find the true ethics of the dust! Christ is an altar for me of the common dust, the clay of my humanity! Yet, so help me God, I would not speak irreverently of that common clay of my humanity; that is the only glory I have. All other things are accidental trappings, to be destroyed in the fire, that eremacausis, the slowly burning fire of God, that is always destroying effete things. The accidental things that separate men are being destroyed in that fire, blessed be God!

When a man in the hour of crisis readjusts things his first business is to find himself anew in Christ in the common fact of his humanity, and to strip himself of all the ornaments and accidentals by which he thinks he rises—and by which he does seem to rise a little way above his fellows. Do you remember what Mr. Dooley said about the skyscrapers of New York? They are called skyscrapers, by everything except the sky! Let that be a parable, and there I leave it. When I want to readjust things in hours of crisis, of sin, or sorrow, or tragedy, my first business is to get to the altar of Christ which is of the earth, and, stripping myself of everything else, put my manhood by the side of His Manhood. That is the first thing, the great thing, the sublime thing. I never climb to God on the steps I have carved. I climb to God when I descend to the dignity of my naked humanity on the earth and in the dust; and when, lying there, I find the Son of Man, for there also I find heaven opened, for He is also Son of God. He will interpret my problem and heal my wounds and illuminate my darkness. There is no approach to God by climbing.

> Heaven comes down our souls to greet,
> And glory crowns the mercy seat.

I glance back once more over all the pages of the past, and find the altar was the symbol of human conditions. When the altar was neglected there was individual, social, national weakness. One of the first signs of true revival was repairing altars and erecting new ones. When the altars were whole, and used, there were times of prosperity.

I leave these larger applications this morning, for I am more occupied with the individual. Unless I take this crisis to which I have come to the altar which is also an altar of sacrifice, then it is going to harm me, whatever its character may be. A new joy having come into your life, my brother —a joy of God, and from God, and intended for you—which does not make you erect your altar, a joy in the experience of which you do not go back for readjustment to the altar, will work you harm, however beneficent it may seem. Let me now speak tenderly, but as faithfully as I know how. Some of you are brooding over a sorrow, nursing it persistently; you have never taken it to your Lord, you have never erected your altar, have never stripped yourself in the presence of the Man Christ Jesus and found in Him the solace of grace, and through Him your way to God. Sorrow like a bird of evil omen, with its black wings outstretched, is blighting your life, and, more, it is spoiling the lives around you. Let us fulfil the symbolism of the past in the light of the new, and erect our altar and find our way into that fellowship with God that comes through Christ.

We have an altar, not in Jerusalem, not in any official place, but outside the camp and on the earth. This altar is for every occasion of life, and especially for those that are marked as special, an occasion of joy or of sorrow, of victory or of defeat, of holiness or of sin.

I have said nothing of the appeal of this passage. I conclude by referring to it and asking you to consider what the writer of the letter said. There are two kinds of sacrifices which we are to offer on our altar. First, praises to God, and, second, "to do good and to communicate forget not," that is the giving of benefits to other men. To erect this altar is always to be constrained, first, to praise God, and then to be driven out on the pathway of beneficent helpful service.

If in this hour of sudden crisis, on this day that stands out from the rest by reason of sudden joy or swift sorrow, I cannot do that which sometimes one feels would be helpful, erect an actual altar and slay a victim and watch the fires burn it, still, let me remember that all the spiritual things suggested by that act are mine in Christ. He is the sacrifice, through Him burns the perpetual fire, and in Him the elemental things of my soul may be restored, purged, lifted, renewed, satisfied. Then let us who have the altar use it to the glory of His name.

CHAPTER XX

THE PRESENCE NEEDED

If Thy presence go not . . . carry us not up hence.
EXODUS 23:15.

IN THE HISTORY OF THE WORLD THERE HAS BEEN NOTHING comparable to the creation of the Hebrew nation and its attempted realization of the theocratic form of government. Moreover, in the history of that nation no time was more wonderful than the period during which Moses was dictator. He was a man of vast learning and singular force of character. To him the greatness of the nation consisted in its relationship to God, and his greatness as a leader lay in the wonderful way in which he was able to keep alive among the people during the period of his oversight this conception of their greatness.

The occasion of the words of my text is to be noted, and that with some care. Three months after the exodus the people came to the wilderness of Sinai, and there encamped, and Moses ascended the Mount. In those lonely heights he saw and heard that before which all former sights and sounds were as nothing. The pomp and splendor of Pharaoh's court, in which he had been nourished, paled into insignificance before the glory of the great King as it was unveiled before his wondering eyes.

During a period of months he spent his time passing backward and forward between the people and God, and during this time he received the Divine constitution of the nation, its laws and its ritual. The Sinaitic peninsula became the theater of revelations that were to affect humanity to the end of time, and Moses was the medium of revelation.

After his last sojourn of forty days in the Mount, he descended to find the golden calf, to find the people hankering after a representation of God—for the people had made the golden calf, not as an attempt to supersede God, but to represent Him. We know the story of this man's fierce anger and sorrow, how he smashed the tables of stone to fragments and instituted most drastic methods of dealing with the people. Then we see him returning from those terrible hours to God, and in God's presence breathing out his soul in a petition that was never finished, and is all the more eloquent and forceful because it was never finished. He said, "If Thou wilt forgive their sin . . ." and the sentence is unfinished; "and if not, blot me, I pray Thee, out of Thy book which Thou hast written." In that hour of solemn and awful communion between Moses and God he was commanded to return to the people and resume his position as leader. God said to him, I will not go up in the midst of these people lest I consume them. I will send an angel. Then follows one of the most wonderful of all Bible pictures, the picture of this man mediating between God and the people, arguing the case with God. We are to remember that the very argument of Moses was inspired by God. At last God said to His waiting servant, "My presence shall go with thee, and I will give thee rest." Then all the pent-up agony of Moses' soul expressed the resolution inspiring all his mediation as he cried out, "If Thy presence go not . . . carry us not up hence."

I want to lead you, so far as I am able, or rather so far as I may be helped, in consideration of this story, and then to leave it to make its own application, to speak its own message to us. We fix our attention on that word which was the response of Moses to the word of God's grace, that word in which there is revealed all the terror which had assailed his soul at the thought that God was about to withdraw Himself from His people. "If Thy presence go not . . . carry us not up thence."

Let us inquire, first of all, the reason for that word. Why did Moses say such a thing, and how did he come to the resolution which expressed itself in that word? Then, second, let us observe the definiteness of his decision, and inquire the reason for it.

First, then, the reason for the decision itself, and the way by which Moses reached it. He took this position because he realized that the presence of God met the people's needs. This is the simplest of all statements, and I have made it so, in order that we may come face to face with the great teaching. Let us go back with this man and find out what he had been learning concerning God that made him decide that progress without God was impossible, for that is the meaning of the declaration, "If Thy presence go not with us, carry us not up hence." We cannot go back on the past, it is too glorious. We decline to go forward on any conditions other than those which have made the past. Progress without God is impossible; retrogression is out of the question. What revelations had Moses received of God that brought him to that decision? For the moment I am going to confine myself to those latest revelations of God that had come to Moses during those months in which he had been holding communion with God on the height of the mountain. I shall go further back presently to find out the process by which he came to the ultimate decision. What did he know of God as the result of those recent revelations?

He had discovered that God was a God of law. He had discovered that He was a God of order. He had discovered that He was a God of gifts. He had discovered that He was a God of love.

He had discovered that He was a God of law, that He

was a God of law because the people needed law. In that wonderful code which, according to this record, he had received in the solemn and high hours of communion he had found a law perfectly adapted and adjusted to the needs of these people. It was a Divine law, coming from One Who knew the whole need of these people, and it was perfectly adjusted to that need. It was a human law in its image of man's weakness. We read these Old Testament Scriptures somewhat carelessly. At least, we are in danger of doing so, and there is a reason for this in that we have grown away from some of the incidental things of these laws; but to read them carefully and intelligently, and in the atmosphere of the hour and in the midst of the conditions of the people, is to realize what Moses realized—as they were whispered in his soul, spoken to him with a voice articulate perchance, or more probably in the high altitude of communion with God—that these were the exact regulations and requirements that these people needed. Think of the people, semi-barbarous, vulgarized by over two centuries of brutal slavery, suddenly led out of slavery into freedom. Is there any more perilous situation? With profound respect, and making no claim to an understanding of the problem, my friends in the United States, men of the North and men of the South, will agree with me that the most terrific hour that came in their history was the hour when the Negroes were freed—and still the problem of the Negro is not solved. Think of these people, then, as freed from two hundred years of slavery. They had never lost the sense of relationship to God and of some Divine purpose in their history; but, nevertheless, they were vulgarized by the brutalities of human oppression. At your leisure, read again the whole code as you find it in Exodus, and observe its perfect adaptation to the needs of these people. Moses had discovered that God was a God of law, adapting Himself to the needs of men, speaking words to regulate their conduct and their relationships, of infinite wisdom.

He had discovered, moreover, that God was a God of order. All this had been revealed in details which seem to us to be so trivial that we read them carelessly. "Let them make Me a sanctuary; that I may dwell among them. According to all that I show thee, the pattern of the tabernacle, and the pattern of all the furniture thereof, even so shall ye make it." Then instructions were given, such as, eleven curtains of goats' hair, the length of each, thirty cubits, and the breadth of each, four cubits; and thou shalt couple them with clasps of gold and loops on the edge! This is the kind of thing which we read hurriedly, and sometimes even smile at, saying, Did God really say all that? He said all that, and I venture to affirm that Moses had been supremely impressed with the orderliness of God, with the fact that when He gave instructions to a people in this stage of development, He descended to the details of loops and clasps and couplings and lengths and breadths and materials. He is not only the God of the infinitely great, He is also the God of the infinitely small, careful not only concerning constellations, but also concerning the order of the leaves on the branches of the trees, so that, if we examine it, we cannot discover anything irregular in nature. If a tent is to be made for a people to worship in, God knows the materials and the couplings. At last, in the final chapter, we find the majestic music of the sevenfold repetition, "According to the pattern."

Moses discovered, moreover, that God was a God of gifts. "And the Lord spake unto Moses, saying, See, I have called by the name Bezaleel the son of Uri, the son of Hur, of the tribe of Judah: and I have filled him with the Spirit of God, in wisdom, and in understanding, and in knowledge, and in all manner of workmanship." What for? "To devise cunning works, to work in gold, and in silver, and in brass, and in cutting of stones for setting, and in carving of wood." Men inspired by the Spirit of God to be goldsmiths and silversmiths, workers in brass and stone, and carvers of wood.

Moses had heard that wonderful word. God would take hold of Bezaleel and fill him with the Spirit to make him cunning to work a work of delicate beauty to which he was called. Fingers hardened with the brutality of brick-making were to be made delicate enough for fine gold work. Moses had found that if God is indeed particular that the order He chooses be observed, He is also One Who gives a new and mystic power by which fingers shall become deft to do the appointed work.

Finally, Moses had found in that agony of argument that God was a God of love, for he had heard God say amid the fiery indignation of His holiness against the failure and sin of the people in the valley, "I will not go up in the midst of thee . . . lest I consume thee by the way." The inspiration of the anger was the tenderness of God's love; the threatened withdrawal was the evidence of His patience and longsuffering.

Thus Moses came into the presence of God knowing that if God remained in the midst of His people to direct, control, suggest, then all their need was met; he was convinced of this thing also, that if God were absent, then only need remained.

There is no suggestion in the story of the withdrawal of God actually, for God never withdraws Himself from humanity, and, speaking within the limitation of human expression, God cannot withdraw Himself from humanity, for in Him men live and move and have their being. The thought is of the withdrawal of the consciousness of God, withdrawal of the sense of His presence. The angel proposed to lead them did not mean the absence of God, but the absence of the consciousness of God in the minds of men; and thus the terror that seized the soul of Moses was that this God—Whose presence had been made known to him, and was symbolized to the people by the thunder and the cloud and the lightning on the Mount, and was now to

THE PRESENCE NEEDED 263

be evidenced in this very law and ritual—should withdraw the consciousness of Himself, and there should be between Him and His people the intermediation of an angel. This terror was born of his profound conviction of the need the people had of God, and of the fact that God perfectly met that need.

How did this man come to this conviction of the sufficiency of God? My inquiry may be answered briefly by declaring that successive revelations of God had been given to him to which he had been obedient, and by obedience to which the capacity had been created within his soul for new revelations. If the story of this man be pondered, it will be seen that God was ever breaking in on him with new methods and with new light. After forty years of shepherd life, forty years of preparation, forty splendid years of loneliness in the wilderness, God appeared to him. When next you think of Moses do not pity him when he leaves the glitter and gaud of Pharaoh's court. It was a great hour when he left all that behind and reached the essential grandeur of the loneliness of the wilderness, and that high sense of the nearness of God that always comes to a man when it is possible for him to escape from the tinsel and show of earthly things. After forty years, one day, as he was leading his flock as a shepherd, he saw a strange sight, a bush that burned with fire and was not consumed, and he heard within his soul a voice that said to him, "Put off thy shoes from off thy feet, for the place whereon thou standest is holy ground." This was a mystic and inclusive revelation, but not the perfect explanation, of the fact revealed. The suggestion was that God is a fire, which does not necessarily consume, but, drawing near to which a man must put the shoes from off his feet, or, in the language of our own day, recognize the need for reverence and submission and awe. Then Moses heard speech, the condescension of God as He took the speech of man and spoke to Moses' soul, revealing the fact of God's consciousness of what had bruised and broken Moses' heart forty years before in Egypt; "I have surely seen the affliction of My people, which are in Egypt, and have heard their cry by reason of their taskmasters; for I know their sorrows; and I am come down to deliver them out of the hand of the Egyptians." Trembling and afraid, Moses had shrunk from the great mission to which he was called, and said, I am not eloquent; and had been rebuked as God said to him, "Who hath made man's mouth?" Following on blindly, blunderingly, yet heroically, Moses had watched the power of God destroy the great nation and deliver an oppressed people. During those three months between the escape from Egypt and the arrival at Sinai, he had found that this God was a God of resource. Draw a contrast, for the sake of the light that comes from it. Think, first, of that night of the crossing of the sea, the sweeping of the wind of God, the holding back of the waters, the mystic awfulness of the stress and strain and storm, the march of the people through the sea; and the breaking of the morning and the music of the great song of victory. Then think of Marah, the bitter well, of the healing tree close beside it, and of God discovering the natural secret to His servant, so that the water was healed. Thus God was discovered as a God of resource, not merely the majestic might that breaks the yoke of the oppressor and divides the sea, but as a God of hidden secrets of healing, and of springs among the rocks, so that waters gushed forth for the quenching of His people's thirst. At last Moses came to Sinai, the culmination of everything that preceded it, where the burning bush found explanation, and all the secrets that lay behind the operation of the Divine power were unveiled. Do you wonder that in this hour of national failure and national sin, when it seemed as though God would withdraw Himself from the people He had so wondrously made,

THE PRESENCE NEEDED

that this man cried out in the agony of his soul, "If Thy presence go not with us, carry us not up hence?"

Now, observe the definiteness of this position. In an earlier chapter of this book we find the word concerning God's personal guidance of this people: "The Lord went before them by day in a pillar of cloud, to lead them the way; and by night in a pillar of fire, to give them light," and, again, "And the angel of the Lord, which went before the camp of Israel, removed and went behind them." Such had been the experience of the past, the pillar of cloud by day, and the pillar of fire by night: symbols, merely, necessary to meet the need of that peculiar people. We see no cloud by day, no pillar of fire by night. We have never seen cloven tongues of fire sitting on the heads of assembled saints. Why not? Because we live in a day of greater light and privilege, when signs that are natural are unnecessary because of the fulness of spiritual illumination. Remember, we are now thinking of that dim and distant time, when these people were, as I have already described them, semi-barbarous, vulgarized by slavery. God fulfils Himself in many ways, always adapting Himself to the immediate need of His people. The supreme fact was the presence of God, and this was suggested to them, and kept before their minds, by that mystic cloud which burned and gleamed in the darkness of the night. The deeper truth is that the Angel of Jehovah was there, not seen but present. We must ever draw a very clear distinction in reading the Old Testament between "The Angel of the Lord" and "An angel of the Lord." Wherever we find the phrase "The Angel of the Lord," we discover that it has quite a separate significance, and refers to an entirely distinct person. It is difficult to say so much without saying a little more. To my own mind, there is no doubt whatever that the One spoken of as "The Angel of the Lord" was the Son of God Himself, Who thus appeared in many a mystic manifestation in the olden days, and Who must never be confused with the angel ministers. Through that figurative, poetic language of the time, the truth is revealed that God had been actually leading, overshadowing with the cloud by day, and shining in the gleaming fire by night.

In this hour of peril and of sin God said to His servant, I will send an angel, and Moses declined to accept an angel, he declined to go forward if there was to be some substitute for God, even in the form of an angel. That would have been retrogression, a going back. That is the meaning of one of the things that Moses said in the course of his praying, "See, Thou sayest unto me, Bring up this people: and Thou hast not let me know him whom Thou wilt send with me." It is as though Moses said to God, I have come to know Thee, through these unveilings and revelations, but I do not know the angel. I know nothing in all literature more wonderful than this, a man saying to God, I decline angel guidance after having known Thy guidance. God answered this man—appalling as seems his daring, so appalling that we almost tremble to put it in that way—by saying, "My presence shall go with thee."

Observe now, most carefully, that to which I referred by way of introduction. Moses did not suggest that they should go back. Retrogression was impossible, the past was too glorious. A little while after, the people suggested that they should go back: "Were it not better for us to return into Egypt?" There was no such thought, however, in the mind of Moses. It was impossible to go back on that glorious past. That I do not now dwell on, but this I do want to insist on: he did not dream of progress without God, "If Thy presence go not with us, carry us not up thence." Better to die here, underneath all the magnificence of this mountain in the wilderness, and be buried, than to cross the Jordan and enter the land that flows with milk and honey without God. "If Thy presence go not with us, carry us not up hence."

THE PRESENCE NEEDED

The deliberate choice of the lawgiver was that, having arrived at that point in the glorious history when the onward march was checked by sin, if God was withdrawing Himself, the best thing was to die in the wilderness. All this is the language of high faith and clear belief.

How terribly we fail here, oftentimes, in individual, church, and national life. If in very deed God has departed from us, then let us cease. Oh, the agony of attempting to go forward along a line of the Divine pathway when God has withdrawn Himself. What insufferable agony—if you will permit me the superlative illustration, as it seems to me—would be that of the preacher who, having seen the vision and heard the voice and known the thrill and power of the Spirit's presence, should try to preach after he had lost his vision and the sense of the presence of God! Can there be anything more terrific, as we look at things in this atmosphere, than a Church of Jesus Christ from which Jesus Christ is absent. That is what Moses meant. The glorious past, the watchfulness over all the long years of slavery, the mighty hand stretched out to work deliverance, the divided sea, and the march, all the glorious past; but if God is going, then let us die here! There lies the land of the future, the program of God, the crossing of the Jordan to the land flowing with milk and honey; but we cannot go if He is going to leave us: "If thy presence go not with us, carry us not up hence."

That supreme conviction and resolution made Moses the man of power that he was, and led him in all the steps he immediately took. I watch the process. What is this strange thing he is doing now? He is striking his tent, the tent of meeting—not yet the tabernacle, that was not yet erected, but his own tent, which had served as a center for their whole life, to which they could come for judgment, the very place from which God had spoken to Moses, and pitching it outside the camp, going away from the people and pitching his tent outside the camp. What was this man doing? Excommunicating a whole nation in order that he might readmit it on true terms! If the people will go back, they must go back by way of confession, and by way of putting away sin. He will receive them in the name of the God with Whom he has been holding communion. That is the way back. Believe me, there are moments when a man can excommunicate a church as surely as a church can excommunicate a man. In this, Moses pitched his tent outside the camp; but the camp was reconstituted around that tent by the way of return and the way of confession.

It was because of his profound conviction of the necessity for God, if the program of God was to be carried out, that he had adopted this method. Notice, again, the argument between God and this man. God said to him: "Thy people, which thou broughtest up out of the land of Egypt," and, reverently yet definitely, Moses flung the burden back on God: "Thy people, which thou hast brought forth out of the land of Egypt."

Such a meditation as this enshrines its own application. To-day we face life with its crowding and overwhelming opportunities of service, and, thank God, the past is full of glory and triumph. The present is difficult. Problems are confronting us. I am speaking, not of the larger outlook of the Christian Church, but of the narrower one of this church. We are all conscious that the hour is electric with difficulty and strain, and yet there lies a future before us, a future grand and glorious in the purpose of God, for His Church is to march victoriously until the very gates of Hades surrender. The program is clear and plain and definite, but for the moment we are halted. What is the supreme need? Finances? No! Numbers? No, a thousand times no! What, then? God. He has been with us; we have known His presence, His power; the demonstration of it has been found in lives renewed, remade, desolate men comforted, hopeless souls made courageous, impure men and women rendered pure. I stand here to-night, ere I go away, saying this: "If Thy presence go not with us, carry us not up hence." I am not suggesting that the presence is withdrawn, but I tremble sometimes lest it should be, lest we run for a time by the momentum of past victories while God is absent. If I could lay a charge on my own soul as I leave this pulpit for eight weeks, and if I could lay a charge on my people, it would be this: Discover whether the glory is passing away. Is it moving out from the threshold as Ezekiel saw it go? Is there a danger that God be withdrawn? I am not going to answer the question. I want to find out. I propose to do it. Will you join me? "If Thy presence go not with us, carry us not up hence." Let us end there. Blessed be God, the past cannot be undone. The one thing you cannot take from me is yesterday, with its glorious revelations of power. The future can be undone, and it is well for us sometimes to pull ourselves up like this, and to deal with God. There I leave it.

CHAPTER XXI

THE FRUIT-BEARING FRIENDS OF JESUS

No longer do I call you servants; for the servant knoweth not what his lord doeth: but I have called you friends; for all things that I heard from My Father I have made known unto you. Ye did not choose Me, but I chose you, and appointed you, that you should go and bear fruit, and that your fruit should abide: that whatsoever ye shall ask of the Father in My name, He may give it you.

JOHN 15:15, 16.

THE WORDS OF THE TEXT ARE FOUND AMONG THE RECORDS OF those tender and intimate conversations of our Lord and His disciples on the eve of His passion, and we cannot better prepare our hearts for considering them than by reminding ourselves of the circumstances under which they were uttered. They were indeed dark days in the experience of these men. Behind them lay those brief but wonderful years of comradeship with this strangely commanding Person, those years of ever-growing wonder as they traveled with Him and listened to Him and watched Him. Ahead lay some dark and unfathomable mystery which filled their hearts with foreboding. He gathered them into an upper room, and talked to them. The first part of the Lord's teaching was strangely disturbed by these men; the second part of it was undisturbed and quiet. He first girded Himself with a towel, and bent to wash their feet, and He was disturbed by Peter's protest. Then, at the Passover feast, the atmosphere became electric, and the teaching was disturbed when He excluded Judas. He was further interrupted by Peter's question, "Whither goest Thou?" by Thomas saying, "Lord, we know not whither Thou goest; how know we the way?" by Philip's outcry, "Lord, shew us the Father, and it sufficeth us"; by Jude's inquiry, "Lord, what is come to pass that Thou wilt manifest Thyself unto us and not unto the world?" Jesus proceeded to teach them, until, hushed into silence, they followed Him as, leaving the upper room, He moved perchance down the slopes of the mountain, or perchance to the temple in the darkness of the night, uttering as He went the great allegory of the vine, and so completing His instructions. We shall be helped to an understanding of the words of the text if we remember the purpose of these discourses. The keynote of all of them is found in the opening declaration of chapter thirteen: "Now before the feast of the passover, Jesus knowing that His hour was come that He should depart out of this world unto the Father, having loved His own which were in the world, He loved them unto the end." He was preparing them for the future, for the immediate future, dark and mysterious, the tragic hours of the Cross, and for the future that lay beyond, when the new light should shine and the new power be realized at the coming of the Spirit. The final discourse of Jesus upon this occasion was introduced, as I have said, by the allegory of the vine, and our text is contained within that discourse, and is immediately related to that allegory. When Jesus said to these men, "No longer do I call you servants . . . but I have called you friends . . . and appointed you, that ye should go and bear fruit, and . . . that whatsoever ye shall ask of the Father in My name, He may give it you," He was but carrying out in definite application in one particular regard the whole figure suggested by His magnificent claim, "I am the Vine, the true."

Two matters demand our consideration. We are arrested first, by the changed relationship and its reasons; and, second, by the resulting responsibility, in itself and as to its possibility.

In the first place let us observe this change in relationship. That the relationship was changed is certain, for the form in which our Lord uttered the words indicates and emphasizes the thought of deeper relationship into which these men were now to pass; "No longer do I call you slaves." The change was not capricious; it was the result of previous training. He called them disciples at the beginning. There came a moment when He called them apostles. Now He called them friends. That is not to say that they had not already been in some sense His friends. That is not to say that they would cease to be disciples. That is not to say they would cease to be apostles. As a matter of fact, their full apostolic work had not yet commenced. They were disciples when first they followed Him, apostles when, after a period of training, He first sent them forth; but now He said to them, "No longer do I call you servants. . . . I have called you friends."

A slave was the property of his master, unable to possess, and so having nothing of his own, unable to elect and so unable to do, on his own initiative. A slave, therefore, was at the disposal of his owner, all his energy must be for the increase of the possessions of the one who possessed him; all his choosing must be in accord with the choosing of the one who owned him. The law of the slave's life is unquestioning submission, blind obedience. Is not all this a description of the relationship these disciples still bore to Christ? Does it not describe the relation that the Christian must ever bear to Christ? Yes, in some senses. We are still His bondslaves, and it is to be noted that ere this discourse was ended He called them so again. In the twentieth verse we read, "Remember the word that I said unto you, a slave is not greater than his lord." That was a reference to what He had said in the past, but it indicated a maintained relationship. They were still His slaves in some sense of the word; yet He distinctly marked a change in relationship when He said, "No longer do I call you slaves." It is noticeable, moreover, that in the apostolic writings the apostles spoke of themselves as slaves, and the apostle who was added to their company, born out of due season, but not a whit behind the chiefest of them, delighted ever to call himself the bondslave of Jesus Christ. Christians are still the bondslaves of Jesus, His property, unable to possess or to have of their own, unable to elect save under the compulsion of His choice, or to do save as doing is putting forth energy on His behalf. Christians are still called on to increase His possessions, and to elect in accordance with His elections. But here we halt. The slave renders unquestioning submission, and blind obedience. That is not the last word about Christian discipleship. It is at that very point that we discover the character of this change in relationship. "I have called you friends," and in a moment we are introduced into another realm of thought which we shall see does not negative the essential values of the first, but rather transfigures them and makes them glorious and beautiful. What are friends? When we begin to think seriously, we realize how we constantly abuse the great word *friend*, how casually and carelessly we make use of it. Sit down some time, and write a list of your *friends*. None of us have very many; we have many acquaintances—and thank God for the whole of them—but few friends.

What is the basis of friendship? Reciprocal and self-emptying love, and, consequently, mutual interest. Find me my friend, and I will say to you, This friend loves me to the forgetfulness of himself, and I love him to the forgetfulness of myself. He is forever seeking my interests, and I am always seeking his, so far as our lives touch each other in this realm of human friendship. Jesus said, "No longer do I call you servants . . . but I have called you friends." The law of life in slavery is unquestioning submission and blind obedience. The law of life in friendship is informed submission and intelligent obedience. The friends of Jesus are submissive, but by no means unquestioningly. They are submissive after they have asked questions and He has satisfied them. The friends of Jesus are obedient, but no longer blindly. He has told them all things. "The slave knoweth not what his Lord doeth"; he has to imagine; the friend knows what his Lord is doing; his Lord has told him. He is rendering obedience no longer blindly but intelligently. In this exposition I am warranted by the whole movement of the story. Did I not remind you of the disturbances in the teaching of the Lord in the upper room, "Lord, whither goest Thou?" Jesus answered, "Whither I go, thou canst not follow Me now; but thou shalt follow afterwards." "Lord, why cannot I follow Thee now?" Is that a slave speaking? Yes, a slave seeking friendship. Never forget this, Christ was not angry with Peter, He answered Peter, "Whither I go ye know the way." Then Thomas said, "Lord, we know not whither Thou goest; how know we the way?" Is that a slave? Yes, a slave getting ready to be a friend, asking his questions. Then Philip cried out almost angrily, almost in protest, "Shew us the Father and it sufficeth us." Is that a slave? Yes, on the highway to friendship. These men did not become friends because they asked questions, but because He was willing to answer them. He made them His friends, they did not make Him their friend. "Ye did not choose Me, but I chose you." The central Personality, full of glory and light, full of surprise and amazement, is neither Peter, nor Thomas, nor Philip, nor Jude, but Jesus. He is seen taking hold of the weaknesses of men and making them the foundations of strength. When He had answered all their questions and removed their blindness, He said, "No longer do I call you servants . . . I have called you friends," for I have admitted you to the secrets, I have told you all things.

Consequently, in friendship we have the fellowship of love as the inspiration and the atmosphere of fellowship in effort. That is an infinitely higher plane on which to live than that of slavery. This is what Jesus' heart is ever seeking, not that we should render Him blind obedience, but intelligent obedience; not that we should give to Him unquestioning submission, but satisfied submission; not that we should drag ourselves after Him as though it were hard work, and imagine that in the dragging there is virtue; but that we should go gaily, gladly, to suffer for His name, for very love of Him; not slaves, but friends, and therefore slaves as never before.

What was the reason for this change? I have already answered this question incidentally, yet it is so important that we shall dwell on it for a moment longer. Jesus distinctly told them why He made the change. "No longer do I call you servants; for the servant knoweth not what his Lord doeth: but I have called you friends for all things that I heard from My Father I have made known unto you." The basis on which our Lord made the change of relationship was, first, His action in revealing God to them; and, second, their new capacity for service resulting from the revelation.

His revelation of God to them we may consider generally and particularly. I shall dwell principally on the particular revelation contained within this very discourse. To this group of men He had made God known. They had found God in Him. Perhaps at the moment they hardly knew it. I do not believe that at this time they could have formulated a creed which would have contained within it a declaration of Jesus' Deity, but they had found God in Him, and by and by they would find out that they had found God in Him. They had learned two things to the full realization of which they came progressively, to the ultimate realization of which the Church of God has not yet come, so vast are they. They had found in Him the revelation of the Divine holiness. They had found in Him the revelation of the Divine love. The proportion in which they were conscious of the Divine holiness and the Divine love through His revelation was the proportion in which they understood Him, and, understanding Him, were prepared to be not slaves alone, but friends. The holiness of God was revealed, not so much in the teaching of Jesus—though there surely it is revealed —as in Himself. Let me speak of Him for a moment as man alone, let me think of Him in His human life only. In Him I see a man who by all His affirmations, those which were definite and specific, and those which were occasional and incidental, revealed the fact that all His life was conditioned within the will of God. Then let me watch His life in order that I may understand the will of God, and so know the God in whose will He lived. As I watch Him in the selflessness of His selfhood, in the awful purity of His familiarity with all human emotions, I begin to understand what His God must be. Whereas that does not exhaust the meaning of the great word spoken to Philip, that word has that value also, "He that hath seen Me hath seen the Father." He that has seen any man has seen his God. Every man reveals his God in what he is himself. Ultimately the soul responsive to his God, if the god be lust, greed, passion, will reveal in his own face lust, greed, passion. In that sense Jesus challenged men when He said, He that hath seen Me hath seen the Father." Those who have seen Him have seen God in what He is; in His sinlessness they have seen the holiness of God. In Him, moreover, they had seen the Divine compassion, the Divine love; and this, not so much in what He was in Himself, but in what He was toward sinning men.

Here again I pause to lay emphasis on something I have already said incidentally, that the Church itself has not yet grasped the fulness of this revelation of the love of God in Jesus as seen in His attitude toward sinning men. Never were His lips disfigured by the curve of contempt. Never did His face convey to sinning men the assumption of superiority. Never did He say a hard thing to a sinning soul. That is what created difficulty in the mind of the rulers of His time. This Man loved sinners, made friends with them, did not patronize them, did not denounce them. Oh, God, that the Church might begin to see this compassion of God as revealed in Jesus. That compassion is not pity that excuses wrong, it is love that dies for wrong. The measure in which we have seen God as Jesus revealed Him is the measure in which we are prepared to be His friends, and therefore the friends of God.

In these final discourses God was revealed by Jesus supremely in His redeeming grace. Take the whole happenings of the upper room. There was, first, the inclusive symbol, when He girded Himself with a towel. That towel was the insignia of slavery. When Peter wrote his letter, he was surely thinking about that upper room when he said, "Gird yourselves with humility as with a slave's apron." The apron, which was the the symbol of slavery, Jesus girt about Himself and washed their feet. That act was symbolic of redeeming grace, stooping, bending, until it had taken the meanest position of all in order to lift men to the height of glory. In that stooping, bending, bowing of the towel-girt slave, Jesus was revealing God. Then followed the exclusion of Judas. There is an attitude of soul which grace abandons! There is an attitude of spirit which grace excludes from its covenant! After that came the inclusion of Peter. Grace said to him, "The cock shall not crow, till thou hast denied Me thrice. Let not your heart be troubled; ye believe in God, believe also in Me." There is an attitude of soul most dastardly, yet having at its center high aspiration and noble desire, which grace includes, fulfilling the high desire by the destruction of the thing that is mean. Grace was revealed in the expository answers Jesus gave to these men. Mark the sequence of them. To Thomas He said, I am the way to the Father; to Philip He said, I am the Father also, for if you have seen Me you have seen Him; to Jude He said, The Father will love and come to those who come to Him through Me.

Now said He to them, I have made known these things concerning God to you, and on the basis of this revelation I call you friends. The revelation of love produced love. There came a day when John wrote a letter in which he said, "We love Him because He first loved us." John knew the fact of the love of God through his Lord. So John became his Lord's friend. The revelation of the Divine love in all its glory created love within the souls of these men. Jesus Himself in the prayer that followed said, "This is life eternal, that they should know Thee the only true God." On the basis of that unveiling of God through Christ these men became slaves no longer, but friends. Therefore they were ever after slaves volitionally, not of compulsion, no longer dragging themselves after Him reluctantly, but rejoicing that they were counted worthy to suffer shame for His name.

So we pass to glance at the resulting responsibility, in both itself and as to its possibility. Our Lord here declared that these men were appointed by Himself to two things; to bear fruit, and to ask whatsoever they would of the Father. These two things must never be separated from each other. The purpose is fruit-bearing; asking is in order to fulfil that purpose. Our Lord had appointed the disciples to bear fruit as branches of the vine, and He had appointed them to ask whatsoever was necessary to enable them to bear that fruit.

The idea is of the branch doing two things which a branch always does in a fruitful vine: it bears fruit, and it does so by demanding from the vine the life that enables it to bear fruit. In any vine on which our eyes may look we may observe the fruit-bearing branch and know that it is asking, demanding, its life of the vine, and expressing the answers it receives in the clusters of fruit it bears.

Nothing can be more important in our interpretation of this particular passage than that we should be harmonious with the whole allegory. When our Lord made use of it He was not using a new figure, He was borrowing an old one. That is the meaning of His claim, the smoothness of our translation of which robs it a little of its impact. What Jesus literally said was, "I am the Vine, the true." That little phrase, *the true*, interjected after the declaration, emphasized the fact that He was borrowing from the past economy. That figure of the vine runs all through the old economy. It is found in psalm and prophecy. Jesus stood at last among these Jewish disciples, and He said, "I am the Vine, the true!" Glancing back to the ancient prophecy in which it is declared that the vine which should have brought forth grapes had brought forth wild grapes we have an exposition of fruit-bearing. What is the fruit the vine ought to have brought forth? God looked for *righteousness* and for *judgment*. Instead of judgment, He found oppression; instead of righteousness, He found a cry! The fruit for which God was looking on His vine was judgment and righteousness. Judgment is not punishment; punishment may be an aspect of it, but judgment is government, true, righteous, just. He looked for judgment, and, behold, oppression. He looked for righteousness, and, behold, a cry. Now said Jesus, "I am the true Vine." By that He meant that through Him judgment and righteousness are coming to the world.

With that general statement in mind, let us observe the

fruit-bearing of Jesus. I shall content myself now with the most general statement concerning it. Will you call to mind the first words that Jesus is recorded to have uttered on the verge of His public ministry? I am not now referring to His boyhood's words, but to those He uttered on the day when He came to John's baptism. John said, "I have need to be baptized of Thee, and comest Thou to me?" Then Jesus said, "Suffer it now: for thus it becometh us to fulfil all *righteousness*." At the end of that public ministry the Greeks came asking to see Him, and He said, "Now is the *judgment* of this world: now shall the prince of this world be cast out. And I, if I be lifted up from the earth, will draw all men unto Myself." The first word of the public ministry declared that *righteousness* was to be fulfilled. At the close He said, "Now is the *judgment* of this world." The Lord looketh down from heaven for righteousness and for judgment, and in the long history of the race He had found oppression and a cry; but, at last, in this Man He found righteousness and judgment, not in Himself alone, but in Him for humanity.

"Suffer it now: for thus it becometh us to fulfil all righteousness." What was this that He said must be done? It was the baptism of repentance. But He had nothing to repent of! He repented for humanity as He bent to the baptism, and completed His repentance in the passion baptism whereby He made possible the fulfilment of righteousness in the case of men who had failed. When did He declare that judgment, the true government of the world, was coming? When He said, "Now is My soul troubled." By the way of the Cross, that for which God and man had looked, and looked in vain, shall come the judgment of the world, its true government; for the prince of the world is cast out, and our Lord being lifted by the Cross fulfils the purpose of God. In all the ministry of Jesus between that initial word and that final word deeds and teaching, tarryings and journeyings, were true to that passion and purpose. He was bearing fruit.

Now to His friends, He said, I have appointed you to bear fruit. We can leave once more all the ampler outlooks and become immediate, practical, simple. How are we to bear this fruit of righteousness and judgment in the world? Not for ourselves is this fruit to be borne. The figure of fruit denies that spiritual selfishness which simply seeks spiritual blessing to consume it on our own desires. The prevailing sin of the Church is that. The fruit we bear is for others, for the world. How are we to bear that fruit? Only as we are brought into such relation with Jesus that we share His self-emptying. The kenosis must be repeated in His disciples if they are to bear fruit. That is fundamental, initial. How shall we express it? By becoming obedient unto death. If we interpret that by the facts of His life we shall see how we are to bear fruit. By our being ready to go into the company of sinners, by our ability to repent on behalf of sinners, by our belief in sinning men, by our justification of them through our belief in them, by infinite patience with them, by the pouring out of our lives for them and into them, we bear fruit. We see immediately that we can never be fruit-bearers in this sense unless we actually begin at the beginning and put ourselves into definite, living, personal, immediate contact with sinning men. There has been a teaching of separation from the world that in some of its aspects has been utterly pernicious. We are not to withdraw from the society in which we are living, but to stay there and bear fruit there. In proportion as we know what it is to have true fellowship with the Son of God we shall seek out the depraved, the lost, the sunken, the bruised and the unclean, and, sitting down by them, we shall bear the fruit of righteousness and judgment for them as we pour out our lives in sacrificial service.

We need a Church reformed to the pattern of her Lord, the self-emptying One Who bears the fruit of righteousness and judgment in a world dying for lack of righteousness and judgment. He came into contact with polluted and spoiled humanity, and while the Pharisees looked on and were amazed and hostile, He received them and made Himself their friend. We have not begun to learn the meaning of true friendship for Jesus Christ until we have sacrificed our sensibilities and our refinements and our preferences as we gather to our heart and life and actual fellowship sinning men and women in order that we may lift and change them by that holy contact.

It is a hard word, and who is sufficient for it? Then let us remember that Jesus said, Not only have I appointed you to bear fruit, but I have appointed you to ask the Father whatsoever you need in order to its bearing. If the condition of fellowship be kenosis or self-emptying and the Cross, the resource for that fruit-bearing is pleroma, that fulness which there is in Christ, for "in Him dwelleth all the fulness of the Godhead bodily, and in Him ye are made full." If the task be a great one, and if from it flesh and sense shrink, let us ask that we may receive that enduement and equipment of the very compassionate cleansing life of Christ that will enable us to bear this fruit in the world to His glory.

We all began our Christian discipleship as slaves. It is a solemn beginning, characterized by a great silence and a great submission, but if we have come no further than that fruit is rare. That is why there are so many degenerate vines in the vineyard of the Lord. Maintained fellowship with Christ brings us into friendship. We come to that in hours when we are oppressed, frightened, perplexed, and we dare ask Him questions, and have such confidence in Him that we dare express our doubts to Him. In response to such questions and such doubts He is able to tell us His secrets and so to lead us as presently to say, "No longer do I call you servants . . . but I have called you friends."

Let us gladden His heart by such intimate friendship that through us He may be able to do what He desires to do for this sad and needy world.

CHAPTER XXII

THE POWER OF THE GOSPEL

For I am not ashamed of the gospel: for it is the power of God unto salvation to every one that believeth; to the Jew first, and also to the Greek. For therein is revealed a righteousness of God by faith unto faith: as it is written, But the righteous shall live by faith.
ROMANS 1:16, 17.

WHEN PAUL WROTE THIS LETTER HE HAD NEVER VISITED Rome. He earnestly desired to do so, and expected that his desire would be fulfilled. That desire was created by the fact of his Roman citizenship, and by his interest in the Christian Church in Rome; and that more especially because he desired that the Church in that city should be an instrument for the evangelization of the Western world. Writing thus to the saints in the Imperial City, he declared that he was not ashamed of the gospel, and he gave his reasons.

The statement that he was not ashamed is in itself interesting. It is the only occasion on which we find Paul even suggesting the possibility of being ashamed of the gospel. I am perfectly well aware that this is a declaration that he was not ashamed, but why make the declaration? I think there can be but one answer, and it is suggested by the words immediately preceding the text: "So much as in me is, I am ready to preach the gospel to you also that are in Rome." The declaration that he was not ashamed of the gospel, with its implication of the possibility of being ashamed, was the result of his consciousness of Rome, of its imperial dignity, of its material magnificence, of its proud contempt for all aliens, of the vastness of its multitudes, of the profundity of its corruption. There was no question in his mind as to the power of his gospel, and yet we detect the undertone of inquiry as he wrote: "I am ready to preach the gospel to you also that are in Rome. For I am not ashamed of the gospel."

It is always easier to preach in a village than in a city, to the sweet, simple people of the countryside than to the satisfied metropolitans. Really it is not so, but the feeling that it is so invariably assails the soul of the prophet of God. In answer to that consciousness of his soul, or perhaps in answer to his feeling that such a consciousness might exist in the minds of the Roman Christians, Paul affirmed his readiness to preach the gospel in Rome also, declaring that he was not ashamed of it, and giving as his reason that this gospel was "the power of God unto salvation." The only justification of a gospel is that it is powerful. A message that proclaims the need for, and the possibility of, spiritual and moral renewal must be tested by the results it produces. A word devoid of power is no word of the Lord. A gospel that fails to produce the results it announces as necessary and as possible is no gospel. Is our gospel the power of God?

Let me say at once that the particular burden of my message this evening has come to me as the result of a long letter which I now hold in my hand, four closely written pages which I am not going to read to you in full, but which I have read again and again for my own soul's profit and examination as a preacher of the gospel, and from which I propose to read a few sentences. The letter refers to meetings which have been held in preparation for the winter's work:

> You were saying on Tuesday evening that men were everywhere inquiring after reality, and I quite agree. We

often hear about the dynamic of Christianity. There are youths and young men—I speak only of those about whose temptations I know something—who have to face temptations, and even this week have cried to the Lord Jesus for help and have tried the best they knew how to overcome, yet have failed. When a young man comes to me and asks where he can get the power to overcome, what am I to say? One did remark to me, "It is not a lack in our religion that it supplies no real power to overcome such-and-such temptations, temptations that cannot be avoided, and that have to be faced?" Men don't want a merely theoretic idea or ideas about the dynamic of Christianity. They want to realize how they can practically appropriate that dynamic. Careful Christian workers want to know how far, and in what way, they may safely encourage those spiritually sick and blind to hope for spiritual help after they have believed for the forgiveness of their sins; and experience shows it must not be a matter of mere inference, for inference would be likely to promise more than what seems to be genuinely realized. To hold out hopes that experience must disappoint is disastrous. Yes, it is reality men are longing for.

I believe that letter expresses the inquiry and the feeling of many souls. I think that my friend has fastened on a word that he knows I am peculiarly fond of, the word *dynamic*. I plead guilty; I love the word, and I use it a great deal, and I do so because it is a New Testament word. It is the very word of my text, The gospel is the power, δυναμις, of God unto salvation. The letter of my friend is practically a challenge of the declaration of my text. The text says, "The gospel is the power of God into salvation." My friend suggests that there are men who have heard the call of Jesus, who have been obedient to it, and yet have not experienced that power. I am not going to argue the points of the letter, but rather to consider the statement of Paul, hoping and believing that in that consideration and in an attempt to understand the meaning of the great Apostle at this point there may be help for honest souls whose difficulty is voiced by the writer of the letter.

However, let me say to the writer of the letter, and to all such, that I agree that there is nothing more important to-day than that the Christian preacher and teacher should be real in the use of terms. But all who are making that demand must recognize the extreme difficulty of reality in terminology when dealing with spiritual forces that can never be perfectly apprehended. Whenever we have to deal with great forces we find ourselves in a similar difficulty. I am not an electrician, but I suggest a question whether the phrase, "to develop electricity," is an accurate phrase. I do not say that it is not, but I ask, Can you *develop* electricity? Is it not, after all, a word that we hazard until we come to fuller knowledge? Is there any man in this house, or in London, or in the world, who is prepared to tell us the last thing about electricity, not only what can be done by it, but also what it is? The moment we get into the realm of great forces which are intangible, imponderable, demonstrated by what they do, we are at least in danger of seeming to be unreal in our terms. We are dealing now with the most wonderful of all forces. At the close of our meditation undoubtedly there will be a sense in which some of the terms used will seem to lack reality. It is not that the force dealt with is unreal, but that it is so far beyond our final explanation that terms cannot be discovered which cover the facts of the case while excluding everything that should be excluded.

Confining ourselves now to the words selected, let us consider, first, the affirmation, "The gospel . . . is the power of God unto salvation"; second, the condition on which the power is appropriated, "to every one that believeth"; and, finally, the exposition of the operation which the Apostle added, "for therein is revealed a righteousness of God by faith unto faith."

First, then, as to the affirmation. Here many sentences

are not necessary. The Apostle declares that "the gospel . . . is the power of God unto salvation to every one that believeth." The power: that is something which produces results, something which is more than a theory, something which is mightier than a law, an actual, spiritual force, producing spiritual results, an actual power accomplishing things. What it is in itself may be a mystery; how it does its work may not be known; but the Apostle declares that it accomplishes certain things, and that we may know by the results it produces that the gospel is more than a theory, more than a law, that it is, in fact, a power. Moreover, he makes the superlative declaration that it is "the power of God." This is the superlative way of declaring its sufficiency for doing certain things. In quality it is irresistible, in quantity it is inexhaustible. Yet he declares further that it is "the power of God unto salvation." This at once defines and limits the power of the gospel. The gospel is the power that operates to this end alone. The gospel is the power which operates to this end perfectly.

The word "salvation" immediately suggests inquiring what the danger is that is referred to, for to know the danger is to know the scope of the salvation. Here, to summarize briefly, the danger is twofold: pollution of the nature, and paralysis of the will. In the presence of temptation men find that their nature is so weakened that they yield, and their will is so paralyzed that even when they have willed not to yield, still they do yield. That is the whole story of the danger. The Apostle declares that the gospel is "the power of God unto salvation," that is, for cleansing the nature from its pollution, and for enabling the will, so that henceforth a man shall not only will to do right, but shall do it.

It is perfectly clear, however, that the gospel operates in human lives only on the fulfilment of conditions. The gospel is not the power of God to every man. "The gospel . . . is the power of God to every one that believeth." The

Apostle here recognized the human possibility, that is, a possibility common to all human nature, irrespective of race or privilege. "To the Jew first; and also to the Greek"; and to the Greek none the less and none the later. The conditions can be fulfilled by men as men, apart from the question of race or privilege or temperament. The gospel can be believed by the metropolitan or the provincial, by the dweller in Rome as surely as by the dwellers in the hamlets through which he had passed, by the learned and by the illiterate. Belief is the capacity and possibility of human life everywhere.

What, then, is this capacity? We must interpret the use of the word *believe* here by its constant use in the revelation of the New Testament. There must be conviction before there can be belief. Belief is always founded on reason. How can they believe who have not heard? The conviction is not necessarily that of the truth of the claim; it is not necessarily conviction that the gospel will work. There can be faith before I am sure that this gospel is going to work. Indeed, thousands of people have a profound conviction that the gospel will work who yet have never believed. The conviction necessary is that in view of the need experienced, and of the claim which the gospel makes, it ought to be put to the test. Jesus said to His critics on one occasion: "If any man willeth to do His will, he shall know of the teaching, whether it be of God." Surely that was a perfectly fair test. He who puts the gospel to the test of obeying it will find out whether its claim of power be accurate. When a man is convinced that in the presence of his need and of the claim which the gospel makes he ought to put it to the test, he has come to the true attitude of mind in which it is possible for him to exercise faith. Faith, then, is volitional. That is the central responsibility of the soul. Faith is not a feeling that comes stealing across the soul. Faith is not an inclination toward the Lord Jesus Christ. Faith is that volitional act which decides in the presence of the great need, and in the presence of the great claim, to put that claim to the test by obedience thereto. Conduct is the resulting expression, which is conformity to the claims made by the gospel, immediate and progressive. Whatever the proclamation of the gospel says to the soul, the soul is to put the gospel to the test by obeying. Invariably in the actual coming of a soul to Christ under conviction of sin everything is focused at some one point; and when that is obeyed other calls will be made on the soul by this gospel, which is one of purity and righteousness, as well as of mercy and of love. Faith is that volitional act which puts the gospel to the test by obedience to its claims. That is the condition of appropriation.

The whole situation is illuminated for the inquiring soul by the explanatory word: "For therein is revealed a righteousness of God by faith unto faith." That is the exposition of what the Apostle has already written concerning the gospel, both as to the nature of the power that is resident in it and as to the law by which that power is appropriated in individual lives. The declaration that there is a revelation in the gospel of the righteousness of God does not mean that the gospel has revealed the fact that God is righteous. That revelation antedated the gospel; it was found in the law, it was found in human history, it was found everywhere in the human heart. Out of that knowledge comes the agony of soul that seeks after a gospel. The declaration clearly means that the gospel reveals the fact that God places righteousness at the disposal of men who in themselves are unrighteous, that He makes it possible for the unrighteous man to become a righteous man. That is the exposition of salvation. Salvation is righteousness made possible. If you tell me that salvation is deliverance from hell, I tell you that you have an utterly inadequate understanding of what salvation is. If you tell me that salvation is forgiveness of sins, I shall affirm that you have a very partial understanding of what salvation is. Unless there be more in salvation than deliverance from penalty and forgiveness of transgressions, then I solemnly say that salvation cannot satisfy my own heart and conscience. That is the meaning of the letter I received: mere forgiveness of sins and deliverance from some penalty cannot satisfy the profoundest in human consciousness. Deep down in the common human consciousness there is a wonderful response to that which is of God. Man may not obey it, but in the deeps of human consciousness there is a response to righteousness, an admission of its call, its beauty, its necessity. Salvation, then, is making possible that righteousness. Salvation is the power to do right. However enfeebled the will may be, however polluted the nature, the gospel comes bringing to men the message of power enabling them to do right. In the gospel is revealed a righteousness of God, which, as the Apostle argues and makes quite plain as he goes on with his great letter, is a righteousness which is placed at the disposal of the unrighteous man so that the unrighteous man may become righteous in heart and thought and will and deed. Unless that be the gospel, there is no gospel. Paul affirms that was the gospel which he was going to Rome to preach.

Then we come to a phrase which is full of light. He tells us that this righteousness therein revealed, revealed in the gospel, is "by faith unto faith," in which phrase he tells us exactly how men receive this power. He has already told us that it is to everyone that believeth, then he gives us an exposition of that phrase. As he has given us an exposition of "salvation" as the revelation of righteousness of God at the disposal of men, so now he gives us an exposition of the phrase "every one that believeth" in the phrase "by faith unto faith."

The phrase is at once simple and difficult. There can be no question as to its structure. Taking the phrase as it stands, and looking at it grammatically apart from its context, it is evident that the second "faith" is resultant faith. The faith finally referred to grows out of the faith first referred to. "By faith unto faith." It is an almost surprising thing how successfully almost all expositors have hurriedly passed over this phrase. What did the Apostle mean? Did he mean that is an initial faith on the part of man which results in a yet firmer faith? That is possible, but there is another explanation. I believe the Apostle meant that the gospel reveals a righteousness which is at the disposal of sinning men by the faith of God unto the faith of man. The faith of God produces faith in man. The faith of God. Ought such a phrase be used of Him? Verily, if faith be certainty, confidence, and activity based on confidence. The faith of God is faith in Himself, in His Son, and in man. On the basis of God's faith in Himself, and on the basis of His faith in His Son, and on the basis of His faith in man, He places through His Son a righteousness at the disposal of man in spite of his sin. That faith of God becomes, when once it is apprehended, the inspiration of an answering faith in man. Inspired by God's faith I trust Him. I act in consonance with the faith that He has demonstrated in human history by sending His Son, and by all the provision of infinite grace.

I take my way back from this epistle and observe once more the Lord Jesus as He revealed God to me, and that is what He always did in dealing with sinning souls. He always reposed confidence in them in order to inspire their confidence in Himself. If Thou canst do anything, said one man to Him; If thou canst . . . ! All things are possible to him that believeth, was His answer. That was the Lord's declaration of His confidence in the possibility of the man who was face to face with the sense of his own appalling weakness. There are many yet more remarkable and outstanding illustrations in the New Testament. The Lord ever dealt with men on the basis of His confidence in them, in their possibility in spite of failure, always on condition that they would repose an answering confidence in Himself. A supreme illustration of this was afforded in the upper room on that last night when He was dealing with the disciples in the sight of His approaching departure. Mark most carefully His conversation with Peter. Peter, demanding to understand Him, in agony in the presence of the gathering clouds, said: Where art Thou going? Jesus replied: Whither I go ye cannot come now, but ye shall come hereafter. Again Peter asked: Why cannot I come now? I will follow Thee anywhere. I will die for Thee! Jesus replied: Wilt Thou die for me, Peter? Verily, verily, I say unto thee, the cock shall not crow, till thou hast denied Me thrice. Let not your heart be troubled: ye believe in God, believe also in Me. If I go away, I come again to receive you to Myself. I go to prepare a place for you.

Take out of that conversation its central value. It is Christ's confidence. He said to Peter, in effect: I know the worst that is in you, the forces that you have not yet discovered that within four-and-twenty hours will make you a denier, cursing and swearing. I know the worst, but if you will trust Me I will realize the best in you. I know the best in you. I shall have perfect confidence in you, provided you will have confidence in Me.

Let me take a superlative declaration. Whatever we think about humanity, Christ thought it worth dying for! He believed in it, in spite of its sin, in spite of its unutterable failure. When He confronted sinning souls He believed in them. He knew their incapacity. He knew that of themselves they could do nothing; but He knew also that in them was the very stuff out of which He could make saints who would flash and shine in light forever. In spite of the spoiling of sin, there was that in them with which He could deal. If I may borrow an awkward word from the old theologians, God believes in the *salvability* of all men. God puts righteousness at the disposal of man by faith in Himself, in His Son, and in the man at whose disposal He places it. If that once be seen, men respond to that faith of God by faith in Him.

Let us come away from the realm of argument into the realm of experience. All true Christian workers, men and women who know what it is really to get into close touch with sinning souls, and into grip with the spiritual life of men, have learned that the way to lift men back out of the slough of despond is to let them see that Christian workers believe in them. The way to lift any woman back again out of the degradation into which she has come is to show her you know she is capable of the higher and the nobler in the power of the gospel of Jesus Christ. "By faith unto faith." By faith a righteousness of God is revealed in the gospel. By the confidence which God reposes in Himself, and by the confidence He has in the possibility of every human life, He has placed righteousness at man's disposal through Christ. No man will ever avail himself of that except by faith. No man can appropriate the great provision save as he responds in faith to faith. As this faith of God in man is answered by the faith of man in God, then contact is made between the dynamic that is resident within Himself, and placed at the disposal of men by the mystery of His passion, and the weakness and incapacity of the human soul.

Such was the gospel of which Paul was not ashamed. Such is the gospel. The accuracy of the theory can be demonstrated only by results. That is the whole theme. I am here this evening to affirm once more—and I do it no longer as theory, I do it as an experience; I speak from this moment not merely as advocate, but as witness—that "the gospel . . . is the power of God unto salvation." However hard and severe the affirmation may seem at the moment, I am nevertheless constrained and compelled to affirm that if the gospel does not work, the failure is in the man, not in the gospel. If that be not true the whole Christian history is a lie. If that be true, then all the thousands and tens of thousands of human beings who for two millenniums have declared what the gospel has wrought in them have been woefully deceived, or have been most mysteriously perpetrating fraud throughout the centuries and millenniums. If it does not work, then that man who says that he has been delivered from besetting sin is a liar, and he is sinning in secret. Either this declaration is true, or the gospel is an awful deception, enabling men to hide secret sin. I pray you think again. If you have imagined that there is no dynamic in the gospel, think again, and examine your own life again, and find out whether or not you have fallen into line with the claims of the gospel and fulfilled its conditions. I assert that it is not enough that man shall hate his sin and cry out for help; he must put himself in line with the power that operates, he must fulfil the conditions laid down. It is not enough to submit to the Lord; a man must also resist the devil. It is not enough to resist the devil; a man must also submit to the Lord. There are men who submit and cry for help, but they put up no fight against temptations. They will never appropriate the power. There are men who put up a strenuous fight against temptations, but they never submit, never pray, never seek help. They will never find deliverance. "The gospel is the power of God unto salvation to every one that believeth." The gospel is that wherein the fact is revealed that righteousness as a power is at the disposal of a sinning man by God's faith in that man, inspiring man's faith in God. If men would discover the power of this gospel they will do so as they submit to its claim immediately and thoroughly.

If this were the time and place, as it is not, I could call witnesses. They are in this house: men who have known the very temptations delicately referred to in this letter, subtle, insidious temptations; but who also know that the gospel has meant to them power enabling them to do the things they fain would have done, but could not until they believed in this gospel.

I would like my last note in this address to be an appeal to any man who is face to face with this problem. My brother, God believes in you, and that in spite of all the worst there is in you. God knows the worst in you better than you know it yourself, yet He believes in you; and because He believes in your possibility He has provided righteousness in and through the Son of His love and by the mystery of His passion. I want you to respond to God's faith in you by putting your faith in Him, and demonstrating your faith by beginning with the next thing in obedience. You also will find that the gospel is the power of God, not theory, not inference, but a power that, coming into the life, realizes within the life and experience all the things of holiness and of righteousness and of high and eternal beauty.

CHAPTER XXIII

WINNING SOULS

He that is wise winneth souls.

PROVERBS 11:30.

THE SLIGHT DIFFERENCE BETWEEN THE AUTHORIZED VERSION and the Revised Version in the translation of this text suggests two different meanings. The Authorized Version reads, "He that winneth souls is wise," and that seems to mean quite simply that it is a wise thing to win souls. The Revised Version reads, "He that is wise winneth souls," and that seems to mean quite as simply that the condition for winning souls is wisdom; winning souls is a wise business; a man must be wise if he is to win souls. When the two ideas are thus suggested we realize that each translation may convey both meanings. The Authorized Version declares, "He that winneth souls is wise," that is, in himself and in his deed. The Revised Version reads, "He that is wise winneth souls," that is, wisdom is the condition for the work, and when that condition is fulfilled, the winning of souls is the inevitable issue. I feel, therefore, that we are justified in treating this text in both ways, as conveying both ideas. Whichever translation we take, whichever idea may appeal most strongly, we recognize that one subject is suggested, that of winning souls, whatever the declaration with regard to it may be. The declaration we shall treat as twofold; first, that wisdom is necessary to the work, and, second, that the accomplishment of the work is demonstration of wisdom.

Let these be the lines of our consideration: first, the subject referred to, winning souls; second, the wisdom which is necessary to do the work; and, third, the wisdom of the work done.

First, then, as to the winning of souls. The phrase is an old one. I do not mean merely by the fact of its presence in the Divine oracles, but by the fact of its use. I think we are compelled to admit that we do not hear so much about it now as some of us did in our boyhood days; but it is still being used, and is by no means unfamiliar to Christian people. Herein lies a difficulty, not insuperable, but quite definite; the difficulty of familiarity with a phrase, and the consequent difficulty of prejudice as to what the phrase may really mean. Here, therefore, we must clear our ground, or we may be lead into false speculations and certainly into misunderstandings of the enterprise which is suggested by this phrase of the Old Testament, a phrase illuminated, transfigured, and glorified by all the revelation contained in the New Testament.

What, then, is meant by winning souls? To proceed carefully with our investigation brings us immediately to another question, What are souls? When we have answered that, we may proceed to inquire, What is it to win them?

What, then, are souls? We have no right to take the word as it is in common use to-day and read into it either the interpretation of that common use, or the interpretation of our own conception of its meaning. We want to know what this man meant when he wrote the word. What did he mean by "souls"? I can answer the question only by looking carefully at the word and seeing its place in these Old Testament Scriptures. Let me immediately say, it is one of the commonest words to be found in these writings. Someone who has had the time to count tells us that the Hebrew word occurs 754 times in the writings of the Old Testament. Of those 754 times, the word is translated "souls" 472 times; on 282 occasions the Hebrew word is translated in forty ways, so that altogether the same Hebrew word is translated in forty-one ways. The predominating translation, however, is the one that we find in our text. If, then, this word was thus variously translated, and evidently as variously used, it is important that we discover its real intention. The word means simply a breathing creature. Its first occurrence, interestingly enough, is in the twenty-first verse of the first chapter of Genesis, which says that "God created the great sea-monsters, and every *living creature* that moveth," living creature meaning breathing creature. As I take my way through the Bible and observe its use, I discover that it became almost constantly and exclusively used of man himself. To take this Hebrew word *nephesh*, and trace it through the Old Testament and tabulate the results carefully, is to have a remarkable aid to the study of the psychology and theology of the ancient Hebrew people. It is used over and over again of man as a person, of man as a being whose existence is due to the fact of life. Thus the word does not refer to the spirit of a man alone, it does not refer to the mind of man only, and it certainly does not refer to the body of man alone; but the word in its common use excludes neither body nor mind, nor that which is essential, spirit; it includes all of them. "He that is wise winneth souls." Here the word "souls" does not mean the spiritual side of man's nature only, or the mental capacities of a man alone; certainly not his bodily powers only. It means the whole man, and man is not a disembodied spirit. The essential in man is spirit, but no man is man in his spiritual nature alone. This old-time writer, having much less of light and less understanding of the value of human life, and less understanding of God's estimate of the grandeur and glory of human life than we have to-day, said, "He that is wise winneth *men*"—using the word generically.

Now we may ask our second question, What is it to win men? Here again the word employed arrests us. I like the word "winneth" and yet there is a sense in which while certainly valuable as it reveals the best method of doing the work, it is not quite accurate as a revelation of the thought of the writer. "Winneth" is a very beautiful word, for it is by the note that woos and wins that men are most often helped; but the Hebrew word here is *to take, to catch*, and that in the widest variety of applications. Here again a little illumination may come to us if we remind ourselves of how this word is rendered in our versions. It is translated elsewhere, to accept, to bring, to buy, to draw, to infold. I would not be at all afraid of taking any one of these words and putting it into my text. He that is wise accepteth souls. He that is wise bringeth souls. He that is wise buyeth souls. He that is wise draweth souls. He that is wise infoldeth souls. That suggests all sorts of methods for doing the work, and every word seems to have some of the music of the gospel of the Lord and Saviour Jesus Christ, and some revelation of the beauty of His methods with men. But the simple meaning is, to take alive. We may get some New Testament light on this in the story of the miraculous draught of fishes (Luke 5: 1-11). Jesus said to Peter on that occasion, "From henceforth thou shalt catch men." That is exactly the thought of my text. "He that is wise catcheth men." Looking at the story in Luke again, I am constrained to say that our translation misses something. What did Jesus really say to Peter? "From henceforth thou shalt catch men alive." The value of what Jesus said did not consist in the similarity of the work these men were called to do, but in the disparity between the work they had been doing and what they would do henceforth. Henceforth you shall catch men alive. They had toiled all night and had not taken anything. Jesus instructed them where they should cast their net, and they cast it, and caught a great multitude of fish. When they caught those fish they took them from the element of life into that of death. Jesus said, Henceforth you shall catch men alive, that is, you shall do for men, the exact opposite to what you have been doing in the case of fish. Those fish you have brought from the element of their life to the element of death. You shall bring men from the element of death unto life. You shall catch men, take them alive; you shall lead them into life; you shall bring them to Me, and so bring them unto life; you shall buy them by putting out your own strength and energy in service and sacrifice to bring them into life; you shall draw them in your fellowship with Me from death unto life; you shall infold them in the bundle of life.

That is the real thought of my text. Let us go back to Proverbs and think of it as a whole. First of all, we have a series of parental discourses on wisdom by a father to his son, then a collection of proverbs made by Solomon during his lifetime, then a collection of proverbs made in the time of Hezekiah, finally, certain speeches by men unknown to us. The whole book is unified by its perpetual contrast of two ideals of life, two methods of life, two conditions in which men live: the way of wisdom and the way of folly, the way of righteousness and the way of wickedness, the way of godliness and the way of godlessness, the way of life and the way of death. In my contrasts I have introduced only one word that is not in the book of Proverbs, the word "Godlessness." All the rest are there, and that is plainly inferred. In the discourses on wisdom, and in the Proverbs these things are put into contrast: wisdom and folly, rightness and wickedness, godliness and godlessness, life and death. Right here, in the heart of the book, the preacher says, "He that is wise winneth souls," that is catcheth men, leading them from folly to wisdom, from wickedness to rightness, from godlessness to godliness, from death to life. This is also what Jesus said, "Henceforth you shall catch men alive," winning them from the element of death and bringing them into the element of life, wherein all the meaning of their personalities will be fulfilled to the uttermost. The work is winning, not spirits alone, not minds only, not bodies simply, but men.

I submit to you—broad, hurried, and necessarily brief as this outlook is on a great subject—that it is a great enterprise to win souls, to capture men and bring them from darkness into light, from death to life. It is a worthy enterprise, that is, it is worth while. There is no enterprise that confronts a man when he stands in the bloom of his young manhood that ought to appeal to him like this. There is no enterprise that presents itself to a girl in the beauty and freshness of her youth that ought to capture her dear heart like this. To win souls, to lead human beings out of darkness into light, out of death into life, out of paralysis and failure and heartbreak into power and victory and joy, is a worthy enterprise. I submit to you, it is an enterprise which brings more satisfaction and delight to the soul than any other. I say to you, my Christian brothers and sisters who have never yet given yourselves to this work, you do not yet know the joy of life. There is no joy in the world like the joy of seeing a broken, soiled, spoiled man or woman healed, cleansed, renewed; to observe the haunting fear in the eyes as first we saw them changed into dancing joy when they have come to Christ and to life. To win souls, to catch men, women, and children, to take them alive, out of the element of death into the element of life—that is a worthy enterprise, a satisfying enterprise, a delightful enterprise.

In his proverb the preacher said, "He that is wise winneth souls." What is the wisdom that is necessary for this enterprise, for doing this work? What did he mean by wisdom? All the book of Proverbs reveals what he meant. The other wisdom book, which came from the same pen, the book of Ecclesiastes, will show what he meant. The third wisdom book of the Old Testament, with which in all likelihood this man was familiar, for it is probably the most ancient of all the Old Testament books, the book of Job, will show what he meant. Wisdom, in the sense in which these books are designated wisdom books, meant simply what we mean by philosophy. In these books we find the philosophy of the Hebrew religion. There is a distinction between the philosophy as discovered to us in these wisdom books and all other philosophies which I will only mention now. The Hebrew philosophy began with the affirmation of God. All others begin with Pilate's question, "What is truth?" Do not misunderstand that passing illustration. I am not criticizing the method of the question, but reminding you that the Hebrew philosophers did not begin with that question. They affirmed God, and proceeded on the presupposition that God is all-wise, that wisdom could be perfectly predicated only of God, that apart from Him there is no wisdom, that in Him all wisdom dwells. From that presupposition they deduced their doctrine of human wisdom. I go back to the beginning of this wonderful book of Proverbs and find a definition. The preface is in the first seven verses of the first chapter; then the writer gives his definition of wisdom:

The fear of the Lord is the beginning of knowledge.

These Hebrew philosophers believed that wisdom in man was the result of man's right relationship to God. God is the fountain of all wisdom, and in proportion as man submits himself to His law and seeks His knowledge and His guidance and direction, in that proportion man is wise. I am inclined to say, in spite of all the centuries that have passed since these wisdom books were written, that it was a very sound philosophy.

I turn to the New Testament and I do not find that conception of wisdom altered. I do find it is illuminated, that a new light is breaking out, because there is a new revelation of God. In the letter to the Romans Paul comes to a point where he breaks out into a great doxology; "O the depth of the riches both of the wisdom and the knowledge of God! how unsearchable are His judgments, and His ways past tracing out!" That is the Hebrew conception of God as the All-wise, but it follows the great apostolic teaching concerning salvation. I turn from that to the Corinthian letter and I find the same man writing to people who are being darkened in understanding by false philosophies in the Corinthian city, and he tells them that God has chosen the foolish things of the world to bring to nought the wise things of the world, until at last he reaches the culmination of his teaching when he declares that Christ Jesus "was made unto us wisdom from God." Then he analyzes the wisdom, declaring it to be "both righteousness, and sanctification, and redemption."

Thus the New Testament doctrine of wisdom is that it exists in God, that man is wise only as he comes into right relationship with God, and that wisdom has manifested itself in a method by which men, blind and foolish and far away and in darkness, may see and return and be enabled. Paul declares that for humanity in its sin and shame the ultimate unveiling of the wisdom of God is in the redemption that He has provided for man in Christ Jesus.

Then I turn to James—the supremely ethical writer of the New Testament, whose very letter is saturated with the Sermon on the Mount, and with Proverbs and the wisdom books of the Old Testament—and I find that he gives us a description of what wisdom is when it is at work: "The wisdom that is from above is first pure, then peaceable, gentle, easy to be entreated, full of mercy and good fruits, without variance, without hypocrisy."

In this passage we have a perfect description of the man who wins souls. If, then, I am to be engaged in this great enterprise I must have the wisdom that cometh down from above. There is a wisdom, says James, that does not come down from above, it is earthly, sensual, devilish, and so he dismisses it. He then describes the wisdom that cometh down from above, and so shows us the wise man as God sees him. This is the man who is able to catch men and lead them from darkness to light. Let us then observe what James says about the wisdom that cometh from above, not in its widest applications, but with our minds fastened on this one subject of the capacity for winning souls. In this declaration three little words must be carefully observed which are not descriptive words but which mark a method: "*First*, pure, *then* peaceable, gentle, easy to be entreated, full of mercy and good fruits, *without* variance, without hypocrisy." My emphasis has brought out the words I ask you to observe: "First . . . then . . . without." "First," that which is fundamental in this wisdom; "then," the attitudes of mind that result; "without," the things that are excluded. What is fundamental? Purity. What are the things that result? "Peaceable, gentle, easy to be entreated, full of mercy and good fruits." What are the things that are excluded when this wisdom masters the life? "Variance, hypocrisy."

The first word needs no comment; the wise man must be "pure." Then the attitudes of mind. "Peaceable" means not merely that the wise man is in himself a man who loves peace, but that he is pacific, that he makes for peace. Immediately the word of Jesus comes to our minds, the word from the great Manifesto, "Blessed are the peacemakers." The next word, translated "gentle," really means patient. The next word, "easy to be entreated," is a great word and certainly admits of two interpretations. This translation is the interpretation of the revisers, and I do not agree with it. "Easy to be entreated," suggests a man who can be approached easily, but I believe it means more, it means persuasive. "Full of mercy," that is, full of compassion. "Full . . . of good fruits," that is, full of the very things these needy people are waiting for. All these things lie within wisdom. They may be remembered by simple alliteration: pure, pacific, patient, persuasive, potential. These are the very qualities that are necessary if we are to win men.

First, pure. I cannot win men from impurity to purity if I am impure. I cannot catch men from the element of death and bring them into life if I myself am abiding in the element of death. I cannot lure men to walk the sunlit path if I hug the place where shadows lie and the darkness is thick. "First, pure." The man who attracts other men to holiness is the pure man. The reason why many people are utterly incapacitated for winning souls is that within their life is harbored, permitted, entertained, something that is impure and unholy. First, pure.

Then peaceable, pacific, making peace. Then patient. Ah, me, how often much patience is needed for winning souls! How they disappoint us, how they break out again and again into the same old sins, and how we are tempted to say, We will wash our hands of them! Never! The wisdom that is from above never washes its hands of the most hopeless, failing souls. Love never faileth. Love is at the heart of the wisdom of God. Then persuasive, knowing how to deal with men so as to lead them to the light. Then potential, replete with compassion, which is the desire to give good fruits, which are the very gifts for which men wait.

This wisdom that is from above excludes *variance*. Here I deliberately go back to the Authorized Version, and prefer its rendering, "partiality." God is no respecter of persons, we are told. That is not so. He is a respecter of persons. The Bible does not say that He is not. The Bible says God is no respecter of faces, and the word was spoken to Jews, who thought that their very faces won them the respect of God! That quality of impartiality is necessary if we are to win souls. We so often have respect for faces; we do have hope of this man, but not of that other man. We look at certain people and come to the conclusion that they are not salvable. Such a conclusion is always a lie, a blasphemy. There is no man on whom Grace cannot work God's perfect will if he can be brought into right relationship therewith.

Again, without hypocrisy, that is, without pretense. In the mystery of the common human mind there is a most remarkable detection of any kind of hypocrisy or cant in a man who is trying to talk about religion. All our influence is killed if our attempt to draw a man to religion is mere pretense.

This is the wisdom that cometh down from above. This is the wisdom that is needed if we are to win men. This winning of souls is not a mechanical business which we can go to school to learn; it is not an easy arrangement which can be taken up by people when they have read a certain number of books dealing with the subject. The capacity for dealing with souls is that wisdom which cometh from above, which is, first, pure, then contains within itself these great and gracious qualities, and excludes partiality and hypocrisy. The capacity to win souls lies in life homed in the will of God, responsive to the grace of God, incarnating the very life of the Christ of God. "He that winneth souls is wise." "He that is wise winneth souls."

It seems to me that I need take no time with the third line of thought, save briefly to refer to it. I need not argue the wisdom of the work. Why is it wise to win souls? Because this satisfies God. God is against the spoiling of human lives and the wanderings of men into the paths that run out into pathlessness. Catch them, catch them alive, bring them back, turn them again into the way of peace, and God is gladdened. It is wise to win souls, for it satisfies God.

It is wise to win souls, for it glorifies man, and that in the true sense. Oh, the wasted wealth of humanity, the powers and capacities and potentialities blighted, spoiled, ruined! Oh, the agony of it! Win them, catch them, renew them! This is great, gracious, and glorious work. To see that which was out of the way turn into the way, that on which rested the cankerworm and the mildew and blight, breaking out into blossom and beauty and flowers and fruit. To see that man whose very face had become the awful sign manual of his lust being transformed into a man whose face is a revelation of the love of God. To see that girl whose eyes, naturally full of life and love, had become hard and scornful and devilish transformed, until from them flashes the glorious light of the eyes of Christ. It is great work, this! It is wise to win souls.

It is wise to win souls, moreover, because by winning souls we hasten the coming of the day of God.

Are we winning souls? Are we catching men? If not, why not? Is it that we have never seen the glory of the enterprise? Or is it that we lack the wisdom necessary? If it be that we have never been winners of souls because we have never seen the glory of the enterprise, then let us get near to Christ, really near to Him, spiritually near to Him. Resolutely forgetting and putting right out of our lives for one short hour all the influences of friends and others, and getting near to Him, and looking from His viewpoint, what shall we see? We shall see the extreme glory of humanity as we have never seen it. We shall see as He sees, that when God in the counsel of His great wisdom said, "Let us make man," He said a great thing. We shall see the consequent tragedy of human undoing as we have never seen it. The man who sees only the ruin of humanity has never seen the ruin of humanity. That man who is impressed only by the foolishness he finds in human nature does not know the tragedy of human undoing. But if behind the face bruised, marred, scarred, and battered, bloated, blasted, we can see the potential image of God, then we shall begin to know the tragedy of sin. Jesus looked through the mask (more than a mask), through the disfigurements of sin to the potential that lay behind. Thus He saw the tragedy of the leprosy. If we can see with Him, then the master passion of life will be to win souls, to have some share in the glorious enterprise of realizing the latent possibilities of humanity, in order to glorify that humanity and in order to glorify the God Who thought it and made it.

If we know the glory of the enterprise and fain would be winners of souls, but are conscious of our lack of the wisdom necessary, then let us return to an earlier word of James in this same letter: "If any of you lacketh wisdom, let him ask of God, Who giveth to all liberally and upbraideth not."

I lack the wisdom, God knows how I lack it, and how I feel I lack it, the wisdom that is first pure, then peaceable, pacific, patient, persuasive, potential, and without partiality or pretense. I lack it, but I am going to ask for it, and when I do so, ashamed that I am so lacking, He does not upbraid me, and He will give it. I, even I, can have it! I can have this wisdom. I also may become a winner of souls.

Shall we not presently get away somewhere quietly and put ourselves at His disposal, that in the power of the wisdom that cometh from above we may share the high and holy enterprise?

CHAPTER XXIV

BE STRONG—AND WORK!

Be strong . . . saith the Lord . . . and work: for I am with you, saith the Lord of hosts.

HAGGAI 2:4.

THESE WORDS WERE UTTERED ABOUT TWO THOUSAND FIVE hundred years ago, yet they come to us and to our day with a pertinence which is almost startling. This is not surprising, for our times have much in common with those of the old Hebrew prophets. There are certain senses—the statement must be made guardedly, and received guardedly—in which the prophetic writings make a profounder appeal to us than do the apostolic writings. Men to-day *know* so much more than they *do*, with the result that they begin to question the things they know. That was the condition in the time of the prophets. Therefore these prophetic writings are powerful in the conditions addressed, in the principles recognized, and in the appeals made. So from this ancient writing we take out these words and find that they are living and powerful words, coming to us not faint and far from that Eastern land and that bygone time, but with an immediateness that gives us to feel they are verily the word of the Lord to us.

In the book of Ezra we have the account of the laying of the stones of the second temple. A decree forbidding the work having been obtained from Artaxerxes, for fifteen years the house of God lay waste, with that almost appalling aspect of desolation, not of a structure battered and bruised and beaten, and in some senses made beautiful by the tempests and time, but of a structure commenced and never finished. At the death of the king this edict lost its authority, but the people did not proceed with the building, urging difficulty, danger, and poverty as reasons. Yet all the while neither danger nor difficulty nor poverty prevented them from building their own houses, and cieled houses withal, houses of beauty and luxury. To such a people the messages of Haggai came, and this brief prophecy of only two chapters tells the story of how he delivered these four prophecies in conjunction with Zechariah, and how the people arose and built the house of the Lord.

In our text three things are found with which I propose to deal: first, the need revealed by the command to "work"; second, the responsibility resting on the people in view of the need; finally, the encouragement which was given to them in order that they might take up that responsibility and meet that need. The need was to build the house of God. The responsibility was that they should be strong and work. The encouragement was the promise and covenant which God made with them: "I am with you, saith the Lord of hosts."

The house of God has been neglected. We can imagine men saying: Why build this house? Why not wait? Why not leave the building to our children? The question was answered by the prophesyings of Haggai and Zechariah. One supreme answer was given to all such inquiry. It was the answer of the final, fundamental fact of all human life, the fact of God. In one of his sermons at our Mundesley Bible Conference my friend John A. Hutton said something which those of us who heard him will never forget, and said it in such a way that we shall never forget. Speaking of the spies who went out to spy out the land of Canaan and afterwards described themselves as grasshoppers, Mr. Hutton said that those men thought they were looking at the facts of the case, but that they were not looking at facts, but looking at circumstances; and he declared that there is but one Fact, and that is God. All other things are circumstances related to that Fact. That is the underlying truth which made necessary the building of the house of God in that bygone age. God is the age-abiding Fact, the ever and everywhere present Fact, and men who forget Him are leaving out of their calculations the supreme quantity, and therefore their findings are inevitably doomed to be wrong. A science that forgets God is blind, seeing only that which is near, and at last boasting itself that it has no interest in anything that is far. The philosophy that excludes God is equally incomplete, and therefore incompetent. Science starts with emptiness of mind, a perfectly proper attitude. Philosophy starts with a question, What is truth? a perfectly fair method of operation. But science proceeding to the discovery of the facts will inevitably finally touch God. The question is whether it will dare to call Him God when it finds Him? Philosophy attempting to account for things and to give us the true wisdom of life must take God into account. The question is whether it will ultimately do so or not. The one fact from which there is no escape is the fact of God. God is not distanced from human life. In Him we live and move and have our being. God is not uninterested in human life. If the great revelation of these sacred writings is to be trusted, there is absolutely nothing in which God is not interested. In passing, let me urge very seriously those of you who have not been reading the Old Testament recently to read it once more, without prejudice, simply to see it as revealing God's interest in the common things of life, the commonplaces of life. It is the Old Testament that teaches you that God puts human tears into His bottle. It is the Old Testament that tells that God knows whether the garment you wear is a mixture of wool and something else or not. The Old Testament tells us that God is interested in the fringes that people wear on their garments. Trivial things, you say. That is our God! He is the

God of the infinitely small as well as of the infinitely great, not alienated from any part of human life, knowing our downsitting and our uprising, our going out and our coming in; near to us in the casual as well as in the critical, numbering the hairs of our head. That is the supreme fact of life, and the fact from which there can be no escape.

> Whither shall I go from Thy Spirit?
> Or whither shall I flee from Thy presence?
> If I ascend up into heaven, Thou art there:
> If I make my bed in Sheol, behold, Thou art there.

What unutterable folly, then, on the part of humanity or of man if it or he leaves God out of calculation.

Because God is the final and fundamental fact in human life, therefore He is the supreme obligation. To do His will is individual salvation, is social salvation, is national salvation. One human life perfectly poised toward God and adjusted toward His good and perfect and beneficent will is a human life realized, fulfilled, and progressively glorious. A society, which the Church of God ought to be, discovering His will, walking in the way of it, obedient to the light that ever shines more and more unto the perfect day, is a society within the boundaries of which there is no lonely soul, for when one weeps, all weep; when one laughs, all laugh. A nation seeking righteousness rather than revenue, eager to glorify God rather than to maintain its face in the world, is a nation great, secure, impregnable, mighty with essential might.

The supreme obligation on human life is its relationship to God, therefore it is important to build His house. In the days in which Haggai exercised his ministry the building of the house was entirely material. The house was the true rallying point for the people, the place of worship, the place where men gathering together did not seek the presence of God, but remembered His presence, recognized His power, reminded their own hearts anew of the abiding fact of His covenant with them and of His perpetual care of them. Moreover, in that ancient Hebrew economy, the house of God was essentially the house of prayer for all nations, as our Lord Himself did say in the days of His flesh, quoting from the ancient prophecies. Then how supremely important it was that the house should be built. There, for fifteen years, having been raised but a few feet in all probability from the ground, the first few courses laid, it had stood desolate, overgrown with verdure, moss-covered, a perpetual revelation of the fact that people who bore the name of God had largely forgotten Him. The supreme need in that hour was not the rearrangement of policy with surrounding nations, not the rediscovery of a lost art, not increase in commerce; the supreme necessity was that the house of God should be built, the sacramental symbol of the nation's relationship to Him.

To-day the house of God is no longer material; it is living, it is spiritual, it is the Church of God, the Church of God which is the house of the living God. In this world of ours the Church of God in the Divine economy is an institute of praise and prayer and prophecy. An institute of praise, a living temple of living souls whose eyes are toward the light, whose faces are irradiated with joy, who are living in the midst of the sorrows and desolations of time as men and women who have found mastery over sorrow and desolation in their fellowship with the unseen and eternal. That is true of the Catholic Church, the whole Church, and in that function of the Church all the things that divide us cease to be, and we realize that the building of the Church of God is of supreme importance in order that there may be maintained in the midst of the sorrows and sins of humanity a living testimony to the gladness and holiness which are possible to men as they live in right relationship with God. Nothing, therefore, can be more important than this building of the Church, the building of it stone upon stone, of living stones brought into touch with the Living Stone, Whose preciousness is made over to them that they may share that preciousness and bear testimony in their glad, pure, consenting life to what the Kingdom of God really means in the world.

Whereas the house of God to-day is no longer material but spiritual, the material is still a very real symbol of the spiritual. When the Church of God in any place in any locality is careless about the material place of assembly, the place of its worship and its work, it is a sign and evidence that its life is at a low ebb.

Let us not, however, lose sight of the larger matter, the necessity for the continuation of the building of the spiritual house of God. There is nothing this nation needs more than that the Church of God itself should be more clearly seen. Therefore there is no work more important than that of the continuity of the building of that spiritual house which, in the life of the nation, is not to be dictated to by the nation, but to exercise its threefold function of praise, prayer, and prophecy, and so contribute to the true essential strength of the national life.

These words spoken in the olden days by the prophet indicated, not only the need, but the responsibility. The spiritual value of this old-time story is here most marked, most definite. These people were to "be strong"; that is the first thing. And they were to "work"; that was the second. These two things cannot be separated. There can be no work apart from strength; there can be no strength, such as the prophet referred to, which does not express itself in work. "Be strong . . . and work."

This charge to the people was a suggestion of their weakness, the weakness that had prevented, and still was preventing, them from building the house of God. We discover the elements of the weakness in the most simple way by looking at the prophecy. In the first place their weakness consisted in the fact that they were careless about this matter. They said: "It is not the time for us to come, the time for the Lord's houses to be built." That is so startlingly modern that I hardly know what to say about it. It is not the time! The modern man will not speak so simply; the modern man will say that it is not the psychological moment. That means the same thing. Whenever, in the presence of superabounding need, man says, It is not the psychological moment, know well that the cleverness of his argument is revelation of the carelessness of his heart. The time is not come; we are waiting for the time, for some moment electric with inspirational opportunity. People who wait for that moment never find it, and do not want to find it.

Another element of weakness to which the prophet drew attention is revealed in the question he asked: "Is it a time for you yourselves to dwell in your cieled houses, while this house lieth waste?" The second element of weakness in the life of the people was luxury and comfort; they were dwelling in their own cieled houses, and perchance discussing ever and anon in their social gatherings the neglected condition of the house of God. The set time had not come to build it; but the time had come to build their own houses, and to ciel them with beauty.

There was yet another element of weakness. We discover it by another question: "Who is left among you that saw this house in its former glory? And how do ye see it now? Is it not in your eyes as nothing?" The third element of weakness was contempt for that very house which lay unfinished, and contempt for any man who suggested that it ever could be restored to its ancient glory. This contempt was born of a great past, of which the people were always talking, and in which they rejoiced, to the neglect of the present, with its terrific responsibility and its glorious opportunity. The collateral writings to this prophecy reveal some of the reasons for the contempt. The sacred fire was no longer burning, the shekinah glory was no longer manifested, the ark and the cherubim were no longer in their places, the urim and the thummim had been lost, and the spirit of prophecy was silent. All these things were absent. The people looked back to the days when these things were there in all their glory, and they held the present in supreme contempt, both as to its conditions and as to the idea that it was possible to restore the lost glory.

I say again, the picture is wonderfully modern. We still have the carelessness which says, The time has not come. It expresses itself often in prayer for revival. The revival is here, if we will but have it so. I pray you talk no more about the indifference of the nation; talk if you will of the indifference of the Church to its own evangel, its own gospel, its own living powers. The set time has not come, so men still say.

Then there is the weakness resulting from comfort. The Church of God to-day is suffering from material prosperity within her own borders. Things which our fathers spoke of as luxuries we speak of as necessities. For all spiritual service we are being rendered weak, anemic, enervated by the cieled houses and the comforts of our lives. The old Spartan heroism of our fathers, the simpler life, and the great poverty, have largely passed away. It is not the time to build the house of God, but it is the time to build our own cieled houses and dwell in them.

Another element of weakness present with us is our perpetual looking back and sighing for departed glories, for the voices of preachers of other days, for the prayer meetings that once were held, for all those peculiar manifestations of the presence of God in past days. The old men are sighing for these, and looking with contempt on the present hour, disbelieving in the possibility of revival and the building of the house of God.

Said the prophet to these men, and now says the word of

our God to us, "Be strong." If we would know what our strength is we may know it by examining our weakness. Over against every element of weakness we are to place an element of strength. Over against carelessness what shall we put? Listen to the voice of the prophet. "Consider your ways. Ye have sown much, and bring in little; ye eat, but ye have not enough; ye drink, but ye are not filled with drink; ye clothe you, but there is none warm; and he that earneth wages earneth wages to put it into a bag with holes. Thus saith the Lord of hosts: Consider your ways." One of the first conditions of real strength will be obedience to that command, the consideration of our ways. The people were living in cieled houses, in great material prosperity. But look more carefully: "Ye have sown much, and bring in little." But they had brought in very much, they were wealthy! "Ye eat, but ye have not enough"; but they always had enough to eat! "Ye drink, but ye are not filled with drink." But they always had enough to drink! "Ye clothe you, but there is none warm." But they always had plenty of clothing! "He that earneth wages earneth wages to put it into a bag with holes." But they had not discovered the holes! Mark the satire of it all. The prophet was declaring that in spite of all their getting they lacked the supreme possession; in spite of all their eating, there was hunger never satisfied; in spite of all their drinking, there was thirst never quenched; in spite of all their clothing, there was chilliness of soul that found no warmth; in spite of all their earning, there was a lack which nothing out of the bag into which they put their wages could provide! How true it all is to-day! The consideration of our ways is, indeed, the first necessity if we would be strong.

The second element of strength under such conditions was consciousness of the weakness of the house of God in its ruin, its devastation, of the fact that it stood there unfinished. Twice over the prophet said with infinite pathos: "This house lieth waste." I wonder when the one hundred and second psalm was written. It seems to me it must have been at a time in connection with this exhortation, or else the prophet was remembering it:

Thou shalt arise, and have mercy upon Zion;
For it is time to have pity upon her, yea, the set time is come.

How did the psalmist know the set time had come? what was the sign for the arrival of the set time?

> For thy servants take pleasure in her stones,
> And have pity upon her dust.

In that hour, when these men really looked at the ruins, and the ruins entered into their heart and created great contrition, the set time came; they were then beginning to feel the element of strength.

Yet one other element of strength is revealed in the story. It is confidence in the promise and power of God: "I will fill this house with glory, saith the Lord of hosts. . . . The latter glory of this house shall be greater than the former, saith the Lord of hosts: and in this place will I give peace, saith the Lord of hosts." When they believed that, they arose and built.

The second part of the responsibility is revealed in the words: "and work." Work was to be opposed to idleness. That needs no argument. Work was to take the place of theorizing. I think that needs, if not argument, at least careful consideration. Far be it from me to speak with disrespect of efforts that may be in themselves most sincere; but sometimes I am appalled at the time we waste in considering things and theorizing about things, calling conferences to consider the situation, attempting, on the one hand, to express Christianity in terms suited to the modern mind forsooth, as though the modern mind mattered; and, on the other hand, to consider the difficulty of the situation.

"Work" is the word of the Lord to us. We cannot travel a hundred yards from this place without finding some opportunity, if our eyes are open, to build the house of God by the capture of a soul, by a kindness, by a word of love, by a ministry of immediate help. In the work of building the house of God nothing is mean; the whole glorifies every part. That least thing you are doing, apparently so unimportant, is of supreme importance when you place it in relationship to the whole.

The last note of the text from the ancient prophecy is one full of encouragement. The prophet not merely drew attention to the need, not merely called to strength and to work; but in the name of God spoke to them this word of God: "I am with you, saith the Lord of hosts." Therefore, the things missing did not signify. These things also might be restored, the very things over which men were lamenting.

All this is most immediate and pertinent. "I am with you, saith the Lord of hosts." There is no need for us to gather together and pray for the coming of the Holy Spirit. There is no need for us to cry in our agony, "Awake, awake, put on strength, O arm of the Lord." They did that also in the days of Isaiah, and God answered them: "Awake, awake, put on thy strength, O Zion." If I may reverently say so, it is as though God had said, Why do you call on Me to awake? I have never been asleep! It is you who are asleep. When today we gather together to pray to God to come among us it seems to me He would say, I am with you, even though you are unmindful of Me; even though you are not responsive to Me, I am with you. If we can but come to a new realization of that living presence and know that we have not to ask or wait for His coming, but that He is here waiting for us, then we shall arise and build. It is not true to say we need more of the Holy Spirit, but it is true to say that the Holy Spirit needs more of us. In that realization of the nearness of our God we shall find strength for all He is calling us to do.

The prophet named God by one of the great titles of the Old Testament, "The Lord of hosts." He is the Lord of all hosts. He is the Lord of His people who are called to work; He is Lord of the enemies who would attempt to prevent them from working, making the wrath of men to praise Him. "If God be for us, who can be against us?" He is the Lord, not merely of the hosts of the earth, but of the hosts of heaven also, the hosts of the spiritual world. He is Lord of all angels, all unfallen ones, and of the spirits of just men made perfect. Angels, and the spirits of the just made perfect under His dominion are filled with praise of Him and inspired by His love, and in some strange mystery which we may not understand are co-operative with His purpose even now. How many of us need the vision that was given to the young man with the prophet of old? Said he, "Behold, an host with horses and chariots was round about the city. . . . Alas, my master! how shall we do?" And the prophet said, "Lord, I pray Thee, open his eyes, that he may see." And the Lord opened the eyes of the young man, and he saw; and, behold, the mountain was full of horses and chariots of fire.

> So to Faith's enlightened sight
> All the mountain flamed with light!

He is also the Lord of the fallen ones. When He was incarnate, how often they cried out to Him: "What is there between Thee and us, Thou Jesus of Nazareth? Art Thou come to destroy us? I know Thee Who Thou art, the Holy One of God." Then came the answer of the One of supreme authority and almighty power: "Hold thy peace, and come out of him." All the spiritual forces of the spiritual world against us are held in check by the power of God; or to put it as I have so often put it here, for I love the truth, I joy in it: Satan cannot touch a single hair on the back of one of Job's camels until he has asked permission of God. If what the nation and the world supremely need is the building of the house of God, what the Church supremely needs is a new vision of God, a new consciousness of His nearness.

> Hell is nigh, but God is nigher,
> Circling us with hosts of fire!

The Lord and Master said to His disciples ere He left them, "Lo, I am with you all the days." In the lonely island washed by the waters of the sea John heard a voice, and the voice said: "I am the Alpha and the Omega, saith the Lord God, which is, and which was, and which is to come, the Almighty." Then he "turned to see the voice which spake," and this is what he saw: "I saw seven golden candlesticks; and in the midst of the candlesticks one like unto a son of man, clothed with a garment down to the foot, and girt about at the breast with a golden girdle. And his head and his hair were white as white wool, white as snow; and his eyes were as a flame of fire; and his feet like unto burnished brass, as if it had been refined in a furnace; and his voice as the voice of many waters."

That was the last appearing of God to man, figurative, symbolic, suggestive, and that to help us to understand Him when He says, "I am with you all the days."

The command and the promise were alike enforced by the words, "Thus saith the Lord." "Be strong . . . saith the Lord . . . and work; for I am with you, saith the Lord of hosts." That is overwhelming in compulsion and confidence. The story has often been told of Livingstone. When all alone, hemmed in by hostile tribesmen, waiting apparently for death, he wrote:

> I read that Jesus said, "All power is given unto Me in heaven and earth. Go ye therefore, and teach all nations . . . and, lo, I am with you always, even unto the end of the world."

Then follow these significant words:

> It is the word of a gentleman of most sacred and strictest honor, and there's an end on't. I will not cross furtively by night as I had intended. It would appear as flight, and shall

such a man as I flee? Nay, verily I will take observations for latitude and longitude to-night, though they may be the last.

When the morrow came he crossed without harm from the midst of hostile multitudes.

With all reverence, may we not say, as God says to us, "Be strong . . . and work; for I am with you"? "It is the word of a gentleman of most sacred and strictest honor, and there's an end on't." So God help us:

> To the work! To the work! We are servants of God,
> Let us follow the path that our Master has trod;
> With the balm of His counsel our strength to renew,
> Let us do with our might what our hands find to do.

CHAPTER XXV

THE WAY TO THE ALTAR

If, therefore, thou art offering thy gift at the altar, and there rememberest that thy brother hath aught against thee, leave there thy gift before the altar, and go thy way; first be reconciled to thy brother, and then come and offer thy gift.

MATTHEW 5:23, 24.

THESE WORDS ARE FOUND IN THE MANIFESTO OF THE KING, and constitute part of the section safeguarding the sacredness of human life. After the enunciation of fundamental principles of character and influence, and the value of law in itself, that Manifesto contains the new laws of the Kingdom conditioning earthly and heavenly relationships. The laws of earthly relationships deal first with the foundations of society, forbidding murder and adultery; then with the pillars of society, insisting on truth and justice.

The sacredness of human life is recognized, and murder is forbidden. The method of the King in the enunciation of His ethic was to put His own commandment into contrast with that of the old economy, not abrogating it, but fulfilling it. In the old economy the word of the law, definitely, sternly, simply, forbade the act of taking life: "Thou shalt do no murder." The new prevents the act by dealing with the mental attitudes which precede it. The King warned the subjects of the Kingdom against anger, for in that there is peril. Anger in the sense of intense displeasure may not meditate revenge at the moment, but it would rejoice if the one against whom it proceeds were to suffer. Yet sterner words fell from the King's lips in condemning contempt: "Whosoever shall say to his brother, Raca," the supreme term of contempt, "shall be in danger of the council," that is, citation before the whole Sanhedrin. But if a man shall say to his brother, "Thou fool," the language of malice, of insult with intention to wound, then the only fit punishment for such as he is that he be taken outside the city walls and cast into Gehenna, the place of refuse and of burning in order to destroy it. The severity of the ethic is apparent. Yet the tenderness of the ethic is equally apparent. Under the old law the sinner is arrested red-handed. Under the new law he is arrested because of those attitudes of the soul which, unless they be held in check, canceled, made not to be, may eventuate in the act of murder. All this is tremendously searching, but the matter is not done with. Our Lord did not end at that point. This preliminary survey has been necessary in order that we may find the atmosphere of our text.

Let me ask you now carefully to observe in this text the word "therefore." "If, *therefore*, thou art offering thy gift at the altar . . ." It would be manifestly unfair to take this text without recognizing its relationship to all that has gone before. It is impossible to read any text which is ushered in by the word "therefore" without inquiring, Wherefore? What, then, is the simple meaning of the text in its first application? Because these mental moods of anger and contempt and malice are forbidden, *therefore*, if any man has given his brother occasion for such moods he is to act at once so as to remove them. If thou art angry with thy brother, thou art in danger of judgment; if thou shalt say to him, Raca, in contempt, thou art in danger of judgment before a higher tribunal; if thou shalt say to him, Thou fool, thou art refuse socially, fit only for destruction. Then turning to the brother man, Jesus said: Therefore, if when thou art coming to the altar thou rememberest thy brother has something against thee which may inspire a feeling of anger, contempt, or malice in his breast, go and be reconciled to him, not for thy sake only, but for his sake, lest he become guilty of sin. That is the first application of the text. We shall return to it in the course of our meditation.

Realizing this to be the first application, we may consider its wider reaches as they include the subject of restitution and reparation in their relation to our acceptance with God.

We shall observe three things in these words of Jesus: first, a supposition, "If, therefore, thou art offering thy gift at the altar and there rememberest . . ." Second, the clear, definite, imperative command of the Lord: "Leave there thy gift before the altar, and go thy way, first be reconciled to thy brother." Thirdly, and finally, the gracious, ultimate welcome: "Then come and offer thy gift."

In dealing, first of all, with the supposition I desire to remark that this was not a doubtful hypothesis; it was the recognition by our Lord of a fact not only generally experienced, but always experienced. Approach to the altar of God always quickens the activity of conscience: "If, therefore, thou art offering thy gift at the altar, and there rememberest that thy brother hath aught against thee . . ."

Let us think of this a little carefully. First, it is interesting to note our Lord's references to the altar. He never referred to the altar except here and on one other occasion, so far as the records reveal. The other occasion is found, interestingly enough, in the twenty-third chapter of Matthew, wherein is chronicled that last terrific address of His in Jerusalem. Here we have the Manifesto introduced by beatitudes, "Blessed . . ."; there, in the last address, we have denunciation, with ringing, thrilling thunder, "Woe . . . Woe . . . Woe . . ." In that first Manifesto, and in that last denunciation, our Lord referred to the altar. It is quite evident that He was making reference to an existing order and that the men who heard Him knew exactly what He meant. The whole religious symbolism of Hebraism was present to their minds. The picture suggested is the common one of a Hebrew man coming to the altar of God, bringing a gift. It will readily be admitted further that if our Lord made reference to the existing order He did so in harmony with the highest, deepest, spiritual intention of that order. It was not a mere passing reference to that which was external, spiritual, formal; it was a reference to that which was internal, spiritual, dynamic, to that true coming of man to the act and attitude of worship which was symbolized by the altar. The reason for reading as part of our lesson the passage from the Old Testament in which we find the first instructions ever given to the Hebrew people concerning the altar will immediately be seen. It is important to remember that those first instructions concerning the altar were given immediately after the enunciation of the decalogue containing the inclusive words of the law. After they had been pronounced, the people besought Moses that they should hear the voice of God no more, but that he alone should speak to them, so filled were they with fear. In answer to that request Moses declared that there was no cause for fear, that the purpose of God was good and gracious. Immediately following that, these simple instructions concerning the making of the altar were given. If an altar was made it must be of earth; or if of stone, of unhewn stone. It was to have no steps. All this was primitive and simple, but suggestive of tremendous spiritual necessities and principles. By the altar men were to be for ever reminded that their approach to God was not on the basis of their own ability or righteousness or cleverness. The altar must be of earth, the commonest material, or of unhewn stone, so that man should not glory in that by which he approached God which was of his own creation. There were to be no steps for the ascent to the altar of God—and mark the word—"that thy nakedness be not discovered thereon," a word unveiling the spiritual fact that if a man climb to an altar for his approach to God he reveals his nakedness and unpreparedness for approach. The altar suggested approach to God by man, and more, approach to man by God, for "in every place where I record My name I will come unto thee and I will bless thee."

The altar, moreover, was the place of sacrifice. Man approaching the altar was coming to God always recognizing, even though he might not be able to explain, the mystery of the whole fact, the necessity for approach by the way of sacrifice. We know how far these people wandered from spiritual comprehension, and remember how in the day of Christ they were almost blind to spiritual values; but when our Lord referred to the altar He was not a ritualist, He was not a formalist, He was referring to all that the altar stood for; man drawing near to God by the way of sacrifice. When He uttered the great word of the Manifesto, He already knew that the time would come when under the constraint of the Spirit, an inspired writer would write, "We have an altar"; that in Himself the way of fellowship was being provided, all the foreshadowed values were being fulfilled; that in Him man would find his way to God, as in Him God had found His way to man. In His Person and through His mission,

> Grace comes down our souls to greet,
> While glory crowns the Mercy-Seat!

With all this in mind, we listen to the supposition of the Lord. Coming to the altar is approach to God. Coming to the altar is coming to the hour and place of worship. Coming to the altar is finding our way into fellowship with God by means of mediation and sacrifice. Coming to the altar is the recognition of the sovereignty of God, of the supremacy of His will. Without any further argument, it is perfectly evident that coming to the altar produces recollection of any violation of that will. No man ever seriously draws near to the altar without remembering.

This is invariable, and it is inevitable. Let it be borne in mind that the wrong done, to whomsoever it was done, whensoever it was done, is fixed in the mind of the man who did it. There are forgotten things that are not forgotten. They are forgotten, I am not conscious of them now; but they are not forgotten, they are hidden away in my mind, covered over by other things. Some of you remember how Scott in *Guy Mannering*, in a very quaint way, refers to the disorderliness of some minds. He says that Dominie Sampson's mind was like "the magazine of a pawnbroker, stowed with goods of every description, but so cumbrously piled together, and in such total disorganization, that the owner can never lay his hands on any article at the moment he has occasion for it." There are minds like that. However orderly our minds may be, there are things buried away in it of which we are not conscious at the moment; but they are there. There is a little expression we often use in conversation and public speech: "Call to mind"; we all know the possibility of calling to mind. No wrong we have committed have we really forgotten; it is there, covered over, much to our own ease, guilty ease, perilous ease, dangerous ease; but it is there. When we approach the altar we remember. There is no need to go far for illustration. Thank God, we do not know each other's secrets, and thank God we need not unveil them to any human being; but in this very hour we have been remembering. One of Watts' greatest pictures is called "The Dweller in the Innermost." It is a representation of conscience, with a star on her forehead, with a trumpet and arrows lying on her knees. The outstanding wonder of the picture is the green, fiery eyes. Yes, but we forget her. We are unconscious of her eyes, and we do not hear her voice, and the trumpet and the arrows seem forevermore to lie on her lap. But when we approach the altar, she looks, and her glance searches us; she speaks, and with trumpet tongue; she acts, and those "arrows are sharp . . . in the heart of the King's enemies." The dweller in the innermost is awakened when we draw near to the altar. This word of Jesus was not a rhetorical allusion, it was the recognition of a psychological activity of which everyone who really knows what it is to draw near to the altar of God is conscious. When men first come to the altar of God they remember sins of the past; and in every subsequent approach, if wrongs have been done, they are remembered. It is so whether we will or not. "O Lord, Thou hast searched me, and known me." It is desirable that it should be so, and if we really know our own hearts, the mystery of them, and the meaning of sin in its vileness and poison and power, then we shall cry out as did the psalmist:

> Search me, O God, and know my heart;
> Try me, and know my thoughts;
> And see if there be any way of wickedness in me.

The supposition being considered, let us hear what the Lord says to a man in that moment when approaching the altar of God he remembers. "Leave there thy gift before the altar, and go thy way, first be reconciled to thy brother." That is the command. We may express all that the command means by saying that the activity of conscience which results from the approach to the altar must be the inspiration of immediate action. Observe with great care what is meant by these words. By them our Lord has revealed the fact that the altar never condones or cloaks sin. The altar is the way to purity, not an excuse for impurity. The intention of the altar is to loose from sin, not to hide it. If for a single moment we imagine that in our coming to Christ we come that sin may be hidden, we do not understand the meaning of Christ's mission.

The altar calls on man to co-operate with God to the utmost of his ability in this moral restoration. The very first value of the altar is that it reminds a man of his sin. The very first value of Christian worship is that it starts the activity of conscience, and compels men to think of the actuality of sin. The first value of Christ's presence in the world is not forgiveness, but conviction. In His presence men know sin. When men come toward God through Him they discover sin. One of the last things of religious and social significance that W. E. Gladstone said was that our age was suffering from a lowered sense of sin. I do not know what he would have said had he lived to-day! We often mourn that men seem to have no consciousness of sin. We are under the spell of certain pseudo-scientific attempts to deal with religion. When a modern scientist tells us that the intelligent man does not think about sin it is a most unintelligent statement. The intelligent man faces every fact of life, and sin is a fact from which there can be no escape. I say that the first value of man's presence before Christ is that he will know himself a sinner. Coming to the altar—for "we have an altar"—we remember the things of wrong, the things of evil.

A consequent value of the altar is that it absolutely refuses to harbor the man who is not prepared to co-operate to the utmost of his ability with God for his own moral restoration. "Leave there thy gift before the altar, and go thy way, first be reconciled to thy brother."

What, then, we inquire carefully and with solemnity, is man's utmost? What can a man do in this hour when conscience is awakened, when his whole life is suddenly arraigned before the penetrating awfulness of the eyes of his own conscience? He can do the thing he knows. That of which conscience has just spoken to him indicates his immediate and only responsibility. That one thing demands immediate action. Go to thy brother directly, immediately, without hesitation, crucifying pride; and, looking into his eyes, be reconciled to him. The one thing that conscience speaks of must be dealt with.

Look, I pray you, at the spiritual significance of all this. The man is seen leaving his gift, and leaving the altar. Geographically, he is traveling from it; but the near way to all the values of the altar is that journey on which he goes to find his brother. He is leaving the altar only geographically; all the while the altar holds him to its own spirit and intention, brings him near to the God Whom he is seeking, and leads him along the pathway that eventuates in purity. The journey away is the near way to the altar.

The limits of responsibility are set further out than we generally think. That which man seeks as he seeks his brother is not his own peace of mind, but saving his brother from those attitudes of mind, anger, contempt, malice, which may make his brother sin. No deeper social note is found in all the teaching of Jesus than this. Why am I to co-operate with God for my own moral restoration? Not alone for my own heart's ease and quietness, but because I am involving the man I have wronged, not by the wrong I have done him, but by the wrong he may do himself if he become angry, contemptuous, malicious toward me. Every journey from the altar that leads back to the altar is a journey to serve someone else and save him. So has God bound us up in the bundle of life. "None of us liveth unto himself"; each one lives unto his brother. Therefore, because the law in the Kingdom is stern, forbidding anger, contempt, malice, therefore take this journey and find thy brother.

The limitations are entirely reasonable. We are to deal with that which is remembered between ourselves and the man we have wronged. I am to go straight away to him; there is to be a meeting between two; I am to make my confession to him, and such restitution as I am able to make, such reparation as lies within my power. Somehow, I am to find my way into his heart.

There are other teachings of our Lord which would warrant us in saying that if that man will not receive me I am not to blame; the Lord will deal with him. But have you ever thought how remarkably rare a thing it is for any human being to refuse to forgive? Sometimes we hear of such refusal, most often in novels, but sometimes also in actual life. Alas and alas! I have known such cases, but they are rare. I have often been amazed to find how a bad man, to whom another confesses sin and asks pardon, is ready to forgive and blot it out. In any case our responsibility ends at that point, and in that direction lies easement from morbid and unworthy regrets.

If I am speaking to some individual soul, and I pray and believe that I am—perhaps to many such—I pray you do not interfere with the Lord's quite clear command. Do not say, I remember that one thing, but then there have been other things; I will try to remember them all. Perhaps I may as well say that the sermon this evening is in answer to the letter of a troubled soul that has reached me from the other side of the world, telling me of agony, of desire to make restoration. The writer said, I beseech you preach on the subject and send me the sermon. That I propose to do. Therefore let me say that the letter is a revelation of false attitudes towards this question of restoration and restitution; perfectly sincere, to be pitied, to be loved into the light, but wrong. The one responsibility concerning restoration in order to be reconciled to God is that we definitely go and deal with the one thing conscience names. To-morrow it may name another thing; then we are to deal with that. Do not let us trouble ourselves with things that in the last analysis are very doubtful, or force ourselves to deal with things in the past with which it is quite impossible that we should deal.

Finally, listen to the welcome. "Then come and offer thy gift." Here we may summarize the teaching by declaring that such immediate action in response to conscience whose activity has been aroused by approach to the altar prepares for the appropriation of the advantages which the altar offers. Let that man come back who has taken his journey, who has, so far as he is able, accomplished its purpose, and let him take up his gift and offer it. The altar is for putting away sin. This man has co-operated with God to the utmost of his ability; his approach is now sincere, open and worthy; let him come.

Now the altar is of value. There is an activity of grace which that man still needs, and of which he never felt the need so profoundly as in the hour when he has done his utmost to co-operate with God toward moral restoration. Never so perfectly before did he know his need of absolution, cleansing of the soul, restoration to fellowship with God. Then, said Jesus, Let him come. He will come now, not as a formalist, but in reality. He will come sincerely, and coming sincerely will be received.

The grace of which the altar is the symbol is now to be received. Grace to deal with the wrong which has been righted, for its stain is still on the conscience of the man; its desolation abides. Grace will now deal with that. As between this man and his brother the wrong has been righted; but only God can right it as between man and Himself. This God does, and that is grace in its meaning and value, in its mystery and its mercy.

Let the man remember that he may now come to the altar not alone for the wrong which he has righted so far as he is able, but also for the wrongs which he cannot right. In the moment when conscience has awakened are some to whom it is too late to go. Thank God for the altar! Without it I could have no hope. There are some to whom we cannot go without involving others, and therefore we must not go. We can make restoration only when it may be between ourselves and those whom we have wronged. The confessions that we sometimes hear in inquiry rooms when dealing with souls about sin, made flippantly, involving another, are never sincere. So far as I am concerned, I have no pity for such, and no dealings with them. The confession of sin is lonely, singular, peculiar. There are confessions I can never make, speaking impersonally and as a representative man, for I have no right to involve others. I can go to the altar. I shall carry with me the shame and the wrong and the suffering of some things to the end; but I can trust God's grace for both myself and all the influence of the wrong I did to others, knowing this, that He will not hold them responsible for that for which I alone was responsible. So we must rest in the grace of God. All the strange involutions and intricacies of wrongdoing we must leave at last at the altar.

Those who in the presence of the altar have no questionings of this kind, no remembrances, need very seriously to consider their religious life. Let us be practical, let us be immediate, let us exclude all the world but this congregation, this sanctuary, this hour, this service. Then let us inquire; This coming to God, is it vanity, or is it reality? If it be reality it rebukes us; we remember! If it be vanity we remember nothing, and pass flippantly through the service—the singing of the hymns, pleasant; the sermon, endured!

To the sensitive soul to whom coming to the altar is reality let me say that continuous approach in sincerity enables us to keep short accounts with our own conscience. The thing rebuked in this service can be set right if we will have it so.

The dire peril of carelessness in such matters as these is that conscience becomes hardened. The dweller in the innermost becomes blind. The altar brings nothing to our remembrance. We never blanch with fear or blush with shame. It is an appalling thing that a man may come to that condition.

There is, however, another peril, the peril of unbelief in

the mercy of God. The conscience becomes morbid and sees things that are not there, multiplies transgressions that have never occurred, and turns certain things in life into sins which are not sins at all in the economy of God. Spirituality is diseased, anemic, weak, trembling, often simply because man will not trust in the incredible mercy of God. Do you remember that supreme line in F. W. H. Myers' poem, one of those lines of poetry of which there are few in our language that come out of the essence of eternal things?

God shall forgive thee all but thy despair.

The only thing God cannot forgive is refusal to trust in His love. "O Jerusalem, Jerusalem . . . how often would I have gathered thy children together, as a hen gathereth her chickens under her wings . . ." Was ever figure so vibrant with the infinite passion of God? "And ye would not." Ye would not trust My love! Ye would not respond to My love! "Behold, your house is left unto you desolate."

I pray you, do not doubt the mercy of God. If you have heard Him calling you to some hard task, some rough pathway, some difficult business between thyself and thy brother, know this; that if thou wilt tramp that pathway, and "lay in dust life's glory dead," then from the ground there shall blossom red, "life that shall endless be." The hard journey leads at last to the altar, and the way of the altar is the way of peace.

CHAPTER XXVI

THE FIRST-BORN

And she brought forth her first-born son.
LUKE 2:7.
Who is . . . the first-born of all creation.
COLOSSIANS 1:15.
Who is . . . the first-born from the dead.
COLOSSIANS 1:18.
The first-born among many brethren.
ROMANS 8:29.

WE CELEBRATE AT CHRISTMAS THE SUPREME EVENT IN HUMAN history, the central act of God in that cosmic order in the midst of which we live. Its importance in the affairs of men is demonstrated by the accumulated results of two millenniums, by the spiritual conceptions which it has created, the moral standards which have resulted from it, and, what is more wonderful still, by the renovation and reconstruction of things spoiled and ruined which have followed. These results, however, are but the beginnings. If we would realize the stupendous meaning of the birth of the One of Whom we speak as Jesus of Nazareth, we need to detach ourselves from the merely local and historic, and endeavor to see it in its place in the economy of God. In order to do this no single word in the New Testament is more helpful, perhaps, than the one which is common to these passages of Scripture, the title "first-born"; and no group of passages is more illuminating.

Before proceeding to the consideration of the teaching of these texts it is of the utmost importance that we most carefully recognize the exact meaning of our word "first-born," and of the Greek word of which in each case it is the singularly apt and beautiful translation.

We may divide our word into two parts, as indeed it is, in its very nature, already divided: *first*, and *born*. In so doing we are at once helped to a true understanding of the Greek word of which it is a translation. The word "first" means foremost, and is variously used in reference to time, place, order, or importance. This we need to recognize, or we may think of it as referring to time only in these particular passages, whereas, as a matter of fact, it has a far more spacious value, and in some cases the reference is not to time at all, but to that which is beyond time, the timeless and the eternal. The root of the word "born" literally means to produce from a seed, but it must be remembered that it always signifies to bear, or to bring forth, never to beget. The word has no reference whatever to those profounder matters of being associated with the function of begetting. Therefore it does not necessarily give any revelation of the nature of the one born. It always refers to that hour, or event, or method, by which something already in being is manifested.

The compound word is used of Jesus of Nazareth in our texts in different relationships, but always with the same significance, as of One born or brought forth, and of His being born or brought forth in order to take a permanent place in relation to the subject under consideration. The statement that Mary brought forth her first-born Son does not necessarily mean that no son had been born of Mary before that, although, in all probability, that was true. That, however, is not the significance of the statement. It means, rather, that the Son born of Mary in that mystic hour was the foremost Son, the One taking precedence of all her other sons. The description, "the first-born of creation," does not mean that He was the first of the creation in time, that He existed before all other creations. It means rather that He is the ultimate of creation, that toward which all creation moved, its goal, its consummation, its final glory. "The first-born from the dead" does not mean that He was the first raised from the dead in human history. Lazarus had preceded Him, and if we are to trust our Biblical record, men in the old economy had preceded Him. It means rather that He was the foremost, taking precedence over all others who rise from the dead, and in that sense was the "first-born of the dead." "The first-born among many brethren" suggests not merely His priority in point of time, but rather His eternal supremacy over even all those who are brought into new life as the result of His great and gracious mission.

The profounder questions of being and of begetting are dealt with or referred to in the context in each case. The first-born of the virgin mother was foreannounced by the angel as "The Son of the Most High," "The Son of God." The first-born of creation is described as "The Son of His love," "The image of the invisible God"; and in His own essential being as the One Who is "before all things," the One in Whom "all things consist." The "first-born from the dead" is the same Person, as the continuity of the apostolic argument proves. "The first-born among many brethren" is with equal clearness described in the context as the Son of God.

Thus in every case the Person referred to is the Son of God in the fullest sense of that term, and the very fulness of the term necessitates limitation in our understanding or interpretation of the word. If that statement appears to be of the nature of a paradox let us consider it carefully. "The Son of God" is a term so full that, when we use it in order to explain it, we must limit it. We must limit it as a figure of speech by declining to limit it as we are compelled to limit the term "son" when we use it on the level of our own experience. As God can have no essential beginning, neither can His Son, Who is of His very nature. Therefore the only sense in which the Son of God can ever be spoken of as begotten is in reference to some new manifestation or activity of Deity.

We celebrate at this season the beginning of the central age in the history of man, that which was initiated when the Son of God was manifested. It is an age of consummation and of initiation, and in both cases the Son of God is declared to be first-born.

The four texts I have selected fall into two groups. The first two deal with consummations: the first-born Son of the virgin mother, and the first-born of all creation. The second two deal with initiation: the first-born from the dead, and the first-born among many brethren.

The first two have reference to the original creation of God. "Let us make Man" was the crowning word of that creation. It was preceded by all the lower forms of being. Jesus, as the first-born of a woman, was the first-born of creation, that is, in the sense of being its goal and its glory.

The second two have to do with redemption. Jesus became a man, a member of the race, involved in sin, and as such He passed to death. Suddenly appearing out of the darkness and mystery of death, He was the first-born from the dead. Man having lost the scepter and possibilities of his own being, a new race is to be created by the process of the Divine activity, and Jesus is the first-born among many brethren.

In the first two the redeeming purpose is seen operative in the realm of creation; in the second two the creative purpose is seen as realized through redemption. Thus the movement suggested by these four passages is one, and cannot ultimately be divided. For the purpose of our meditation, however, we may follow the suggested division, being careful so far as possible to observe the relation maintained between the creative purpose of God and His redemptive work, between the redemptive purpose of God and its fulfilment of the meaning of His creative activity.

Let us, then, consider these four passages, not in anything like full or exhaustive treatment, but in order to think of what they suggest concerning the Son of God as the first-born in regard to creation, and as the first-born in regard to redemption.

First, then, the Son of God as the first-born in regard to creation. The words written by Luke in his gospel are full of simplicity, and yet full of sublimity; "She brought forth her first-born Son." In that birth we are brought face to face with One Who is the crown and glory of humanity. According to these Divine records and revelations, man was made in the image and likeness of God. Whether it is necessary for us to accept the interpretation of the Biblical statement which affirms that man in those earliest experiences had come to the fulness of that image and likeness may be a very doubtful and debatable question. Personally, I should say that Adam did not realize that great ideal in all its fulness of experience, but potentially only. In the Bible, before the story of sin, we are face to face with primitive man, with man, that is, in his probationary state, not yet having come to full realization of the dignity and glory of his being, not yet realizing within his own experience what it is to be in the image and likeness of God. Whether that be so or not, the declaration here is that one "born of a woman"—I quote Paul's words from Galatians—is a Son Who is first-born, that is, One Who realized in Himself the Divine purpose and intention, One through Whom, therefore, is revealed in the universe of God, to the heavens above and to the earth beneath, the thought that was in the mind of God when He said, "Let us make man in our own image, and in our likeness." All who preceded Jesus in time, even at their highest and best, had been but hints and prophecies as to the meaning and purpose of God in humanity.

We must remember that this word was written by Luke concerning the birth of Jesus after the completion of His life, after the crucifixion, beyond the resurrection, after there had come to the disciples the illuminating glory of the Pentecostal baptism. Luke was writing of the whole fact of Christ as he knew it as the result of that Pentecostal illumination, and with the sense of the whole life of the Man Jesus on his mind. When his pen wrote the story of that birth, he wrote it thus: "She brought forth her first-born Son." She brought forth the Son of Man, Who takes precedence and preeminence above and beyond all other of the sons of men in that He was in Himself the crown and glory of humanity. On that day, in the manger in Bethlehem, was born the archetypal Man, God's Man, Man according to the Divine counsel, the Divine purpose, the Divine possibility, the Divine power. Perhaps I may illustrate what I am attempting to insist on concerning the hour in which this was written in the most simple way by saying that I do not think Mary would have used these words at that moment. I do not think the worshiping shepherds would have understood Who was born at that moment. Even if Mary pondered in her heart this strange and wonderful thing that had happened by the grace and favor of heaven, as most certainly she did, I think she had no true apprehension of Who her Son really was in this great movement of the Divine activity. Presently, beyond the life of purity, patience, beauty, and power; beyond the awful tragedy of the death in which that life so resplendent in glory seemed to go out and be eclipsed; beyond that strange, transforming resurrection hour setting its seal on the truth of His own teaching, and transfiguring the mystery of the Cross; and beyond that hour of illumination which appeared when the Holy Spirit came for the interpretation of the Christ—looking back, those who had thus come to know Him said, He is the "first-born Son," the crown and the glory of our own humanity. In Him humanity came to its own, to use the phrase we so often employ in other applications; in Him humanity realized itself. He was, and is, the first-born of the race.

That consideration must be supplemented by another. If in Him the ultimate glory of creation in the purpose of God, which is man, was realized, the whole story of the birth of Jesus reminds us of the fact that this did not happen as the result of a process of creation. There was some arrest, some change, some new and interfering activity on the part of God in order that there might appear this crowning glory of humanity in a Man. This One born was begotten by neither the will nor the act of humanity, but by the will and activity of God in a strange mystic brooding and mystery of the Holy Spirit, by which operation motherhood was sanctified and purified for its sacred office, so that the angel announcing the coming of the Babe did say to her, "That which is to be born shall be called holy, the Son of God."

When Paul came to write his Colossian letter—the purpose of the letter being that of showing the infinite resources of the believer on Christ—it was necessary in the course of it to speak of this selfsame One, of His peculiar glories, and His relationship to the whole cosmos; and Paul described Him as the first-born of creation. Let us again remind ourselves that that phrase is the exact description of the true place of man in the cosmos. Man is the ultimate in creation. For the purpose of a meditation such as this, it does not at all matter what view we may hold of the process of creation, that is, if we admit that this order is a *created* order. It does not signify whether we think that the creative process was that of long eons through which creation moved ever higher and higher until it came to its ultimate, or whether we believe that these things came originally into being by some stupendous word of God, immediately producing results.

Either view equally demonstrates the glory and majesty of God. To my own understanding the more wonderful and splendid idea is that which—and it is not out of harmony with Genesis, but is consonant with scientific investigation—that which by long, and to our thinking, slow, processes creation climbed higher and ever higher, until it reached its goal in man. Even if men deny the Creator, they are compelled to admit that the last and final glory of the cosmic order is man. That is exactly what the Apostle meant when he wrote of Jesus as the first-born of creation. He saw Him as the One to Whom the whole creation moved, its ultimate goal, the destiny of everything. It was probably a slow-moving process, but it went ever and ever on, until at last Man appeared. That is the Divine order. Here, of course, we must be very careful to allow the Biblical revelation to flash on our thinking, and to correct it; for the Biblical revelation is not that of man finally evolved into separate being, but that of man ultimately created by an act in which the spiritual and material were united in order that the possibilities of the material might be fully realized; and in order that the glory of the spiritual through the material might be fully manifested. In other words, all creation is an expression of God. No flower decks the sod but that is a revelation of the Divine. No single tint of the rainbow or fleck of color on the petal of a flower but speaks of God. In His temple all things say, Glory! That was a great word of the Psalmist. When Isaiah saw the vision of the uplifted throne he heard also this majestic song, not the song of holiness alone, but this also: "The whole earth is full of His glory." All creation is an expression of God. But its foremost born, its ultimate expression, its last and final word concerning God is expressed in man. The first-born of the virgin is the final Man, the goal and glory of humanity. In that sense He is the first-born of creation, the foremost One, the last and final voicing of the glory of God in and through creation.

Yet here again we halt. As we have already seen, this Man whose birth we celebrate at Chirstmastide was not born as the result of what we describe as natural processes. Here was a strange new intrusion on the part of God into affairs and facts which He Himself had originally created and ordered, and which have ever been under His government. The writer of the Colossian letter is careful to tell us in this very connection that Christ is before all things: that is the language of time. He also declares that in Christ all things hold together, or consist. That is the language of continuity.

Let us face the mystery: He Who came, the first-born of creation, the goal to which the whole creation moved until He came, came not by the movement of creation toward Him, but by a new order of God, a new act of God, a new overruling of God. By the power of God He came, the Creator, Who is before all things; He came, the Sustainer, in Whom all things consist. Thus we stand in the presence of a Light that blinds and a glory that is as darkness to our finite minds; in the presence of that kenosis, that self-emptying of which I never can think without remembering that most awe-inspiring, and yet most illuminating, line of Charles Wesley: "God contracted to a span." The first-born came, not by processes of creation, which God originated and governed, but by a new touch and new intrusion, by a new activity of God. In that is evidence of the redeeming purpose of God in His coming. Man cannot redeem his own kind. Man is of the creation entirely, and, while causing, also shares its failure. God only can redeem; He is beyond the creation. The creation is of Him, but in Him is no failure. He Who faileth never, bends to that which fails and touches it anew with power, and enters into it by His own mysterious self-emptying. That is the deeper truth concerning the birth of Jesus.

Thus we come to that of which the mystic light has been on all our earlier considerations. The Apostle directly writes that Christ is not only first-born of creation, but "first-born from among the dead." The arresting word here is the word "dead." It suggests a condition that ought not to be in human life. Into that condition—a condition expressed in the words, "In the midst of life, we are in death"—He came. He was crowned with glory and honor in order that He might die, not after He had died. Let us read the Hebrew letter very carefully at this point. It does not affirm that Christ was crowned with glory and honor as a result of His dying, but in order that He might die. That is one of the supreme words of revelation: "Crowned with glory and honor, *that* by the grace of God He should taste death for every man." The ultimate crown on the brow of God is that which crowns the Living One Who stooped to die to redeem men. He came into the condition of humanity resulting from sin, lived in the midst of it, passed down into death itself. We can never now celebrate Christmas without realizing the Cross in the midst of it all. I was greatly impressed yesterday with a little poem in a daily newspaper. It may be imagination merely, but listen to it:—

> On the night when Christ was born,
>   In the starlight's gleaming,
> Sharp-speared thorn boughs in the shadow
>   Stirred with troubled dreaming
> Of a cruel, piercing crown,
> Of a King in death bowed down:
>
> On the night when Christ was born,
>   And the glad song breaking,
> Reeds about a marish pool,
>   As with long heart aching,
> Wailed with pain of that far hour
> When a reed should mock His power.
>
> On the night when Christ was born,
>   To a bleak moon clinging,

> Stood a grey, ungladdened wood
>   With the olives flinging
> Writhen shadows—watchers dim
> Of the tree which beareth Him.

Whoever wrote that had been very near to Christ. That is a poetic fancy, but it is nearer to truth than much prose and argument. "The whole creation groaneth and travaileth together in pain."

I want that same poet to write me three more verses about the Cross, telling how those thorns blossomed with the roses of eternity, of how the reed at last became the iron rod of government, of how after a little while the olive wood became the material of the throne of eternal Deity. The cradle and the Cross must always remain close together in our thinking.

We see Him passed to that condition of death, and then we see Him as "first-born from the dead," manifested beyond death as the Living One, passing out of its gloom to the glory of the everlasting day. First-born of dead ones, taking pre-eminence over all others—behold Him!

In the context will be found this suggestive phrase: "The Kingdom of the Son of His love." That is a picture of the issue of all the wonder. It means that He Who is the first-born from the dead is He Who will yet realize all creation and establish the great Kingdom of God. Through His Church, His Ecclesia, His called-out saints, He will make the desert blossom as the rose, heal the salt marshes, give the world its final bloom, and make the whole creation the anthem of the glory of God.

Let us pass to the last suggestive phrase, "The first-born among many brethren." Immediately there rises before the mind a picture of a new race upspringing as the result of His birth, His dying, and His resurrection. From the Roman epistle let me select some illuminative phrases and sentences, for the moment stringing them together like pearls without the complete statements of which they form a part: "Who shall deliver me out of the body of this death? . . . Through Jesus Christ our Lord." "The law of the Spirit of life in Christ Jesus made me free from the law of sin and death." "Heirs of God, and joint heirs with Christ." "All things work together for good." Through these sayings we gain a picture of the new race delivered from death, through the Spirit of life set free from the opposing forces of life, heirs of God, joint heirs with Christ, conscious that, in the midst of forces, the grind of which sometimes is terrible, but the direction of which is of God, all things work together for good. In the midst of creation the new race is broken, bruised, groaning, travailing in pain; and that new race is groaning and travailing in pain together with creation. The groaning and travailing have to do with birth; they constitute the birth pangs of a new creation out of which at last the Divine purpose is to be realized and fulfilled. Of that race Christ is first-born, "the first-born among many brethren."

We are not celebrating a small matter at this holy season. We are celebrating the coming into time and human history of the eternally first-born. The hour is mystic and marvelous, the hour in which He came in splendid lowliness, bowed to our level, even though it was the level of sin and of death, in order to lift us to His level, which is the level of holiness and age-abiding life.

Thus we take our four texts, and from them we hear the music of hope, of courage, of victory.

We shall gather in our homes, and the bairns will be about us. We shall not check their merriment, but rather laugh and play and romp with them. The glory of all the glad news will be that on the faces of our children we shall see the light that comes from the cradle of the Babe. The first-born Son is our ground of hope when we look into the faces of our children.

Then we shall pause a moment in the merriment, and

think of that of which all our newspapers speak every day, of the whole creation groaning and travailing in pain. We cannot read a newspaper without seeing this, if the light of God illumine our reading. Look again. Shining between the lines of the paper is the mystic message of Christmas; Christ is the first-born of creation, and that is the prophecy of the hour in which the groaning shall cease, the travail be over, and God's great triumph be come.

We look at death. I would speak with all tenderness. Some of us will know more of the pain of death at Christmas than ever before. A place is empty! No, it is not empty. Look again, oh ye who are crushed and broken of heart. Look at the vacant chair. Behold, it is occupied by the First-born from among the dead. Now we know that those who sleep with Jesus will God bring with Him.

Lastly, we look at ourselves, and that is the most tragic look of all! Oh, the failings of another year, the deflections from the path of faith, the terrific sense of things that master me. Look again! Cease looking at yourself! "Behold the first-born among many brethren," and in that beholding find assurance in His face that at last He will perfect that which concerneth you. So while the bairns are laughing and angels are singing, let us sing our carols and keep our Christmas. It is a great festival! It is the Festival of the First-born!